Consequential Strangers

ALSO BY MELINDA BLAU

Families Apart: Ten Keys to Successful Co-Parenting

Loving and Listening: A Parent's Book of Daily Inspirations for Rebuilding the Family After Divorce

Secrets of the Baby Whisperer

Secrets of the Baby Whisperer for Toddlers

The Baby Whisperer Solves All Your Problems
(the above written for Tracy Hogg)

Parenting by Heart

Nurturing Good Children Now

The Second Family
(for Ron Taffel)

Watch Me Fly
(for Myrlie Evers Williams)

Our Turn: Women Who Triumph in the Face of Divorce
(with Christopher Hayes and Deborah Anderson)

ALSO BY KAREN L. FINGERMAN

Aging Mothers and Their Adult Daughters: Mixed Emotions, Enduring Bonds

Growing Together: Personal Relationships Across the Life Span
(coedited with Frieder R. Lang)

Consequential Strangers

The
Power of
People Who Don't
Seem to Matter
. . . But Really
Do

Melinda Blau
and
Karen L. Fingerman, Ph.D.

W. W. NORTON & COMPANY
NEW YORK · LONDON

Printed in the United States of America
First Edition

For information about permission to reproduce selections from this book,
write to Permissions, W. W. Norton & Company, Inc.,
500 Fifth Avenue, New York, NY 10110

For information about special discounts for bulk purchases, please contact
W. W. Norton Special Sales at specialsales@wwnorton.com or 800-233-4830

Manufacturing by The Courier Companies, Inc.
Book design by Chris Welch
Production manager: Andrew Marasia

Library of Congress Cataloging-in-Publication Data

Blau, Melinda, 1943–
Consequential strangers : the power of people who don't seem to
matter— but really do / Melinda Blau and Karen L. Fingerman. — 1st ed.
p. cm.
Includes bibliographical references and index.
ISBN 978-0-393-06703-3 (hbk.)
1. Interpersonal relations. 2. Social interaction. 3. Identity (Psychology)
4. Strangers. I. Fingerman, Karen L. II. Title.
HM1106.B53 2009
155.9'27—dc22

2009010721

W. W. Norton & Company, Inc.
500 Fifth Avenue, New York, N.Y. 10110
www.wwnorton.com

W. W. Norton & Company Ltd.
Castle House, 75/76 Wells Street, London W1T 3QT

1 2 3 4 5 6 7 8 9 0

In loving memory of
Skylar Sonn Tancredi
March 18, 1992–August 12, 2006
who understood the power
of consequential strangers.
His far-reaching connections
continue to comfort our family.
—MB

With gratitude to Bryce and Lily
who have brought me love and happiness.
—KF

CONTENTS

ACKNOWLEDGMENTS

This book is a story within a story: It could not have been written without the help of my consequential strangers. Some shared their experiences, others contributed ideas; many offered both. Foremost is my collaborator Karen Fingerman, who coined the term and encouraged me to parse it. The consummate scientist—insightful, thorough, and conversant in fields other than her own—Karen led me to ideas and theories that might have taken years on my own to discover. Any distortions of the research are mine, not hers.

Many other scholars have contributed to this book, but three in particular have provided the academic groundwork on which it rests. They have each been uncommonly generous with their time, thoughts, and willingness to critique: Mark Granovetter, who thirty years ago identified the power of weak ties; Calvin Morrill, whose groundbreaking ideas about public sociability underscore the power of casual relationships; and Barry Wellman, whose social analyses and research have illuminated the force of technology in our social lives.

I am indebted as well to a number of other professionals—scientists and clinicians, business leaders and social observers, editors and journalists. Their ideas, research, and personal stories also inform this book. They took time out of busy schedules to talk about their own work and to suggest other avenues that might be explored; or they shared their insights, reactions, and support via email: Rebecca Adams, Marya Alexander, Irv Altman, Laura Anker, Toni Antonucci, Dave Balter, Mahzarin Banaji, Russ Bernard, Marilynn Brewer, Barbara Brown, Gorden Brunner, John Cacioppo, Walter Carl, David Chastain, Richard M. Cohen, Sheldon Cohen, Ellen Conser, Sue Ellen Cooper, Nila Dasgupta, Bella DePaulo, Heidi Donovan, Bonnie Erickson, Reinier Evans, Bob Feldman, Marc Feldman, Claude Fischer, Richard Florida, Kathie Friedman, Diane Garcia, Pema Garcia, Kenneth Gergen, Naomi Korn Gold, Steve Gold, Keith Hampton, T. George Harris, Scott Heiferman, Arlie Hochschild, Bernie Hogan, Helen Horowitz, Neil Howe, Marco Iacoboni, Lanita Jacobs-Huey, Charles Kadushin, Loraleigh Keashly, Fred Kent, Ellen Langer, Nan Lin, Lyn Lofland, Ed Madera, Rachel Maddow, Margo Maine, Alexandra Marine, Dina Mayzlin, Doug McAdam, Don McKensie, Bob Milardo, Allison Munch-Rotolo, Oscar Muñoz, Gary Namie, Ray Oldenberg, Tony Orum, Scott Page, Ray Pahl, Sally Panalp, Bill Patrick, Christine Pearson, Steve Pedigo, Letty Cottin Pogrebin, Tom Rath, Tim Rees, Jennifer Richeson, Brent Roberts, Karl Ronn, Mark Rosenbaum, Catherine Sabiston, Tom Sander, Eva Schiffer, Michael Schrage, John Shannon, Kennedy Smith, Walker Smith, Graham Spanier, Bonnie Strickland, Michael Sunnefrank, Bob Sutton, Richard T. Sweeney, Ron Taffel, Peggy Thoits, Jonathan Vance, Jorge Vanegas, Anita Vangelisti, Michael Ventura, Michelle Visca, Harry West, Christine Williams, Steve Wright, Robert Wuthnow, Craig Wynett, and the wizards behind the curtain at Zingerman's, Paul Saginaw and Ari Weinzweig.

Beyond the ivied walls and the think tanks, of course, are the real-life dramas that most resonate with readers. Some interviewees' anecdotes ended up on the cutting room floor, but their insights and honesty bolstered this book nonetheless: Chuck Adams, Jane Adams, Jayant Agarwalla, Max Aguilera-Hellweg, Chude Pam Parker Allen, Allyson Beatrice, Dana Behar, Mary Benes, Tim Bishop, Barbara Biziou, Jourdan Biziou, Paul Blake, Anthony Dias Blue, Wally Briggs, Gail Burak, Rob Camarata, Anavel Caparos,

Raymond Chau, Joe Chernov, Erin Childs, Martha Cincoski, Sara Cummings, Doug Davis, Grover Dear, Zhu Xiao Di, Kenny Ellis, Bill Farris, Nelson Fellman, Jan Felshin, Edrie Ferdun, Kasha Ferrin, Ken Fox, Minnie Franco, Helen Garfinkle, Karima Gebel, Cynthia Gibbs, Ed Gotbetter, Henry Graff, Barbara Green, Carolyn Green, Mary Walker Green, Judith Gronim, Laura Halliday, Renee Harris, Mark Hewitt, Pat Hickock, Sheila Hoffman, Yolanda Holtzee, Joan Horton, Christine Hourihan, Jim Hourihan, Michael Hussin, Bertha Josephson, Jim Kates, Jeanne Kelly, Margaret Kierstein, Peter Kohlsaat, Marjorie Knott, Leah Kunkel, Ellen Law, Tom Lazarus, Kenhee Lee, Ellen Lefcourt, Donna Lenhardt, Scott Levy, Karla Lightfoot, Sylvia Mackey, Robin Maltz, Astrid Matthysse, Dottie Mayhew, Stephen McCeney, Carla Messina, Gail Miles, Peter Moore, Alex Muñoz, Linda Osborne, Ken Osman, Mike Patterson, Raquel Perez, Murray Pincus, Joanne Robert, Rita Ross, Daryl Roth, Karen Robinovitz, Toby Rosenbaum, Sue Rubenstein, Sylvia Rubin, Joan Seager, Yuna Shaughnnessy, Tina Silverman, Gunjan Sinha, Suzanne Slesin, Judith Snow, Jane Stein, Rick Stein, Jill Stern, Theo Stites, Susan Strayer, Jack Tantleff, Melody Townsel, Kathy Travis, Cay Trigg, Linda Tucker, Elaine Ulman, Susan Valentine and our fellow yoginis, Dorothy Varon, Carol Watchler, Joan Weigele, Reggie Weintraub, Jonnie Wesson, Denis Wood, Chris Wright, Sherry Wright, and Shelly Zimbalist. I have excluded names of people who preferred pseudonyms and whose identities might be revealed if listed here, but I am no less grateful for their contributions.

Writers need feedback—and reality checks—along the way. At the risk of repeating names, I need to thank, in particular, Helen Garfinkle, Jane Stein, and Bonnie Strickland, who (going above and beyond the call of friendship) read most, if not all, of the book in various draft stages. Others who critiqued the proposal and/or portions of the text include: Russ Bernard, Barbara Biziou, Marilynn Brewer, John Cacioppo, Walter Carl, Sheldon Cohen, Ellen Conser, Connie Evans, Jan Felshin, Edrie Ferdun, Ronda

Fingerman, Lois Fisher, Elena Gatti, Bonnie Goebert, Mark Granovetter, Keith Hampton, Bertha Josephson, Margaret Kierstein, Paula de Koenigsberg, Susan Kravitz, Ellen Lefcourt, Carla Messina, Patrice Morhart, Allison Munch-Rotolo, Sue Rubenstein, Sylvia Rubin, Lorena Sol, Sandra Sonn, John Stein, Theo Stites, Elaine Tata, Peggy Thoits, Linda Tucker, Joan Weigele, Reggie Weintraub, and Barry Wellman.

No one has read more of this book (or read the proposal more times!) than our intrepid agent, Eileen Cope. Eileen and I go way back. Although I've acknowledged her editorial skills, candor, and smarts in previous books, she truly brought those gifts to bear on this project. She is a writer's dream, sometimes pushing, sometimes reining in—always demanding the best. She wisely led us to Amy Cherry, this book's champion and artful editor. Amy is among a dying breed—very hands-on, very responsive. I also thank both women's assistants, Alexandra Bicks at Trident Media and Erica Stern at W. W. Norton, who helped nudge the book through the long process of production, along with Nancy Palmquist, managing editor, Amy Robbins, our excellent and supportive copy editor, and Chris Welch, who designed these pages.

Last and certainly not least are the people closest to me who allow me to pick their brains and to go on and on about consequential strangers. Many of you are listed above, but I know you all know who you are, and I am truly blessed to have you. And a special thanks, in alphabetical order, to Henry, Jen, Jeremy, Lorena, and Sam, whom—to use Tom Antonucci's definition of the innermost circle—I can't imagine life without.

—Melinda Blau

First, I would like to thank Melinda Blau. She is a writer's writer. When this project began, we planned a quick sortie into the arena of peripheral relationships, with the goal of writing a book in twelve months. Melinda persisted for over two and a half years of in-depth interviews, voracious reading, and tenacious writing and rewriting to produce this highly polished finished product. All of the credit goes to her.

I share Melinda's gratitude to our agent, Eileen Cope, who initiated me into the field of commercial writing with patience and wisdom. Her mentorship throughout this process has been invaluable. It also has been a pleasure to get to know Amy Cherry, whose upbeat attitude, quick turnaround, and insightful feedback on every chapter truly shaped this work. I also thank Erica Stern, Alexandra Bicks, and Amy Robbins, who provided great help in the preparation of this book.

To the list of scholars Melinda has already thanked, the following individuals enlightened my understanding of consequential strangers, answered specific queries, or contributed to ideas in this book directly or indirectly: Rebecca Adams, David Almeida, Victoria Bedford, Eric Bermann, Kira Birditt, Rosemary Blieszner, Niall Bolger, Brant Burleson, Deborah Carr, Laura Carstensen, Susan Charles, Ann Crouter, Roberto Drago, Phoebe Ellsworth, Scott Feld, Melissa Franks, Helene Fung, Frank Furstenberg, Patricia Griffiths, Elizabeth Hay, Heather Helms Erikson, Janis Jacobs, Janice Kelly, Neal Krause, Frieder Lang, Eva Lefkowitz, Shelley MacDermid, Erina MacGeorge, Jennifer Maggs, Meghan McDonough, Robert Milardo, Laura Miller, Sara Moorman, Dan Mroczek, Terri Orbuch, Wayne Osgood, Karl Pillemer, Lindsay Pitzer, German Posada, Harry Reis, Rena Repetti, Karen Rook, Joyce Serrido, Susan Sprecher, Rob Stawski, Jill Suitor, Danielle Swiontek, Lillian Troll, Bert Uchino, Joseph Veroff, Alexis Walker, Kipling Williams, Sherry Willis, Jeremy Wood, and Steven Zarit.

Many people who supported me during this process reside outside the great metropolises. Consequential strangers and friends in small college towns (West Lafayette, Indiana, State College, Pennsylvania, Urbana, Illinois, Bloomington, Indiana, and Irvine, California) deserve my thanks. I am grateful to the "Yeazell clan" in Cincinnati for family time, diversion from work on weekend visits, and ever-sweltering August birthday parties. My parents in Des Moines and my sisters have never faltered in providing support and, more importantly, chocolate, which have sustained my career.

I initially came to the topic of consequential strangers via an interest in what scholars refer to as "peripheral ties." My husband and children are my "core ties." My list of acknowledgments (and my life) would not be complete without them.

—Karen Fingerman

INTRODUCTION

The Birth of a Notion

> A human being is part of a whole, called by us the "universe," a part limited in time and space. He experiences himself, his thoughts and feelings, as something separate from the rest—a kind of optical delusion of his consciousness. This delusion is a kind of prison for us, restricting us to our personal desires and to affection for a few persons nearest us. . . . We shall require a substantially new manner of thinking if humanity is to survive.
>
> —*Albert Einstein*

Every day we interact with people who influence our lives in small and great ways but who are not part of our inner circle: a yoga teacher, a waitress, a gym buddy, a pet sitter, a former coworker, a "friend" on Facebook, dad's army chum, the proprietor of a favorite clothing store, a professional contact known mostly by phone. Each of these relations is different from the other, but they all are consequential strangers—people who are so much a part of our everyday life that we often take them for granted.

This book is the result of a collaboration between two consequential strangers—Melinda Blau, a journalist, and Karen Fingerman, a social scientist and professor at Purdue University. If writers tend to write what they know, creative scholars also study and develop theories based on their personal experiences. We can read about other people and see how various ideas and research findings play out in their stories, but most of us "get" the importance of consequential strangers by examining our own lives. So it was for Blau and Fingerman.*

The Journalist

For Blau, it was her move from Manhattan in 1990—years before she and Fingerman would cross paths. When people in her new locale—Northampton, Massachusetts—asked if she missed New York, she replied, "No, I miss New Yorkers." She had in mind Kathy, a fellow tenant she often chatted with in the lobby of their building, and Henrietta, the septuagenarian writer whom she respected and learned from but saw only for coffee after their class at the New School. She missed popping in on Stanley and Leon, the celebrated butchers on Madison Avenue who had given her children slices of bologna and watched the two of them grow up. She remembered how Helen, the Korean greengrocer, would set aside a box of Concord grapes for her every autumn. The collective presence of this wide-ranging array of people punctuated her daily comings and goings in Manhattan. Eventually she realized that "New Yorker" was code for an entire category of casual relationships that had virtually disappeared from her life.

To remedy her sense of isolation, Blau launched what she, for lack of a better term, called her "acquaintanceship campaign." She wasn't in the market for friends. She needed informal relations. So whenever she interviewed someone in the area who sounded interesting and open, she'd invite the person to coffee. She felt

* Here and throughout the book, we use the editorial "we" but refer to our individual selves in the third person. For interviewees, we use an asterisk (*) to denote a pseudonym, in which case some identifying details may have been changed as well.

vulnerable putting herself out there, but at least had the cover of her profession. In this way, she met a handful of new people—among them, a psychology professor, the editor of a local paper, and a woman she interviewed for an article about divorce. She also accepted her landlord's invitation to have lunch with "some people you might like."

Some of those tentative connections went no further than a first "date." Some led to other new acquaintances. A few became good friends. Most, happily and appropriately, stayed on the periphery of her social circle and yet contributed to her sense of belonging in Northampton. They made Blau's life richer and more interesting, often giving her opportunities and connections she'd never have imagined. She finally had people she could ask whether a particular restaurant was good or which doctor had the best reputation. And when the city dug up her front lawn to repair a burst water main and she was out of town, there were people she could call for help.

The Scholar

In the mid-nineties, Fingerman, who had spent much of her career studying adult relationships, was beginning to pay attention to nonintimate social ties in her academic work. What do these outsiders do for our sense of self? How do they satisfy our competing needs for individuality *and* connection? Why do we need to notice these important yet overlooked relations? But it was soon after the birth of her first child that she truly came to terms with their significance—mostly by accident.

In 2000, Fingerman experienced every cliché of new motherhood—a deep and abiding love for her baby, the stress of figuring out how she would combine work and family, and the realization that she might never wear a bikini again. But she also had feelings no one had forewarned her about. Her world had narrowed. In this new universe, only three people existed: Fingerman, her husband, and her baby. Initially their time was intense and joyfully focused within the confines of their tiny family. Fingerman loved the cocoon they'd built around themselves. But she also missed aspects of her former life, which included volunteer work at the local soup kitchen, travel to academic conferences in Europe, and brown-bag lunches during which she and her graduate students discussed new ideas in the field.

When Fingerman returned to teaching, she settled happily into a new routine. But one afternoon, as she drove into the entrance of the day care center parking lot to retrieve her son, she had an epiphany. The scene was familiar enough by then. Every day between 5:00 and 5:30 p.m., fifty or so vehicles drove in and out of the small lot behind the center, which normally held no more than fifteen cars. The overflow forced some parents to park on the sidewalk. Yet no one stole a space. No one honked. Tempers remained in check. As each parent began to exit the lot, he or she waited patiently for drivers in the lead to inch their way out of the narrow entrance. Marveling at their civility, Fingerman understood the reason for their restraint: their connections. They were neighbors, colleagues, care providers, the university librarian, and each knew the other at least tangentially. She began to think of them as "consequential strangers."

Fingerman then started to notice the myriad ways in which people on the periphery sustained her sheltered family. Metaphorically, her husband and baby were always at the center of her vision, but other, less intimate relationships were on the blurred edges. As her child grew, she met other parents at the playground who knew about gymnastics and music classes for toddlers. There were people whose services she used, people on whom she depended for haircuts and legal advice, and the woman who rang up her iced tea each afternoon at the cafeteria. The story her research was beginning to suggest certainly seemed true in her own life: *People outside one's circle of family and close friends mattered as well.*

This Book

The collaborators first met by phone in 2003 when Blau called to interview Fingerman about a mother-daughter study she had published. Over the next few years, the two exchanged emails and phone numbers and kept in touch electronically, opening windows for one another into their respective worlds of journalism and research. In 2005, Fingerman emailed Blau a chapter she had recently published about peripheral relationships. As the first sheet of paper spit out of her printer, Blau's eyes lit on a phrase in the title that seemed to leap off the page.

This book is an exploration of that phrase—"consequential strangers"—people who don't seem to matter, but really do. In Chapter 1, we talk about the ascendance of peripheral social ties—why most of us haven't thought much about their importance until now and why we need a "new vocabulary" to describe the people in our lives, language that enables us to acknowledge and celebrate more subtle levels of intimacy.

We then pull back the camera in Chapter 2, to look at an aerial view of the social landscape so that we can see how each of us—in our everyday comings and goings, in business, in our communities, and in cyberspace—travel in our own social "convoy." Understanding these connections enables us to harness the power of consequential strangers—a power that is now essential to personal and organizational success.

Chapter 3 looks at how these bit players broaden our sense of self and link us to information and other resources we can't get from our intimates. They are more likely to challenge our worldview and to add novelty, dimension, and color to our lives, and to take us "beyond the familiar." Likewise, when it comes to well-being, the subject of Chapter 4, we need to marshal *all* of our social ties in order to stay healthy or cope with an illness—our own or a loved one's.

Chapter 5 looks at "being spaces"—places where relationships first unfold, such as the gym, the beauty salon, a favorite coffee shop or tavern, a playing field, and other environments that are conducive to letting outsiders in. And lest we appear to sound like Pollyanna, Chapter 6 makes the point that although most consequential strangers serve a positive function in our lives, they are not always good to us or for us.

Finally, in Chapter 7, we look toward the future. If the Millennial generation, now rising into adulthood on the heels of Gen X, is any indication, consequential strangers will only become more important. Our lives and our locales have become increasingly diverse. Recognizing the importance of these easy-care relationships, understanding what they do for us, and finding the "hidden solidarities" in our everyday social ties is key to survival in a complex society.

The research in this book, drawn from a variety of sciences, affirms the importance of everyday connections—and not just with our intimates. Therefore, this is a different kind of "relationship book." It won't teach you the rules or give you ten keys that will make you more attractive, loved, or successful, but it will make you think. It will change your definition of what an "important" relationship is. And it will make you more aware of the people you encounter on the job, in your neighborhood, wherever you play and pray, in public arenas, and in cyberspace. You may be skeptical: How could these casual relationships have such an impact, for better or for worse? Read on.

You will see how having a diverse collection of consequential strangers helps you develop a more flexible self, one that is better positioned to take action in your life, even in the face of adversity. You will come to understand the paradox of the periphery: Those we know less well are more likely to keep us informed and excited about life. And by the time you get to the last page of this book, you will look at these seemingly unimportant people in your life with new eyes. They might be slightly or very different from those in your inner social circle, but each gives you something unique—a new opportunity, a different way of looking at a problem, an unexpected kindness, an experience you might otherwise never have had.

Perhaps this is what J. K. Rowling had in mind when she delivered the commencement address at Harvard University in 2008 and suggested that the graduates consider an alternative definition of "imagination." In addition to being "the uniquely human capacity to envision that which is not," said the woman who gave us the indomitable and yet humble young wizard Harry Potter, imagination also is "the power that enables us to empathize with humans whose experiences we have never shared." At the end of her speech, Rowling added, "We do not need magic to change the world. We carry all the power we need inside ourselves already: we have the power to imagine."

It is our hope that this book will inspire your social imagination.

Consequential Strangers

1

The Ascendance of Consequential Strangers

On this shrunken globe, men can no longer live as strangers.

—*Adlai E. Stevenson*

The Joel 100

When humorist Joel Stein, a regular contributor to *Time* magazine, read the proposed 2006 list of influential people, he decided his editors should "get out of the building more." Chinese businessman Huang Guangyu, Egyptologist Zahi Hawass, and Balenciaga designer Nicolas Ghesquière meant nothing to *him*. "What about people who actually affect us?" wondered Stein in his annual send-up of the Time 100.[1]

And so, the Joel 100 was born.

Who *did* matter? Of course his loved ones, but including Stein's wife, mother, and father, there were only eighteen of them. The rest were acquaintances, some obviously more important to him than others but probably not people he'd invite home for Thanksgiving dinner. Forty were people who, in varying degrees, furthered his career, like the producer who gave him his first job as a sitcom writer. Another fifteen or so were individuals whose services and advice the thirtysomething Stein couldn't live without: his lawyer, his agent, his CPA, his account executive at Citibank, his eye doctor, and the copy editor who "makes me look smart by fixing my mistakes." He also listed former landlords, his renter, a mortgage broker, and the couple who sold him his house and "had the guts to move in across the street"—a handy resource when he had plumbing questions.[2]

The Time 100 was published in the May 8 issue of the magazine, and Stein's essay, "Meet the Other 100," appeared on the last page. To read the entire (annotated) Joel 100, readers had to go online. Some did. A few weeks later, in fact, the magazine published a letter from Nelson Fellman, a seventy-five-year-old retired PR executive from Voorhees, New Jersey:

> Joel Stein's "Meet the Other 100" gave me a great idea: to make a list of the people who matter most to me. I wish I had started that list a long time ago. . . . I never took the trouble to tell a high school teacher or a business mentor or a beloved grandfather what a significant influence each had on my life.[3]

Stein was shocked that anyone would bother to look at "a weird online list of people in *my* life," no less feel inspired by it.[4] He has a point, considering that he also included his hairstylist, the man who delivered his bottled water, and the service advisor at the Mini Cooper car dealer who showed him how to hook his iPod into his car. Another buddy made the list because "a guy who knows a lot about good ethnic restaurants is worth his weight in *pupusas*," and a waitress because she gave him tips on braising short ribs. And in the number 15 spot was Dora, the proprietor of Yuca's Taco Stand, who "smiles as if she knows me." Stein admitted an ulterior motive: Once she saw her name in print, perhaps Dora would also throw in an extra taco.

Stein didn't anticipate that his tongue-in-cheek essay would be taken seriously, no less strike a nerve. But the Joel 100 reflected an unspoken truth: Who we really care about are the countless everyday people who touch our lives and influence us *personally.* The editors of *Time* methodically singled out particular scientists, politicians, environmentalists, and inventors who changed the world, but those people are total strangers. Readers identified with the Joel 100 because it was a roster of intimates and *consequential strangers.*

The fact is, each of us has a unique collection of consequential strangers like those on the Joel 100—people outside our circle of family and close friends. They range from long-standing acquaintances to people we encounter on occasion or only in certain places. They cut a wide swath across our lives, and yet each is linked to us in some way and fills a specific need.

In fiction as in real life, consequential strangers are everywhere, even in the funny papers. *Single Slices,* drawn by political cartoonist Peter Kohlsaat, has two guys sitting at a bar, one saying to the other, "It's not quite a relationship . . . it's more of a inclinationship." Some of the most memorable characters in television sitcoms emerge from supporting roles: Eldin, the beefy laid-back handyman on *Murphy Brown,* who doubled as a babysitter, or Rosario, the wisecracking Salvadoran housekeeper on *Will & Grace.* And just about everyone fits the bill on *Seinfeld* or *The Office,* and especially the gang at *Cheers,* the fictional tavern where "everybody knows your name."

The term "consequential strangers" captures a fascinating paradox about casual relationships: *They are as vital to our well-being, growth, and day-to-day existence as family and close friends.* Admittedly, the word "stranger" is counterintuitive when defining people who have an impact. How can they be strangers? The point is, they are not; they are entirely different. A stranger is someone you don't know and can visually identify by "category"—a man, a waitress, a person of Asian descent. A *consequential* stranger is someone you also know something *about* and with whom you are actually "acquainted."[5] If you think of your life as an ongoing drama, your intimates are the featured players, and consequential strangers assume supporting roles. A good narrative needs both. What would the Jimmy Stewart character in *It's a Wonderful Life* have done without the townspeople who came to his rescue?

Expanding Our Vocabulary of Relationships

If—until now—you've never thought about, or appreciated, these supporting players, in part it's because many of them skirt the edges of your social consciousness. You might even take them for granted . . . until you begin to jot down names for your holiday card list. Scanning your social brain, you come up with people you don't necessarily think of as "important," certainly not compared to your loved ones. But somehow it feels like a good idea to send season's greetings. One of Fingerman's studies helps explain why.

She asked a group of volunteers about each holiday card they had received that season—whom each card was from, their relationship to the sender, and what getting the card meant to them. She also questioned their card-sending habits and attitudes. And to gauge their "social embeddedness"—how connected they felt to others—she had them rank statements such as, "I feel part of a group of people who share my activities and beliefs," and "No one cares for me." People at the younger end of the age continuum—under forty—tended to view their holiday greetings as a means of maintaining or building ties, while those at the other end were more likely to see them as a link to their past. But for both groups, the more cards they received, the more socially embedded they felt. And it was not merely a matter of hearing from their intimates. Of the more than 1,400 cards analyzed, over two-thirds were from people in different pockets of the respondents' lives—colleagues and teachers, service providers, acquaintances from the past, and people they hoped to get to know better. In other words, while it staves off loneliness to hear from loved ones during the holidays, an additional sense of security comes from being connected to people who help us feel like our world extends beyond the boundaries of home.[6]

If you tend to underestimate the significance of people on your holiday list at other times of the year, it also might be because practically every article and book, every therapist, and every relationship guru in the media focus almost exclusively on "primary relationships"—your partner, children, parents, and siblings. When Fingerman and a colleague analyzed six years' worth of academic papers—nearly a thousand articles in the most important psychology and sociology journals—she found that *fewer than 10%* of relationship studies covered nonintimate ties, such as neighbors, teachers, clergy, and church members.[7]

Given this overwhelming bias, then, why would you give a second thought to Sara in your meditation group, Frank at the dry cleaner's, or the Smiths whom you run into at the local repertory theater? But those are precisely the kinds of people who populate our lives. They usually outnumber our intimates. On Joel Stein's list of one hundred individuals who affected his life, for instance, 82% were consequential strangers. And when Nelson Fellman sat down to compile his own list, by the time he got to number 35, more than half were acquaintances who in some way affected his life, including a woman he mentored and the corporal in the army who taught him how to play chess.

Clearly our loved ones matter. People who lack close relationships are susceptible to physical and emotional problems. Because intimates are critical to our survival, they are naturally valued more by our culture and, not surprisingly, have garnered the most attention. But that's not the whole story. While those closest to our heart are synonymous with home, consequential strangers anchor us in the world and give us a sense of being plugged into something larger. They also enhance and enrich our lives and offer us opportunities for novel experiences and information that is beyond the purview of our inner circles. Indeed, after all this focusing on the peaks and valleys of close relationships, we must widen the lens to acknowledge the *entire social landscape.*

It's not just the dearth of research on peripheral ties that limits our awareness. We also lack the vocabulary, says sociologist Calvin Morrill, one of a small, growing cadre of scholars in various fields who focus on social life *outside* the home. Morrill points out that to characterize personal ties as either "intimate" or "nonintimate," "primary" or "secondary," doesn't capture the vast sea of connections that fall in between. "We need to move beyond this simple (and in some ways misleading) dichotomy," says Morrill, "to recognize a range of relationships that exist in between these two extremes and function in many important ways for people."[8]

In actuality, all of our social ties are part of a fluid continuum of relationships. Consequential strangers occupy the broad region between complete strangers on the far left and intimates—our strongest connections—on the far right. Just beyond friend territory are your more valued consequential strangers—your close acquaintances. They are usually people you've known longer or see more often, perhaps know more about, like your boss or your hairdresser. You depend on them or have a significant and mutual give-and-take that affects the quality of your life. Among these closer acquaintances might be people who will morph into more intimate relationships over time, becoming good friends, even lovers. In contrast, your casual relations that fall near the "stranger" end of the continuum don't occupy as important a place in your heart. It's unlikely that you feel the same way about your mailman or a waitress at your favorite deli as you do about the high school teacher who convinced you to apply for a scholarship or the neighbor who came to your rescue when you had a flood in your basement.

Many of our consequential strangers are associated solely with the neighborhood or the office, the train station, a store, the bank, the library, the gym. Calvin Morrill refers to these kinds of connections as "anchored" relationships—those that develop over time and are limited to a particular place or activity. Some of them are toward the intimate end of the continuum; others simply punctuate our daily existence, reassuring us that we're not in alien territory.

As human beings, we harbor an innate desire to connect to others who make us feel safe. We seek ways to feel surrounded by people who are familiar. Thus, many anchored relationships are touchstones of our daily or weekly routines. We unconsciously anticipate the presence of these people, so much so that *not* seeing them or encountering them in a different place can be jarring. You run into your mechanic and his family at the mall and initially experience that frustrating where-do-I-know-him-from feeling. Suddenly you recall him in grease-stained overalls at his body shop, and you remember how he came to your aid a few months earlier when your car wouldn't start.

Each of the decisions we make—where we live and work, what we buy, what we do in our spare time, how we commune with a higher power (or not)—can thrust us into a whole new cluster of consequential strangers. Say you get a dog for the first time. You suddenly notice neighbors who have dogs, too. Depending on where you live, you begin to frequent the beach, the dog park, or "the path," as it's known in Northampton. You know that most mornings at around 8:15, you'll run into the trim, long-legged runner whose yellow and black Labs tear through the forest alongside him, the three women with their three quintessentially country dogs (a Lab, a golden retriever, an English setter), and the older woman with the porkpie hat. You know the dogs' names but not the owners'. After weeks or months of passing each other almost every day, you might finally look in the dog's direction and say, "I know this is Max, but I'm embarrassed to admit I don't know *your* name." You introduce yourselves, perhaps walk part of the way together, but there's usually no reason to exchange emails. This relationship is *of* the path. Most of your conversation is about the dogs ("Did Bogey get bigger?" "I love his haircut") but occasionally you'll discuss something that's bothering you that you haven't shared with anyone else. And, to your surprise, she'll offer a suggestion you've never considered. Although most of these "dog people" will forever remain in consequential stranger territory, they can be a surprising source of solace, especially when your dog is sick or dies. Unknowing (and probably pet-less) close friends might say, "Don't worry. You'll get another one," but you can count on your dog-walk comrades to truly understand.

Some consequential strangers appear onstage with great regularity, like coworkers and weekly tennis partners, but if you've changed jobs or moved away, they are probably no longer front and center. Still others are barely more than blips on your social radar right from the beginning: a school parent who picks his child up when you do and same-time-next-year acquaintances, such as a competitor at a business conference, a craftsperson at an annual festival, assorted characters in a vacation community. Each time you meet, you make small talk and glimpse into their lives and learn bits of their history. You learn that Delilah works for a record company and loves to ski, that Renaldo is divorced and has traveled extensively in India. You probably don't think about these bit players when they're out of sight, but they all become part of your "social convoy"—a caravan of the various connections you make as you travel through life. They are resources, available when the need arises. Delilah might come to mind when you're trying to get tickets to a concert, Renaldo if you suddenly find yourself doing business with a company in Mumbai.

You might refer to these people on the periphery as acquaintances, buddies, companions, pals, compadres, cronies, fellows, mates, or any of a dozen other terms.[9] You might identify them by their role—"my doorman," "my acupuncturist." Or you might use "friend" for everyone you know, as in "my friend from church." It's the label of choice in America, suggests sociologist Claude Fischer, who asked 1,050 adults in Northern California to list and classify their relationships. Of the more than 19,000 relations they named, 59% were described as "friends." When only nonrelatives were considered, that figure rose to 83%. "Friends" were most likely to be individuals who lacked a specific role (such as neighbor or coworker), were of the same age, were people the respondents socialized with, and were known for a long time. Fischer concluded that "friend" is a term we use loosely to describe an array of social ties, but not necessarily only our closest ones.[10] Some of our so-called "friends" are actually consequential strangers.

In the end, it doesn't matter what you label a person. The issue is what goes on *in the relationship* and what is exchanged between the two people.[11] As Supreme Court justice Potter Stewart famously remarked when asked to define pornography, "I know it when I see it." Although your yardstick for measuring your relationship may be different from other people's, in most cases *you* know the difference between someone who belongs in your inner circle and a casual acquaintance. Among other indications, the latter may be replaceable; our closest friends usually are not. Indeed, when 234 widows were asked to describe their social networks seven times during a period of one year, the women listed the same *number* of social partners but not the same cast of characters. Their intimate partners remained fairly constant, but people on the periphery varied from one interview to the next.[12]

It's certainly not an insult to call a person a "consequential stranger." These are vital social connections—people who help you get through the day and make life more interesting. They might not know you as well as those in your inner circle, but they might have many similar qualities. Our acquaintances, in fact, often provide some of the same things we expect from intimates: fun times, a sense of history and continuity, emotional support, spiritual lessons, and, quite possibly, aggravation. When Nelson Fellman compiled his list, for instance, he included the bully who beat him up in high school—an unpleasant but meaningful character in his life. In our neighborhoods, workplaces, and organizations, we sometimes encounter "bad" consequential strangers.

Still, most peripheral relationships are beneficial and pleasurable—among other reasons because we usually can take our toys and go home when we're no longer having fun.

Studs Terkel, Pygmalion TV, and the Strength of Weak Ties

The late Studs Terkel appreciated consequential strangers. One of the most respected chroniclers of our time, his insights and curiosity about people were honed in his mother's boardinghouse on the Near West Side of Chicago where a medley of characters held forth in the lobby, talking, arguing, and revealing aspects of their histories.[13] Terkel took it all in and, in his own words, later "earned a living as a listener," culling ideas from the lives of everyday people. In the preface to his first oral history—*Division Street: America*, a compendium of life in Chicago—he explained how he found his interviewees:

> A tip from an acquaintance. A friend of a friend telling me of a friend or non-friend. A nursed drink at a tavern where a high-rolling bartender held forth. A chance encounter with a bright-eyed boyhood companion. An indignant phone call from a radio listener. A face, vaguely familiar, on the morning bus. A stentorian voice, outside City Hall, calling out my name.[14]

Perhaps it's obvious that to create an in-depth study of how urban life affects people, Terkel had to step outside of his inner circle. But all of us do. The challenges of modern life require more than our loved ones can give. Whether it's cutting through a maze of information about a particular disease, figuring out how to best invest the funds in our 401(k), or deciding whether a hybrid car makes sense, we need what consequential strangers offer: a fresh perspective, different ideas, and connections and know-how that extend beyond our familiar.

One of the reasons for the enduring success of *Pygmalion*-inspired reality shows like the long-gone *Queer Eye for the Straight Guy* and *The Biggest Loser* is that they're based on this counterintuitive principle: Our intimates love us, but they're too close to see our true potential. Perhaps you've seen the episode of *What Not to Wear,* one of the more recent entries in the genre, where slick big-city fashion experts Stacy London and Clinton Kelly transform Glenda, a forty-five-year-old mother of two from Fort Lauderdale, Florida. She's a court reporter who has "great skills" but doesn't know how to dress for the job. Glenda won't take her mother's advice to cut her hair, but she allows a "professional" to give her a new do. She can't imitate the stylish friend who nominated her to appear on the show, but she listens carefully to the fashion gurus who teach her how to "dress her age." The pros have no preconceptions about her, but they do have the expertise—and emotional distance—to show her another way. At one point when Glenda demurs, claiming that a particular necklace "isn't me," Kelly responds, "That's okay. We like to push people past their comfort zone." They can because they're from a different world.

Think about the people closest to you. If they're around the same age, they probably read similar books and periodicals, have some of the same songs on their iPods, and tend to agree with your political views and ethics. In contrast, although you naturally share some common ground with your consequential strangers—perhaps you both own motorcycles or suffer from insomnia—these lesser relations can be of a different class, religion, ethnic group, or sexual orientation. They might work in a different field, live in another part of the country or even in another country. Accordingly, they have access to different kinds of information. This principle, known as "the strength of weak ties," was first identified by sociologist Mark Granovetter over thirty years ago. When he asked workers who had recently changed jobs whether they had found their positions through a friend, he began to notice a strange pattern: "One after another corrected me. They kept saying, 'No, he was only an acquaintance.' Then it started to come together."[15]

His interviewees' responses reminded Granovetter of a study of junior high schools. "The authors found that you could link to more people through seventh and eighth best friends than through first and second best," Granovetter recalled recently. "This was buried in a technical article that drew no general conclusions, but to me it sounded quite interesting. It brought to mind what I had learned in college chemistry about hydrogen bonding: Weak chemical bonds tie large aggregations of molecules together, thus providing the main overall cohesion."[16]

Perhaps job hunting worked the same way. Although most people believed it best to rely on close personal contacts because they would be more inclined to help, Granovetter suspected that *distant* relations might have access to information that's different from what we normally receive from family and friends. He was right. A subsequent study, conducted in Newton, Massachusetts, supported this contrarian hypothesis: The vast majority of job-helpers were closer to the stranger end of the relationship continuum: old college chums, former workmates, or onetime bosses with whom the employee still had sporadic contact. In other words, leads came from consequential strangers. "Usually such ties had not even been very strong when first forged," Granovetter reported. He also found that chance meetings or mutual friends sometimes reactivated those old contacts. "It is remarkable that people receive crucial information from individuals whose very existence they have forgotten."[17] *People who don't seem to matter.*

Who among us hasn't heard of someone who switched careers entirely at the suggestion of a casual acquaintance they just happened to run into? Take Frank Harrington, for one. In his thirteen years with a semiconductor manufacturer in California, he managed to move up the ranks but became increasingly discontented with company politics and the constant confrontations. His unhappiness led him to recall a conversation six years earlier with a "family acquaintance" who suggested he might like nursing. The idea—from someone with whom he had only a passing relationship—"resonated immediately" and set him on a different career path.[18]

The benefits of weak ties are not limited to job information. One researcher found that African-American women in an impoverished Chicago neighborhood secured opportunities for their children beyond what was available to them locally. These savvy mothers were not merely conscientious or strict (which they were), they had strong family support from sisters, aunts, and extended kin. But they were also adept at *community bridging*. They used church members and others outside their immediate environment to get their children into libraries, admitted to parochial or magnet schools, and involved in after-school programs, scouting, or other organizations that ultimately bettered their lives.[19]

Such lessons are passed on to the children. California filmmaker Aleks Muñoz, who is movie-star handsome and a "great connector," as one of his acquaintances described him, credits his parents with developing his social acumen.[20] In the blue-collar neighborhood of his San Jose childhood, some of his friends were in gangs; some of his cousins, too. But Muñoz didn't have time to get into trouble. "I was a bit overscheduled, but I liked it." The convoy of his youth included teachers, coaches, buddies on the swim team, and fellow thespians. His swim instructor taught him about photography. The teacher who led the choir introduced him to jazz musicians and history. His theater coach and English teacher gave him an appreciation of great literature. "Even while it was happening, I realized the benefits of that kind of social networking," he recalls. He still relies on weak ties. His writing mentor is an older screenwriter who swims laps at the same indoor pool. His manager is a woman from the neighborhood where he coaches a Little League team. His work in prisons, teaching filmmaking to young offenders, has led to kudos and, not so incidentally, contacts in the movie business.

Granovetter's theory also explains the success of people who deal in nefarious schemes, such as drug dealers, sex traffickers, and terrorist cells. All rely on weak ties to push their products and agenda. Lesser social connections also play a role in certain illegal immigration practices, as a recent Dutch study showed. Of people seeking asylum from war, political prosecution, or poverty who migrate to the Netherlands from Iraq, the Sudan, and the former Soviet Union, a whopping 94% are smuggled out of these countries. The migrants depend on casual acquaintances to find what they consider a "good" or "trustworthy" smuggler. For instance, one Iraqi who had made it as far as Istanbul waited three days for a particular smuggler recommended to him by the friend of his nephew. Surprisingly, these migrants rarely referred to their guides as "smugglers." Instead they describe them in ways that indicate the person is more than a stranger to them and certainly consequential. "I would not call him a smuggler," clarified one migrant. "At the border I was allowed to walk with this man for four hundred dollars and then he was so kind to hand me over to people who brought me to the nearest city for free."[21]

That weak ties can be applied to a range of activities and yield an assortment of benefits doesn't surprise Granovetter. "My main interest was weak ties' role in connecting people to circles they would otherwise not have access to or information from. But," he acknowledges, "it is also true that even acquaintances who do not serve this function for us may be our main fount of sociability and help us define our own identity as well as making the texture of daily life more pleasurable."[22]

Historically, humans may always have had some form of weak ties. From what anthropologists can tell (based on observations of modern-day foraging groups), early societies were comprised mostly of small bands of closely knit relatives who lived apart from other groups but were also socially flexible. When resources were scarce or when they needed to find mates, our distant ancestors had to establish ties *outside* their gene pool in order to survive. Members of a particular group might spend significant parts of the year visiting relatives in other bands, or they might join another group. But back then weak ties tended to develop into something more intimate, or served mostly to facilitate strong ties. In settled agrarian communities, too, subsistence farmers were primarily engaged with their family members. It was only when we began to grow more than we needed that the more modern interactions with consequential strangers—who remained at the level of weak ties—probably began. The need to trade with distant customers required more continual exchanges between people who did not know one another well. And in the past two hundred years this trend accelerated. The demands of industrial economies *require* connection to people outside the family.

Thus, weak ties have never been as numerous, or as important, as they are today. Jobs are no longer accomplished by groups of relatives. Projects can be executed by people in different companies or countries. People who work full-time—and approximately 82% of employees do—are likely to spend more time with acquaintances than with their closest relations.[23] We also rely on lesser connections to service our needs, from personal grooming to maintenance on the many gadgets we own. We even encounter consequential strangers at our own family gatherings—a spouse's uncle, a father's new partner, a sister's mother-in-law. And thanks to email, cell phones, BlackBerries, and social media software that allows us to keep track of our tribes, we are better equipped to wrangle this unprecedented array of weak ties.

The Culture of Continuous Connection: Part I

In 1997, when only 30% of Americans were online, Theodora Stites, an eleventh grader at Northfield Mount Herman in western Massachusetts, was given a laptop so that she could access the school's newly installed internal server, dubbed "SWIS" (school-wide information system).[24] As Stites and her fellow students began to make their first forays into cyberspace, Michael Schrage, a scholar at MIT, was putting the finishing touches on "The Relationships

Revolution," an essay commissioned by Merrill Lynch to educate its clients about the impact of the Internet.[25]

Around this same time, several hundred miles to the north in a suburb an hour from Toronto, Keith Hampton and his undergraduate research assistant, posing as his fiancée, drove through the entrance of a new housing development advertised as "a five-year trial of unique communication technologies, at no extra charge to residents." On the way to the sales office, they passed an old-fashioned chuck wagon bearing a large canvas banner: CANADA'S FIRST INTERACTIVE NEW HOME COMMUNITY—WELCOME PIONEERS.[26] Hampton, a twenty-four-year-old Ph.D. candidate, was there on a tip from his advisor, sociologist Barry Wellman. "The goal of my visit," recalls Hampton, "was to see how the sales staff was selling the development, what they were offering, and for me to get an idea of what I might be getting into if I decided to do my dissertation on it."[27]

Viewed together, these three unrelated stories that began in 1997—a teenager's introduction to the Internet, a scholar's analysis of the digital future, and a sociologist witnessing the birth of one of the world's first "wired" communities—shed light on the single most powerful force propelling the rise of consequential strangers: the culture of continuous connection.

Schrage saw it coming. In "The Relationship Revolution," he had the temerity to suggest that although computers had already begun to transform the way we stored, sent, and manipulated data, anyone who believed that the digital revolution was merely about information was shortsighted. It was the *emotional* component to which people would respond—the human connection. "Significant advances in technology have always altered how we perceive ourselves and our relationships," he wrote. After all, Ma Bell didn't urge us to "reach out and inform." If executives wanted to be prepared for the impact of technology in the future, Schrage warned, they had better focus on *relationships*, not merely information.

Stites and her fellow upperclassmen exemplified his theory.

Despite their teachers' advice to turn off the chat feature when studying or writing papers, the students saw their laptops primarily as instruments of connection.[28] "We emailed teachers and 'SWISed' each other," she explains. "We also had profiles and could see who was online." Stites recalls how exhilarating it was to navigate a screen filled with little chat boxes—her first taste of virtual gossip and online flirting. Occasionally she also talked to strangers on Match.com. "I remember thinking it was a really weird thing that I could talk to people—some of whom I hardly knew—on my laptop. That changed my life."[29]

Teachers fretted and fielded phone calls from parents, many of whom didn't even know what the Internet was. To adult eyes, the kids were at their computers *instead* of socializing. Research flamed their fears. One widely publicized Internet study in 1998 found higher levels of isolation and depression among early users, who seemed more devoted to their computers than their loved ones.[30] Words like "predator," "stalker," "spam," and "flaming" were taking on new meanings. Reports of faked identities also fueled the debate: a girl like Stites could pretend she was a boy—or worse. But on the other side were champions of the Internet, trumpeting its potential for limitless good. John Perry Barlow, an advocate for electronic freedom and songwriter for the Grateful Dead, likened it to "the capture of fire."[31] The utopians believed we would willingly share ideas and resources, treat each other as equals and with respect—all members of the same happily unified cybervillage.

This debate started relatively early in the Internet's history. Both camps' predictions were necessarily based on the experiences of a handful of tech-savvy pioneers. The masses hadn't yet arrived at the party.[32] At least, not until "Netville."

Netville, as Hampton and Wellman dubbed the new interactive community in Toronto, was a social scientist's dream, an unparalleled opportunity to observe the everyday impact of the Internet on a neighborhood—and on average people, not early adapters and techies. The residents, ranging in age from twenty-five to sixty-eight, were solidly middle-class, 90% were married, 61% had children living at home. Asked why they chose Netville, the majority ranked cutting-edge technology *fourth* after affordability, location, and interior design; more than 15% said that it didn't factor into their decision at all.[33] The typical house had three bedrooms and a study, and cost around $228,000 in Canadian dollars (slightly less than the average price of a new home in the area—somewhere around $355,000 in today's Canadian dollars).[34]

Around half of the Netville buyers had no interest in being part of the "smart home" experiment, providing an ideal control group. The remaining homeowners were connected to an experimental broadband service that was *three hundred times* faster than dial-up. The wired residents had uninterrupted access to NET-L, the neighborhood email list. A computer/desktop videophone enabled them to contact a local network of health care practitioners, tap into an online jukebox with more than a thousand CD titles, and "borrow" from a library of educational and entertainment CD-ROMs. They also had instant access to weather reports, home shopping, news, and automated banking. (If this sounds like everything we routinely do with computers and iPods today, remember that this was the late nineties.)

For two years Hampton lived and worked out of a basement apartment he rented from a Netville resident. Eighty-eight percent of neighbors were employed full-time, many as teachers, social workers, police officers, and middle managers in big corporations. In the process of gathering data for his dissertation, he became one of Netville's own. He walked the streets, made acquaintances, was invited to barbecues, and attended neighborhood meetings. The experience, as his mentor Barry Wellman had predicted, was "a window into the future."

Although only 8% had bought in *because* of the high-tech amenities, those who opted for a smart home quickly adapted. During a province-wide teachers' strike, parents emailed each other to make playdates. Instead of posting flyers when a pet disappeared, they put the word out electronically. Following a series of break-ins, they went online to alert their neighbors to keep an eye out for suspicious lurkers.[35] And when they ran into each other on the streets, instead of discussing "the weather," as casual acquaintances tend to do, the wired residents had a far more fascinating topic in common: their high-tech toys.

The Culture of Continuous Connection: Part II

Fast-forward to the early years of the twenty-first century. The Internet (a term used here to include all manner of digital and wireless technologies) was moving more rapidly than any other technological innovation in the history of humankind. Even as the dot-com bubble exploded and fortunes were lost, Internet usage had skyrocketed—in part because almost everyone who had gotten a taste of the new medium saw its potential for connection. And Schrage was right: Technology had transformed our relationships. (Think of your own life at the time. Compared to five years earlier, how many people did *you* know who had email? And how often were you now checking your virtual in-box or searching the web?)

Theodora Stites was in college. Her computer was on all day and all night. Google and Napster dominated her freshman year, and Friendster reigned in her sophomore year. Unlike earlier Internet "communities" which brought like-minded strangers together, these new sites enabled users to connect with *people they knew*—and who their friends knew. Stites explains, "For the most part, the connections were first made in person. I'd meet someone once or twice at a party and give them my email address. I met one guy on a plane and we stayed in touch for years. Through email, you build up knowing what's going on in that person's life."

This wasn't merely a college phenomenon. The same thing was happening among the wired residents of Netville. For all the high-tech gadgetry available to them, they favored email, the applications that allowed them to reach out and touch friends from their old communities as well as their new neighbors. They were living what Wellman and Hampton termed "glocalized" lives, carrying on "conversations" regardless of whether the person was around the corner or a thousand miles away.[36]

Decades earlier, it was shown that only a small percentage of people's social ties typically involved someone next door or down the block.[37] Netville was an exception to this rule, because technology made it easier for residents to connect. Emailing broke the ice—neighbors already knew something about each other when they met on the street. The reverse was true as well: casual conversations often led to follow-up emails and continued interactions. As a result, wired residents recognized *three times as many* of their neighbors as their "unwired" peers. They also talked to their neighbors twice as often, and visited 50% more of them.[38]

Another curious outcome, not seen in similar middle-class housing developments in the area, was that the wired Netville neighbors didn't retreat to the privacy of their spacious rear patios. Instead they dragged out plastic chairs and park benches, creating makeshift porch settings. Sitting in *front* of their houses, they could keep an eye on their children and chat with passersby.[39] So much for the notion that technology alienates.

The Internet not only promoted good neighboring, it also made it easier to take collective action (a strength we would see applied in the coming decade to various political causes). For example, Netville experienced the kind of problems that crop up in all new developments—roads weren't paved in a timely manner, grass wasn't planted on schedule, pipes froze, air conditioners broke down. It's typical for a few "rabble-rousers" to pressure a developer to remedy such problems by putting up flyers or going door-to-door to mobilize their neighbors. But the developer told Hampton that in his experience only around 20% of residents join such a crusade. In Netville, more than 50% did.

"In some cases," Hampton recalls, "one person would literally send hundreds of emails, one for each 'defect' in their house—plaster missing on a wall, nail pops, and so on. Emailing led to conversations on the street, block parties, meetings, dinners, as well as phone calls and faxes to the developer. He told me that he felt very overwhelmed by the unexpected volume of communication." Such was the strength of weak ties abetted by technology. The developer vowed that he would never build another "smart" community.[40]

He didn't have to. A few short years later, most of us would be living in Netvilles of our own making and with more weak ties than our grandparents could have imagined.

Michael Schrage's tomorrow has arrived. We the users, along with—and because of—the entrepreneurs who continue to dream up new sites and software, use the Internet as an instrument of connection, not merely information. The proliferation of online communities and the growing popularity of social networking sites speak volumes about our need to connect to a variety of people, not just our loved ones. Far from squelching our social instincts, digital technology has forever changed how we "do" relationships *and* increased our aptitude, and hunger, for connection. Like the telephone, the Internet has become but another, albeit much more quickly diffused, mode of connection. We blog, we "IM," we text, we Skype, we send winks and pokes. We have our private conversation in public. If, as many social scientists agree, everyday interactions are vital to making and sustaining our connections, we now have a host of "relational technologies" that offer, for better or worse, what researchers call "perpetual contact." We're "in touch" 24/7.[41] We talk to each other in transit, when we're at the airport or on the train, or in whatever down moments we feel bored.

Seeing Theodora Stites in 2007, at home on her couch, clicking away on her laptop—a nightly ritual—brings to mind a question Schrage asked executives only a decade earlier: "What happens when everybody in the company has their own homepage?"[42] Stites has several—on MySpace, Facebook, Twitter, Cyworld ("big in

Asia"), to name a few. "I need to belong to all of them because each site enables me to connect to people with different levels of social intimacy." Stites, now twenty-five and living in Williamsburg, a hip gentrified section of Brooklyn, doesn't look like the kind of young woman who would have trouble finding a date on a Saturday night, nor is her social life limited to relationships in cyberspace. She merely uses technology to manage her web of connections. "A girl I know from college is friends with my friend from college's best friend from Minnesota. They met at camp in seventh grade. The boyfriend of my friend from work is friends with one of my friends from high school. I note the connections and remind myself to IM them later."[43]

Stites doesn't think about the Internet any more than she thinks about the air she breathes. At this writing, she is an account planner at an advertising agency where she works and researches in "the digital sphere." Every now and then her cell phone rings, alerting her to a text message from Dodgeball.com, a service that lets its members know that a "friend," "friend of a friend," or "crush" is within a ten-block radius, thus bringing their virtual social life into the real world, which, despite early fears, is apparently the case for most of us.[44] She also has an account with Twitter, a perpetual news feed, summarized in 140 characters or less, of the various players in her life. *Suzy's at the dentist. Lance tried a new restaurant. Steve finally chose Costa Rica over the Bahamas.* Not surprisingly, the concept of consequential strangers resonates with Stites: "Everyone I meet, everyone I sit next to. Sam from the subway. It's very easy to get someone's information and bring them into my network."

But what of the rest of us? We may not all be in Stites's league, but 77% of adults in the United States use the Internet—93% of them from home, 52% from work.[45] Still, some worry that the so-called "digital divide" has left poor, uneducated, and older Americans on the have-not side of the Internet fence. At the same time, new evidence suggests that not only are these groups gaining access, they also can reap great benefits. In 2004, i-neighbors.org was launched, allowing anyone in the United States or Canada to create a virtual neighborhood association with services similar to those introduced in Netville. The site was part of a study conducted by Keith Hampton to see whether the Internet would create new opportunities for social and community action. Over 6,000 neighborhoods signed up. Predictably, the majority were exclusively middle-class and suburban. But a surprising 28% were in "truly disadvantaged" areas with a high degree of poverty, unemployment, and residential instability—factors that typically thwart citizens' ability to mobilize. As in Netville, their digital connections helped residents in these marginal neighborhoods get acquainted and coalesce around mutual concerns. This, in turn, put them in a better position to take collective action.[46]

"Anything But Socially Isolated"

The bottom line in terms of consequential strangers is that most of us are constantly interacting with *someone*, and potential new relationships are everywhere, including cyberspace. But how does the culture of continual connection mesh with recent headlines declaring that Americans are more isolated than ever? A few summers ago, every newspaper, TV, and radio station—here and abroad—reported the conclusion of a 2006 study indicating that our inner circles had shrunk. Compared to 1985, when the average number of confidants was three, today we have only two people—typically, family members—in whom we can confide, and some have no one at all.[47]

The twin themes of alienation and isolation are trotted out every few decades, it seems, as each new generation ponders how large-scale social change affects ties with relatives, friends, neighbors, and workmates. To be sure, we are slogging through contradictory times, suspicious of government and politicians but willing to entrust our credit cards and our deepest feelings to disembodied others.[48] But as Mark Twain might have put it, reports of the death of sociability are much exaggerated.

It's true that adults are having fewer children, and they're living alone or in smaller groups—singles now outnumber married people. Well-paid workers are actually putting in longer hours—and many others *feel* like they are, due to harried home lives, long commutes, and the fact that work follows them home.[49] Either way, we have less time to nurture our close relationships. Whether we actually *have* fewer people to turn to, however, depends on how you define a person's "network" and how you frame your question.

That 2006 study assigned a very narrow meaning to the phrase "core confidants" and asked *a single question:* "Looking back over the last six months, who are the people with whom you discussed matters important to you?" Even the sociologists who conducted the study acknowledge that the question itself is open to interpretation. To some people, the war in Iraq is an "important matter," to others, a languid sex life is.[50] If, instead, you ask about "people you talk to often or get substantial help from," and also include slightly less intimate relationships, you get entirely different results. A Pew Internet & American Life Project survey in 2004 found that we have *fifteen* of these more broadly defined relationships, and sixteen lesser, but still "somewhat close," ties.[51] In the view of Ann Hulbert, one of the few journalists to look at other data and present a more nuanced analysis of the 2006 study, "the [Pew] findings left Americans looking anything but socially isolated."[52]

But what about consequential strangers—our social contacts who are situated on the fringe of those close and somewhat close ties? In 2000, Harvard political scientist Robert Putnam concluded that there, too, we are lacking. Since the sixties, he argued in *Bowling Alone*, fewer of us have joined unions, fraternal societies, or PTAs. Such organizations provide us with acquaintances and, therefore, "social capital"—connections that lead to opportunities and resources, and, more germane to the point of his book, promote civic involvement. His critics have rightfully noted that Putnam focused on traditional associations whose memberships are now out of favor with younger generations. And although he acknowledged that Baby Boomers and Gen Xers seem to prefer small, less structured groups—in real life and online—he dismissed them because they promote self-centeredness rather than a desire to serve the greater public good.[53]

Arguably, we are a society in flux, having lost the continuity provided by institutions. But that doesn't mean that *all* of our social ties are fraying. Informal or ad hoc groups, as well as cliques and circles, whatever their raison d'être, are social venues that *we choose*—we float in and out of them as our schedules and moods allow; and in them, we meet a multitude of consequential strangers. Small groups, says Princeton sociologist Robert Wuthnow, "provide a kind of social interaction that busy, rootless people can grasp without making significant adjustment in their lifestyle." A Gallup survey commissioned by Wuthnow in the early nineties found that at one time or another 40% of us have been members of small groups in at least one of the three broad categories: religious (Bible study groups, adult Sunday school classes), self-help (AA and its offshoots, disease-focused groups), and activity-oriented (sports, hobbies, and other interests).[54] The years haven't change his view: "Our social relationships have not so much declined as taken on new forms."[55]

Some of our modern social arrangements, and the relationships we develop, can't be pigeonholed into the familiar categories we've relied on in the past.[56] For example, how do you compare a Knights of Columbus meeting with the monthly in-person "forums" sponsored by the Entrepreneurs' Organization, a 6,600-member international community of business owners? The participants, whose average age is thirty-nine, shut off their cell phones for three hours and just listen to each other. They might talk about the difficulty of having to fire an employee or the burden of having to always be in charge—responsibilities that somehow seem less onerous when shared.[57]

For that matter, how do you classify the Heartbeat Salsa Group in Hartford, Connecticut, a diverse group of Latin dance lovers who met through a website—Meetup.com—in 2006? At their weekly "styling" class, participants learn "body rolls, leg sweeps, hand flicks, hip and shoulder rotations, arm movements, and of course, 'the booty.'"[58] Or the 501st Legion, an organization of Star Wars "costume enthusiasts," also known as "Vader's Fist"? They convene in full space-villain regalia for their meetings and parades but also make appearances at charity events.[59] And what about the annual One-Armed Dove Hunt that draws amputees from all over the country who keep in touch with each other via email throughout the year? The event, according to thirty-six-year-old Doug Davis, whom you'll meet in Chapter 3, "really broadens my horizons."[60]

These are all examples of modern situations in which consequential stranger relationships develop and flourish. Calvin Morrill and his colleagues deemed these typically overlooked "ties that do not fit traditional definitions" so important that they devoted an entire book to studies of relationships that develop in public. The sociologists who contributed to the anthology covered venues as diverse as a strip joint, a singles dance, a right-wing discussion group, and a "floating community" of people who sit in the bleachers during the amateur softball season. They are certainly not the kinds of organizations Robert Putnam had in mind, but considering the benefits reaped by the participants, the editors concluded that "personal relationships in public may offer opportunities for creating niches of social capital that have largely been overlooked and are somewhat unexpected."[61]

We are not living the Greatest Generation's lifestyle. We don't work for one company; we don't limit ourselves to one career, one religion, nor even one family. Most of us traffic in a variety of worlds—family, work, organizations, volunteer groups, spiritual gatherings, web communities—and in each realm, interact with a different assortment of people. Traveling through life, each of us amasses an assemblage of relationships that meet our needs and expand our horizons. We are living in the age of "networked individualism," a term coined by Barry Wellman to describe a significant social transformation that began decades ago but has been accelerated by digital technologies: *Where we were once connected through institutions, we are now linked as individuals.*

Social observers tend to draw a sharp distinction between the good old days and the last several decades. It is widely accepted, for example, that most people were once part of "dense" networks in which everyone knew each other. The pharmacist courted your aunt; the mayor grew up with your father; the members of your club drank at the same bar. Your loved ones and acquaintances were pretty much predetermined by who your parents were, where you lived and worked, and whatever traditional organizations you joined. While there is some truth to this characterization, Mark Granovetter questions whether the contrast is actually so dramatic between the "good old days" and now: "It's not clear that the old world ever quite existed anywhere, except in some community studies." He explains that sociologists who studied ethnic enclaves, for example, were out to make a case against urban renewal which was wiping out low-income neighborhoods in favor of middle-class housing. So they tended to focus narrowly on their subjects, painting them all with the same brush, without "seeing the importance of consequential strangers."[62]

Whatever the extent of these differences, it is clear that network density has declined and that most of us are now part of loose-knit webs of people who don't know each other.[63] We are not necessarily interested in joining an organization of preformed social ties as we are of mobilizing our own set of connections. Instead of being one of many who comprise the whole—say, in a family or a company—each of us is in charge of our own social convoy, an unbounded collection of predominantly consequential stranger relationships. Our "communities" and connections are no longer geographically determined, nor have they declined. They have just spread out, and we hold them in our minds.

2

The View from Above

> My network [is] comprised of smart alecks, dorks, hipsters, divas, preachers, itinerant musicians, flatulent geniuses, moms who loathe soccer, nice boys with hopeless goatees, a couple ladies in wigs, a red-haired grandma who likes ice cream and men who'll play piano for her, several people with way too many dogs, one nymphet who won't stop saying "hella," at least nine people called "Matt," one guy who's terrified I'm talking about him right now, the old man at the Chinese restaurant who finally smiled back at me after six years. . . . I like the idea of what Kurt Vonnegut, Jr. has called a "karass"—a group of people who, without even realizing it, are working together to do God's will. . . . Those are the connections you earn.
>
> —*Merlin Mann, founder and editor of 43Folders.com*

Vonnegut's Prophecy

"If you find your life tangled up with somebody else's life for no very logical reasons, that person may be a member of your *karass*," says the narrator of *Cat's Cradle*, Kurt Vonnegut's 1963 cult classic. Like Vonnegut himself, the narrator is a writer from Indiana. He travels to a remote Caribbean island with his fellow Hoosiers in a more formal type of grouping—a "granfalloon." Other than being from Indiana, the narrator has nothing in common with them. His real connections are formed in a "karass," which is "as free-form as an amoeba" and "ignores national, institutional, occupational, familiar, and class boundaries."[1]

That scenario was pure fiction, of course. But Vonnegut got it right. Four decades later, a qualitative change in our social landscape mirrors his vision. The "community" that means the most is *not* a traditional bounded social grouping, like Daughters of the American Revolution or the General Electric company. Rather, it is a loose assemblage of characters we collect from various realms of life and pull into our personal sphere. In the age of networked individualism, we each form our own karass, an aggregate force that both punctuates life *and* causes its twists and turns.

Social network analysts—scientists who map and measure the patterns and flows of relationships—would agree. Although individual traits such as personality or educational attainment affect how you fare in life, that's only part of the story. We might like to think of ourselves as independent agents, marching through life to our own iPod soundtrack, but our *relationships* propel us as well. To understand how, we need to widen the spotlight and shine it on an entity bigger than a single self: the individual community in which you are the focal point. It's the view from the *center* of the karass, the vantage point of every Tom, Dick, or Harriet.[2]

The problem is, networks are like traffic jams.[3] You can easily see the cars that surround you—your intimates. However, it takes a helicopter to view your entire entourage—your "social convoy."[4] So take a moment and mentally position yourself *above* the road. You can see yourself motoring along the highway of life, accompanied by your loved ones, your closest friends, and the various acquaintances you pick up along the way. A handful of people travel alongside you for miles and miles, perhaps for the whole journey. The peripheral people, neither family nor close friends—your consequential strangers—are often there for a particular segment of the trip and tend to serve *specific* needs. They might help you through rough passages, lead you to important resources such as information or others who can help, or provide comic relief when it's most needed. Because your convoy changes as you change, some travelers drop back for a while or fall so far behind that you barely see them in your rearview mirror. Some members of your convoy, such as coworkers or fellow volunteers, also know *each other.* They form a distinct "cluster"—a group within your convoy. Imagine them riding together in a minivan.

Our convoys represent our history and our potential. Seeing our lives from this aerial view allows us to better understand the situations we're in, the decisions we make, the way we solve problems. How we are linked to others—what we get, give, and learn in each relationship—helps explain why some of us have access to better information and new ideas and why we don't flounder in the face of an unexpected circumstance or when a new stage of life suddenly forces us to take a different road. The view from above can also illuminate our own spheres of influence; we travel in other people's convoys as well.

In short, life is as much a function of *whom you associate with* as who you are, and the ability to bring people into your convoy when you need them is a key coping mechanism in a complex world. This perspective, as shown in the examples that follow, can be applied to the challenges individuals face or to the workings of institutions, organizations, and even countries.[5]

A Lady Who Launches

The convoy approach was popularized by psychologist Toni Antonucci, an expert on lifespan development who thought it an apt metaphor for the array of relationships each individual possesses and, in varying degrees, holds on to throughout life. In grad school, Antonucci wrote her dissertation on "attachment" theory, which stresses the importance of early caregivers in developing trust. Having a secure "attachment figure" encourages a baby to crawl away from the safety of that person's side toward a shiny object across the room. At the time, Antonucci recalls, attachment was applied almost exclusively to mother-child relationships. Why couldn't it be extended to adulthood? Antonucci reasoned that the social convoy does the same thing for adults, giving them "a secure base" that allows them to explore and to take risks.[6]

To understand how this works, meet an eclectic and very sociable New Yorker, Karla Lightfoot, an entrepreneur in her early forties who never spends two days in a row doing the same thing or seeing the same people. In her spare time, she teaches yoga, takes pole-dancing classes, and socializes with a wide assortment of consequential strangers. Attractive and infectiously upbeat, she exudes a grounded optimism about life. She also chats with just about anyone who crosses her path. There's the produce guy at Whole Foods, the cashiers, and especially her doormen. She knows a little about each of them, their families, and what's going on in their lives. "There's more than just this exchange of my walking out of my building every day. I feel like we're all connected, and the more that we can tap into that, the more connected we become."[7]

Among her current business projects, Lightfoot leads a series of "incubator" workshops for Ladies Who Launch (LWL), an organization that helps women start and grow businesses. "The workshop is designed to help you expand and clarify your vision and boost your creativity," she explains, "but we also talk about seizing opportunities that are already in front of you. I guess we're teaching them to keep their eyes and ears open to consequential strangers."

That's exactly what Lightfoot does in her own life. Once a client herself, she enrolled in the incubator a few years ago to explore what she might do with "compassion couture," two words that had come to her one morning while meditating. The LWL brainstorming sessions and the support of other women over the course of four weeks helped her turn the phrase into a business: an online site that offers T-shirts emblazoned with faux-jewel aphorisms such as "Be present" and "Choose peace." Other profitable connections flowed from the subsequent monthly networking meetings where she could schmooze with other graduates of the program. One steered her to a boutique that placed a $14,000 order for her T-shirts. Another, the owner of a creative services company, hired Lightfoot to handle new business development.

Coming full circle and now working several hours a week as an LWL "facilitator," Lightfoot continues to broaden her convoy. "At every course I teach, I meet at least two or three new people and end up furthering the relationship. It's about sharing whatever you have and people being able to ask for what they need." She has since landed two other freelance jobs.

It wasn't always this way. Her early career path was far more traditional. "After college, everyone I knew was going to law or med school, business school, or getting into investment banking." Those were the respectable choices for a young woman who had grown up in a "relatively affluent" household and attended private schools in Chicago. Her mother was a school principal, and her father a dentist. Although she initially tried to defy convention by taking a low-paying job in fashion, she later moved on to the hospitality and sales industries but never felt creatively fulfilled in corporate America. "I kept opting for the stability of an organization. It never dawned on me that *I* could develop something on my own."

That lightbulb finally went off in 2001 when her book *The BAP Handbook: The Official Guide to the Black American Princess* came out. The project had actually started as a joke several years earlier. Lightfoot and Ginger Wilson, a Chicago attorney and an old friend, were having a good laugh about how often acquaintances asked them, "So how did you end up going to Wellesley?" or "How did you learn to ski?" Less insulted than amused by the fact that so many whites had apparently never met upper-middle-class African-Americans (or at least ones who skied), Wilson suggested that they write a book about it—one that would poke fun at themselves in the spirit of *The Official Preppy Handbook* but also answer such questions once and for all. "We wanted people to understand how we grew up," says Lightfoot, "without the book being a political statement."

Lightfoot culled two additional coauthors from her convoy. Both were consequential strangers—one a woman she had met in a Princeton LSAT review class, the other someone she knew from high school. Coincidentally, as Lightfoot and Wilson were wondering who might publish the finished manuscript, they received a call from one of Oprah Winfrey's producers asking them to share their memories of an old friend, Ennis Cosby (Bill's son), whose short life and senseless murder was the topic of an upcoming show. Backstage, they found a few minutes to talk to the powerful TV star about their book. Sufficiently impressed, she suggested that they contact her publisher. When the book came out, the ten-city publicity tour plunged Lightfoot into an unfamiliar but appealing world: "Meeting all those journalists who freelanced for a living—something that had never occurred to me—I thought, I could do *that*."

Today she says without a hint of arrogance, "I'm blazing the trail for how a lot of people want to live their lives." She describes herself as an "entrepreneurial matchmaker." A network analyst would call her a "bridge"—someone who spans otherwise unconnected people or groups and can "broker" a new tie.[8] Right now she's planning a business venture with one of her fellow pole dancers. She also intends to introduce four consequential strangers in her convoy who've never met each other: Two of the women import wines, one hosts wine and cheese pairings, and another is writing a wine blog. Lightfoot will start by sending each one a "you-four-should-meet" email. Perhaps a new business opportunity will come of this, perhaps not. Either way, Lightfoot enjoys the process. "Being able to understand and tap into my convoy in a way that supports everyone is the most fulfilling thing I do."

As temperament goes, you might think of Karla Lightfoot as an extrovert—an acquaintanceship artist. You might also observe that she is a young woman born with advantages that give her an edge. Or that she's spiritually in the right place, openhearted and curious about people. And each of those descriptions of Karla the *individual* would be true. But there's also Karla the *social being*. Her success and satisfaction with her life are not merely by-products of personality or privilege; they also derive from her connectedness. As a child, she certainly had the benefit of a "secure base," as Toni Antonucci would put it, but she has been building on it ever since.

Deconstructing the Convoy

Most of us are inherently aware of our convoys. We may not use the term, but we know that our "networks" or "webs of relationships" are important. We also display artifacts of connection. For example, the Rolodex, arguably obsolete in the digital age, still appears on many executives' desks. It is a visual "reminder," says Joel Podolny, dean of the Yale School of Management, "to themselves and an announcement to others about who they are and what they have achieved."[9] Even out-of-date names are cherished; each one represents a bit of history, evidence of the route one's convoy has traveled. Likewise, *Fortune* columnist "Stanley Bing," the alter ego of CBS executive Gil Schwartz, found himself unable to delete contacts from his BlackBerry. Instead of erasing old girlfriends, favorite watering holes, or the name of a man who once sold him a car, he paused "to haul back the sights, the sounds, the stomach acid each [entry] engendered."[10] This natural inclination to take stock socially is undoubtedly one of the reasons so many millions of us have become members of social networking sites such as Facebook: they act as inventories of our social connections, especially our weak ties.

Without realizing it, most of us practice rudimentary social network analysis on our own, albeit without the benefit of the complex computations and algorithms scientists use (and which are beyond the scope of this book). We list all but the most peripheral members of our convoys when we're contemplating a milestone event, like a fiftieth birthday or a retirement party. And when we give gifts, we—unconsciously or perhaps purposefully—order our relationships. We ask ourselves, who gets the well-thought-out and often more expensive gifts? Who gets cash? Who gets socks or scarves or one of those ten-dollar impulse-buy gadgets stores stock around the holidays?

Perhaps we're all social scientists at heart. Karla Lightfoot, for one, describes her convoy the way network analysts might: "I have a group of a dozen or more women who are friends—but only two or three are really close. It's kind of like a series of circles. There are people I've grown up with, people I went to school with, and they're in the inner circles; then it starts to expand to my acquaintances." Her sister and parents are also in the inner circles, while various members of her extended family are farther from center.

It's the same for most of us. When pressed, we can describe our own social "circles" and also those in which we travel. The phrase "social circle" was first used in the mid 1920s by Georg Simmel, a sophisticated and well-connected man himself, according to one of many scholars who has since studied the famed sociologist's work.[11] Simmel used the term to describe how individuals coped with mass society, especially in large cities where they didn't necessarily know their neighbors nor could they count on being known. Circles are loose-knit and based on free choice, not geography. Unlike formal groups, they have no boundaries; and the connections are by virtue of similar interests or pursuits. In modern societies, people typically belong to more than one circle. The importance of circles, in Simmel's view, was that they allowed us to pursue our own interests but also to be "in association" with others.[12]

It's no accident then that Toni Antonucci uses the image of a circle. She gives participants a bull's-eye drawing with "you" in the center. In the innermost circle, you are asked to place "one person or persons that you feel so close to that it's hard to imagine life without them." In the second, you put "people to whom you may not feel quite that close but who are still very important to you." And in the third, "people whom you haven't already mentioned but who are close enough and important enough in your life that they should be placed in your personal network." Because Antonucci was concerned primarily with intimate relationships, she used only three concentric circles in her own studies, which she first launched in the 1980s. She acknowledges, however, that peripheral ties—fourth-circle relationships—also help adults face challenges and try new ventures.[13] (More recently, researchers have used as many as five circles to look at people's personal networks.)[14]

It's a challenging, eye-opening—and possibly time-consuming—experience to analyze your entire social convoy. Subjects in these studies often want to place names on the lines *between*, rather than in, a particular circle. But, as one researcher put it, "People are really jazzed about seeing their networks laid out."[15] We suspect that's because the aerial view enables you to see that you're not a lone driver on the road. Everyone who has been instrumental—or detrimental—at various points in your life is right there. You see which connections have lasted, which have dropped by the wayside. And it becomes clear that your life is not merely a string of events; it is a cavalcade of *people.*

"People are better or worse equipped for relationships because of their social histories," Antonucci stresses. Members of your convoy can protect you and help you find your way, even when your most significant relationships are floundering. "We know that having a lousy relationship with a spouse trumps everything, but some people are able to partially offset that with other relationships."

Although the experts admit that there is still a great deal to learn about how personal convoys work, it is clear that some are more protective than others. Whether or not your convoy provides emotional sustenance and makes your life happy, secure, and more interesting depends on a complex interplay of factors. *Size*, for one. If you're like the thousands of people in the United States, Japan, Germany, and France who have participated in convoy studies over the last three decades, you'll put one to five people in the innermost circle and include anywhere from ten to thirty people in the first three. Occasionally a consequential stranger like your hairdresser might end up in the third circle as well. And if you add a fourth circle to include all your peripheral relationships, you'll end up with anywhere from twenty to over five thousand names in all.[16]

Size matters, but it isn't everything, among other reasons because people have different social needs. A convoy of ten or fifteen, including consequential strangers, might be more than enough for one person, a cause of depression and loneliness for another. Equally important is the *composition* of your convoy and the *types* of relationships in it. Is your convoy mostly relatives, mostly friends, or mostly consequential strangers, or some sort of mix? Having loving relatives and close friends to call on is great, but even better if you have acquaintances as well from all walks of life. Thus, while a network of predominantly strong ties usually trumps a bevy of weak ties, the best is a constellation that combines the two.[17] In short, a diverse, or "integrated" convoy gives you more options.

For example, when Karla Lightfoot needs support, information, or an "in," she can look to relations that currently reflect her various spheres of involvement, but she can also call on her old school chums or dredge up contacts from her past. Because this rich font of resources is available to her through her convoy, she is far less concerned with "security" these days and more willing to venture into the unknown. "For me, it's about having that sense of community. Whenever I need anything, and it's not something I can get from my older sister or parents, then I know I have this whole network of people who are willing to help me in business or with something very personal."

The people in your convoy also play particular *roles*, meet certain needs, and, not so incidentally, bring out different sides of you (more on that in Chapter 3). Therefore, another way of thinking about your convoy is to ask yourself how you get what you need: From whom would you borrow money? Discuss a problem with? Ask for advice about your career? Act silly with? Whom do you call (or contact online) when you feel like losing yourself in a game of Scrabble? Answers to such questions shed light on where you get various types of support (see Appendix I). Most of us now turn to a variety of people to meet specific needs—in much the same way that we shop at boutiques rather than at general stores.[18] And that, experts say, is a good thing, because we have a greater reservoir of specific resources to draw from.

Finally, there is the matter of *density*. What percentage of people who know you also know each other? Although most people's convoys nowadays are loose-knit, they also contain dense clusters—the groups in the minivans. The densest clusters are typically comprised of family members. However, a circle of close friends who have age, lifestyle, and values in common also can be very tight-knit. When writer Ethan Watters described the interconnectedness of his "urban tribe"—compatriots he'd collected during his twenties and early thirties—he was actually talking about its density:

> Certainly, each of these people had a relationship with me, but they all had distinct relationships with each other. There was a web of love affairs, friendships, rivalries, work partnerships, and shared homes. Connect any two of those twenty-five people and you would find a history of activities and hundreds of hours of conversation that held shared secrets, gossip, and all manner of insight about the world. Those relationships created an intricate web of lives that added up to more than the sum of the friendships.[19]

The *bonding* ties that are characteristic of such a dense cluster can be invaluable in terms of trust and emotional support, but they can limit you as well. Social norms are more stringently enforced in close-knit groups. Explicitly or not, there are rules about how to behave and who belongs. Watters, for example, found that even among his group of otherwise freewheeling friends it was hard to bring in an outsider. At one point he felt he had to choose between a new girlfriend and the members of his tribe. It was like bringing a fiancée to an intimate family gathering for the first time—

everyone was suspicious and territorial. Such is the price you pay for being part of an in group.

In contrast, consequential stranger relationships provide us with more expansive *bridging* ties. They may not be as warm and fuzzy, but they tend to expand your horizons because they are linked to other groups. Even in a close-knit urban tribe, Watters observed, friends of friends skirt the periphery. They're the weak ties who connect the tribe to other people and groups, allowing for an exchange of information and ideas that wouldn't be possible if the group had no outside contacts. The best of both worlds, then, is a loose-knit network that *contains* dense clusters. It enables you to feel the security of being an insider while having the flexibility to move between your various social circles.[20]

Naturally, your convoy is shaped as well by who you are—age, gender, personality—and also by your situation and locale. Women and outgoing people tend to have larger networks. Singles, those without children or nearby relatives, and people with higher education and income tend to have more "free-floating" relationships.[21] And if you have multiple interests or a job that necessitates social contact—say, in sales—you're also more likely to have an integrated convoy, containing consequential strangers from the various arenas in which you work, play, and pray. However, even people whose lives are far less complex can amass a supportive and diverse convoy over time. For example, twice-married Dottie Mayhew, a retired waitress in her late fifties, is soft-spoken, a little on the shy side, doesn't use a computer, and doesn't like big changes, which is probably one reason she enjoys life in tiny Medaryville, Indiana, population 549. And yet she maintains contacts that date back to her first marriage and former job, interacts with various people in her community, and has consequential strangers in her convoy whom she met through her husband and three daughters.

Dottie Mayhew never gave much thought to her convoy until the day her daughter Ashley had her second seizure. A few weeks earlier, the sixteen-year-old had collapsed and was rushed to the hospital. She was on a ventilator for three days and underwent a series of tests, but doctors couldn't find anything wrong. "They said that sometimes teenagers have onetime seizures and never have them again," recalls Mayhew. The doctors were wrong and so were the drugs they prescribed. A few weeks later, when her daughter blacked out again, Mayhew reached for the phone and called Joan Seager, Ashley's gym teacher and lifesaving instructor. Mayhew was privy to few details about Seager's personal life: "We didn't go out to dinner together. I didn't know any of her family." But that didn't matter. "I knew that Joan was trained, and that she only lived a mile away. She came over right away and sat on Ashley's bed with her. She took her hand and rubbed her forehead."

Ashley's seizures became progressively worse and, despite multiple hospitalizations and treatments, the attacks persisted. "Joan always came right over," says Mayhew, who over the next five months lost count of Ashley's sudden and mysterious blackouts. Each time, she feared the worst, and finally it happened. One day, as yet another seizure took hold of her, Ashley began to turn blue. She had stopped breathing. Instead of dialing 911, Mayhew again called Joan Seager. She knew the gym teacher could get there faster than an ambulance from the nearest hospital, which was in Winamac, twenty-five minutes away. Two of Ashley's classmates, who knew of her condition and had also taken Seager's lifesaving course, heard the distress call over the police radio. By the time they arrived, Seager was already doing rescue breathing. The boys pitched in, and together, the three consequential strangers saved Ashley's life.[22]

The Horizon Factor

Except for unbreachable rifts such as divorce, our inner circles tend to be stable, whereas fourth-circle relations are more transient—and expendable. We often lose sets of acquaintances when we switch jobs, become parents, end a relationship, go back to school, or make other major life transitions. What is perhaps less intuitive is that *time* itself—our subjective sense of how much of it we have—is also a key factor in our social choices.

Forty-six-year-old Raymond Chau runs a creative department for an ad agency. Born and educated in Hong Kong, he still lives there with his American partner of twenty years. Chau's innermost circles are reserved for his partner, family members, and a few close friends. But like many in Hong Kong, his work responsibilities account for the majority of his waking hours. Accordingly, the bulk of his social convoy consists of consequential strangers: coworkers as well as clients and various other colleagues in the ad business who "just pass through" his life.[23] A few years ago, though, Chau's focus switched almost entirely to his inner circle. To understand why, you have to know a little about Hong Kong and its recent history.

In the thirteen years preceding July 1, 1997—the date of the proposed "handover" that would end 156 years of British rule in Hong Kong—everyone wondered whether the Chinese government would clamp down on the laissez-faire monetary policies that had caused the city to thrive and its residents to prosper. The Tiananmen Square massacre in 1989 further heightened the level of anxiety. Personal freedom was also on the line. "You identified with the Chinese because you're part of China," Chau explains, "but when you saw them shooting their own people, you wondered what Communist rule would mean." Not surprisingly, Hong Kong lost one twelfth of its population during this period of uncertainty. Chau never considered leaving: "My close circle, people I care about most, stayed with me, so I wasn't too worried."

As feared, the city plunged into economic chaos immediately after the handover, largely a result of financial instability that started in Thailand and affected most Asian countries. The handover only complicated matters. Property values went into a dramatic free fall.[24] Unemployment soared, Chau recalls, and anyone who didn't emigrate was desperate to hold on to his job. Hong Kong had long been a city of workaholics. "A lot of people here have two meals [a day] with their colleagues," says Chau. "Then they go home and come back again to work. My field—advertising—is particularly bad, but so is accounting, banking. Even doctors work nine- or ten-hour days." And it's not just the striving class. Chau's brother, a driver, works six days a week. The post-handover uncertainty only made Hong Kong more competitive. "A lot of it was about staying later than the boss," recalls Chau. "Gradually, that became a habit for everyone."

In 2003, just as the economy was beginning to right itself, Hong Kong faced yet another crisis: the SARS epidemic. "It was far worse than the handover," recalls Chau. "Hong Kong almost came to a stop. You didn't know who might be a carrier since they had no idea how it was transmitted." Luckily, Chau was between jobs at the height of the epidemic and rarely had to leave his house. When he did, he refrained from using public transportation. Acquaintances were no longer on his radar. He kept in touch only with his family and a few close friends by phone or email. On Saturdays, he "joined" his father via video webcam. "It was like during a war."

Research explains Raymond Chau's social choices during the SARS epidemic: When personal circumstances like aging or illness, or a situation outside our control—a political shift or a widespread epidemic—make it feel as if the end might be near, it reminds us of the finitude of life, and we shift *away* from consequential strangers. In other words, the composition of our convoys is shaped by our needs. Although we usually need and seek *both* comfort and novelty, at certain times the balance tips in one direction or the other. When we're faced with the prospect of any type of ending, such as a move, we tend to prefer emotional sustenance and a sense of the familiar. So we hunker down with those we hold closest to our hearts, people we know well and can depend on. But when we feel like we have all the time in the world, we crave information and novelty—it's the stuff that makes life interesting. So we turn to consequential strangers who can teach us new tricks and help us get ahead. We're even willing to put up with someone who makes us nervous or uncomfortable—a crotchety professor—if she can open the right doors.

This idea—known in academic circles as "socioemotional selectivity theory"—was conceived by Laura Carstensen, a psychologist at Stanford University. Initially her goal was to figure out why older people often had small convoys comprised mostly of intimates. Instead of accepting the widespread assumption that older folks disengage socially because they are getting ready to die, Carstensen devised an ingenious experiment to show that it is "anticipated endings," not age *per se*, that account for most seniors' diminished social circles. What is particularly fascinating is that Carstensen also demonstrated that social choice can be rather easily *manipulated*.[25]

In the earliest of these experiments, groups of volunteers were told to imagine themselves in two different scenarios. In the first, they found themselves with a spare half hour. With whom would they choose to spend time—a member of their immediate family, a recent acquaintance with whom they had a lot in common, or the author of a book they had read? Predictably, people in the oldest group (between sixty-five and ninety-two, average age seventy-two) opted to see a family member, most younger participants picked a nonintimate—a consequential stranger or a stranger they knew something about. But then the respondents were told to imagine that they were busy making preparations to move across the country in a few weeks and had managed to free up thirty minutes for socializing. Now whom would they choose? The second scenario forced them to think about leaving family and friends behind. Given this limited horizon—their "last few weeks"—the younger participants' answers were virtually the same as the seniors'. They, too, preferred to spend time with a family member.[26]

Interestingly, seniors' answers could also be manipulated by changing the script. A group of older respondents were given this what-if: Your doctor has just called to let you know that a medical breakthrough will add an extra twenty years to your life. Given such an *expanded* horizon, seniors were no more likely than young people to fill their spare time with a family member.[27]

Carstensen and her colleagues have since replicated this research with a variety of populations, and the results have been consistent. For example, the responses of AIDS patients were—not surprisingly—in line with those of older people. And in the aftermath of September 11, old *and* young respondents showed a preference for close social partners—family or good friends.

The theory holds in less individualistic cultures as well. Like their American peers, younger people in Hong Kong characteristically opted for more informational contacts *unless* there was some type of external threat—in this case, the handover. The older cohort characteristically chose the comfort of close social partners *unless* they were given an expanded time frame.[28] And when Carstensen and her colleagues looked at the impact of SARS, the findings mirrored Raymond Chau's social choices at the time: People of all ages sought security and succor over novelty.[29]

Chau's advertising firm did a survey of its own in the wake of the epidemic, asking people what was important to them. Priorities had definitely shifted. Being alive and staying healthy were suddenly more important than work and money. "It was a huge change," notes Chau. "Everyone wanted to spend more time with their family."

How long did that last? Chau's firm didn't do a follow-up, but looking at Hong Kong today, he observes, "Generally people are back to their old way of life, working hard as ever, putting in long hours." Initially the economy had hit "rock bottom," says Chau, but in the twelve months following the epidemic, property values and stocks shot up and kept improving. He notes that "the sense of prosperity and money"—a proxy for the future—overtook "the sense of crisis," which foretold a more limited horizon. "Now

SARS seems so remote." Carstensen's follow-up survey supports Chau's observation: When SARS ended and travel advisories were lifted, Hong Kong residents of all ages were more likely to choose acquaintances over intimates. Consequential strangers were back on the social agenda.[30]

These findings make sense if you think of episodes in your own life such as illness or even welcome occurrences like a graduation or promotion. All are events that signify an end to life as you've known it. Chances are, such times encourage you to cling ever more tightly to your loved ones. Or perhaps you have had a kind of *Big Chill* experience at the funeral of a good friend who died "too young." You vow to stay in touch with the old gang, people who knew you when. . . . Invariably, though, such promises are short-lived. It's not that you're callous; it's because your needs change, and therefore your motivation. Once fear and grief subside, your horizon expands, and you again seek out excitement, advancement, and new experiences, rather than just sticking with the familiar. The fact is, most of the time we need and want *both* kinds of relationships. We can't live without intimates, but we also can't go quite as far without the consequential strangers in our convoy.

Collaborating Across Boundaries 101: The Peripatetic President

Almost every year during orientation week at Pennsylvania State University (or at least this is how the story goes), an eighteen-year-old calls home to report that "some weird old guy" is sleeping in a room down the hall. The alarmed parents are relieved, not to mention surprised, when they learn that the interloper padding around in his pajamas is none other than the university's president, fifty-nine-year-old Graham Spanier, one of the savviest and most respected leaders in higher education. Spanier routinely spends the first week of school living in a freshman dorm. Talk about collaborating across boundaries![31]

"There are books written about how you have to preserve the royalty of the presidency," says Spanier, who manages some 38,200 employees on 24 campuses. "That's not my style." Rather than ruling from the top, he positions himself *at the center*—an approach that not only allows, but gives an edge to, an administrator who dares to step down from the ivory tower. Although he is at the head of a huge institution, Spanier runs the university as if it's his personal convoy, and he's forever adding new consequential strangers to his entourage.

Meeting Spanier, a strapping fellow with a wide smile, you can tell he's not in it for the "edge." He's having fun; he says he'd find it "boring" to sit behind a desk all day. Which is why in May you'll find him on a magical mystery tour through Pennsylvania with new faculty members, not merely to visit other Penn State campuses, but also to see the Harley-Davidson and Hershey factories and historic sites like Independence Hall. "We stay in residence halls," he explains, "and between stops we get to know each other." On any given day during the school year, you also might catch Spanier's magic show in the student union. At the gym, you're likely to find him playing racquetball with a student or a member of his staff. He and his wife, an English professor on campus, are defending champions of the intramural league. At football games, he sometimes dons the Nittany Lion costume and marches in the halftime show. On Saturday nights, he's downtown playing the washboard with the Deacons of Dixieland. He also answers his own email. "It's a way of connecting with people and breaking down some of the barriers that exist with my position."

Little in Spanier's background foretold his nontraditional approach to administration and education. The eldest of three children, he grew up in a neighborhood of working-class immigrants on the South Side of Chicago. His mother was a receptionist and secretary. His father loaded and unloaded trucks, ran a dry cleaning store for a time, and finally became a postmaster. His dad was "modestly involved in the community" in ways that so many fathers of baby boomers were: he was a scoutmaster, a precinct committeeman for the Democratic Party in 1960 during the Kennedy campaign, and a member of the Rotary Club.

Watching his parents struggle, Spanier knew early on that he had to forge his own connections. He "worked continuously" from the time he was nine, babysitting, mowing lawns, working as a pizza chef. "I developed this style of leadership in high school and college. I was involved in just about everything. I had the inclination early on to soak up everything and everyone around me and to then choose the best of what I saw." He excelled in sports, music, and academics, was the first in his family to go to college, and held jobs as a radio announcer and bank teller. "But I never felt like I was a big shot. I thought you had to work hard and prove yourself. If anything, because I didn't have the privileges that other people started with, I never took anything for granted. I think people are looking for connections—intimate and less significant ones. Anything that leaders can do to break down those barriers more makes them more effective."

Spanier's "style" and the relationships he maintains cut a wide swath across the usual boundaries of place, interests, age, and class. He has his lieutenants and other high-level administrators in his inner circle. But it is his ability to keep in touch with an even wider range of consequential strangers—and to see how they live and listen to their ideas and passions—that makes him a superior leader. Of course, in the vernacular of social scientists, an institution like Penn State would be considered a "bounded" network, a "granfalloon" defined by its specific membership—its employees and its students. But by also connecting with acquaintances *outside* the university, Spanier not only gains a unique perspective on the institution he oversees, he has a view and resources that go well beyond its walls.

The wisdom of collaborating across boundaries is apparent in corporate America as well. Jack Welch, the highly respected former CEO of General Electric, pointed out in the company's 2000 annual report that effective corporations are essentially "boundaryless" because they factor in, and consider as part of the company, all the recurring relationships with people who are technically not part of the organization—customers, suppliers, business owners, even other companies. In a sense, Welsh turned a classic granfalloon into a far more expansive and flexible karass. The annual report goes so far as to attribute various innovations at GE to the inspiration of *other* companies, such as Toyota, Wal-Mart, Motorola, and Cisco. Welch ran the organization the way Spanier runs Penn State, informally and openly, so as to create "a culture that breeds an endless search for ideas that stand or fall on their merit, rather than on the rank of their originator, a culture that brings every mind into the game."[32]

The Swiffer Story

If you dig into the biographies of the most successful products on the market, you'll find that they were created in a similar atmosphere. For example, no two people have precisely the same recollections of "Mop 2000," Procter & Gamble's code name for Swiffer—which today claims a whopping 80% of the "quick-clean" category of household products. Nor can anyone pinpoint exactly who or what sparked the notion of "a diaper on a stick," as Swiffer was first known. (One exec pointed out that it was actually a *Maxi Pad* on a stick—an image that probably made its predominantly male creators flinch.)[33] Most agree, though, that Craig Wynett, a guy whom certain executives at P&G once refused to hire because he wasn't "corporate" enough, was the one who made it all happen.

The story began in the early nineties when Wynett, successful as an independent consultant on a few P&G projects, was finally asked to join the company as brand manager for Vicks cold products. One of his earliest suggestions was for the division to broaden its reach by developing a pain-relieving heat wrap that would utilize oxidized iron powder, the same substance used in glove warmers to generate warmth. Wynett was able to see past the boundaries of his own division, but his boss shot him back a memo that read: "You must have too much free time on your hands."

The memo, which Wynett still keeps in his drawer, was emblematic of a serious problem at P&G, a company described a decade ago as "unwilling to lower its prices and unable to distinguish itself as an innovator."[34] Sassy upstarts in Silicon Valley had begun pumping out game-changing new ideas, often through online collaboration, while P&G lumbered along. It took years for innovations to squeeze through the corporate pipeline. Wynett's boss was typical of the old-school breed of managers. Skittish about venturing beyond their familiar domains, they tended to concentrate on short-term profits rather than take on riskier projects.

Durk Jager, then chief operating officer of P&G, and Gordon Brunner, chief technology officer, recognized that the company's flagging image and disappointing sales called for extreme measures. They first cleaned house, so to speak. For example, the Home Care division hadn't produced a new product in decades. Mr. Clean, an overnight sensation when it was introduced in 1958, now had robust competition and slim profit margins. So Jager and Brunner took away the ailing division's *entire R&D budget*, informing employees that they could earn back their funding *if* someone came up with a "big idea." Jager and Brunner also created the Corporate Innovation Fund, which was earmarked solely for new product development and, they hoped, would fast-track innovation.

Timing is everything, and Craig Wynett was finally in the right place at the right time. Born in Atlanta, the son of a couple who ran a tiny ad agency, he was a natural entrepreneur who earned spending money as a kid by bundling firewood in plastic sheets. With the shake-up rumbling through the company, Wynett went directly to Jager. Hordes of bright minds hadn't *yet* come forth with new ideas, he suggested, because a fund in and of itself cannot stimulate innovation. P&G also needed an internal group, untethered to any one division, to "dig out" embryonic ideas and take them a step forward.

Wynett was put in charge of Corporate New Ventures (CNV), an idea factory *within* the company. Management experts refer to such entities as a "knowledge market"—a way of driving innovation in a corporate hierarchy where the most radical ideas typically exist in the lower echelons.[35] Wynett answered directly to Jager and Brunner. Information would no longer flow only from the top down. Instead the new system would bypass the usual practice of filtering suggestions through one's immediate superior. In essence, the creation of CNV flung open the door to the executive suite, allowing anyone with a fresh idea to sit down with the top brass. Employees who were shy about presenting ideas in person were encouraged to send them via the company's intranet. The idea was to re-create—metaphorically—the old P&G lunchroom where, to site one example, a scientist in the food division once chatted with a production manager in the laundry division. Out of their banter emerged the notion of combining flour, sugar, and shortening and running the concoction through a soap mill to make it "fluffy." And so the first Duncan Hines cake mix was born. But in those days, R&D was housed in one building, and employees from every division ate together. Procter had since become so big and globally dispersed that employees with different sets of know-how rarely crossed paths. What they needed, Wynett realized, was a way to bridge the divisions and thereby share their expertise.

In a sense, Procter & Gamble did an end run around corporate bureaucracy by creating CNV. Wise executives and administrators intuitively grasp an essential truth: By inserting top management in the *middle* of a dynamic force, they are in a better position to harness its energy and to tap resources that might elude them in a traditional hierarchy where people with bright ideas are often hidden away. When the company itself is seen as a convoy, with management at the center and the various divisions as clusters of consequential strangers riding alongside, status is less important than ingenuity. This more flexible structure allows individuals to jockey into different positions depending on what's needed. Locating administrators or executives in the center of the convoy allows *everyone* easy access—a veteran staffer or someone who recently joined the company, a hotshot or a quiet thinker—and gives them all a chance to communicate and collaborate.

Granted, you probably won't hear the terms "convoy" or "consequential strangers" in an M.B.A. seminar, but management gurus of late stress the importance of lower-level employees—a CEO's weak ties. The business world is saturated in leadership advice, these experts say; it's time to look at "followership" as well. "Look at why big companies die," suggests an executive at Best Buy who embraces this notion. "They implode on themselves. They create all these systems and processes—and then end up with a very small percentage of people who are supposed to solve complex problems, while the other 98 percent of people just execute. You can't come up with enough good ideas that way to keep growing."[36]

In your personal convoy, the people closest to you travel close to the center, near "the boss," perhaps in the executive limousine. Their presence is comfortable, their views predictable. If you depend only on them, though, you limit yourself, because the "ahas" tend to come from vehicles in the outer lanes, your consequential strangers. So it is in a company. In a variety of industries, dense networks in which everyone relies on the colleagues they know best, are associated with "substandard performance." But workers who are able to broker connections across so-called "structural holes"—entrées into another group or division—reap a bounty of new information and additional resources. Enterprises that operate in this way therefore tend to be more innovative and more productive.[37] Craig Wynett has seen the effect firsthand: "The best of P&G is on the periphery," he observes. "The seams, as we call them, are where the interesting things are—the novel ideas." Which is exactly where the Swiffer was hiding.

In the wake of Jager and Brunner's scouring, Home Care was

scrambling to earn back its R&D budget. They surveyed consumers and went into their homes to watch them clean with different kinds of mops. Scrubbing floors, they learned, was the most hated of all household chores. Strip mops worked better than sponges but—uh-oh—a *clean* mop with *tap water* worked better than anything. That was a bitter pill for employees who believed they produced the best floor cleansers on the market.

"There's gotta be a better way to clean a floor," agreed Wynett when Home Care consulted him about developing a new kind of mop. He didn't do much mopping at home, but when he did, he hated it. The worst part was that the longer you mopped, the filthier the water became, and the more counterproductive the task. The trick, everyone concurred, was to design a mop that would *trap* the dirt instead of sloshing it around the floor. And here the story gets a little cloudy—and that's a good thing, according to Wynett, who believes that you accomplish much more "if you don't care who gets credit." Wynett brought together members of P&G's convoy who typically stayed in their own lanes—scientists who worked with hard-surface solutions and researchers who developed nonwoven materials, as well as marketing experts and advertising people. He made sure that consumers weighed in at several points in the development process, too—a practice that has always been part of P&G's corporate culture and which is even easier today, thanks to the Internet.

Wynett also believed in expanding the convoy to use outside contractors. He once again hired Design Continuum, the product development firm that had contributed to CNV's first success, ThermaCare—heat wraps filled with iron powder—the idea Wynett's former division head had dismissed. The "Wet Jet" prototype was cobbled together in DC's Boston offices using a swivel-headed dry-wall applicator purchased at Home Depot and a liter-sized soda bottle filled with water and fastened upside down to its five-foot shaft. In its report to P&G, the firm suggested a whole "family" of products—including a dry version.[38] But before anyone had a chance to patent the device, Wynett learned that a Japanese rival—the Kao Corporation—had obtained a patent for a dry mop that was remarkably similar. In yet another departure from its usual practice of selling only products developed in-house, P&G licensed the Kao technology—and called it the Swiffer Dry Mop. In a sense, Kao—a competitor—joined P&G's convoy, too.

Management research conducted by Professors Avan Jassawalla and Hemant Sashittal at the Jones School of Business, State University of New York, bears out the wisdom of this approach. Analyzing several high-tech companies in upstate New York—firms whose very survival depends on the rapid development of new products—they found that the most innovative companies attracted employees who welcome diversity. Everyone brings different talents to the table, and out of such collaborations something new and better invariably emerges. However, Professors Jassawalla and Sashittal also caution that many companies are at the other end of the continuum. In such organizations, coworkers "act and organize as if they were afflicted by a deeply held sense of paranoia." They head for the safety of their "silos of like-minded, like-skilled individuals who distrust others."[39]

Wynett grants that it's not easy to get people to collaborate across boundaries or to see "the hidden relationships between things." Change didn't happen overnight, but success helped. Buoyed by the sales of ThermaCare and Swiffer, the company devoted ever larger sums of money to the development of big ideas. CNV has since ministered to a range of other category-defying products that have not only made P&G investors happy, they have changed consumers' habits. The approach is not merely a matter of old-fashioned "group think" nor of simple "networking," a concept that has been around since the 1940s. It involves positioning yourself at the center, paying attention, and pulling from a variety of consequential strangers. It means crossing boundaries. But, Wynett stresses, "having the ability to benefit from the convoy means knowing how to listen and go deep. That's hard work. Thinking is unbelievably expensive—the brain constitutes 2% of our body mass and uses 20% of our calories. But it's possible for anyone to change the way they see the world."

The Lessons of Bolgatanga

It's no exaggeration to say that some of the most critical issues confronting society today depend on a fresh perspective and the ability to collaborate with consequential strangers who might see the same problem from a different vantage point. Eva Schiffer demonstrated this in Bolgatanga, an arid border town in the upper-east region of Ghana. The thirty-three-year-old social scientist was sent there to advise the White Volta Basin Board, a "multi-stakeholder governance organization responsible for overseeing local water resources." In plain English, Schiffer had to somehow coax a common vision out of seventeen wildly different people who had both a role and an interest in how water was used—a problem we see in our own backyard as well.[40]

A native of Düren, a small town in central-west Germany, Schiffer is a lovely sprite of a woman in wire-rimmed glasses. Her first taste of Africa was a three-month stay in rural Namibia where she did field research for her Ph.D. Now employed by the International Food Policy Research Institute, the Washington, D.C.–based agricultural think tank that dispatched her to lead the team in Bolgatanga, she dresses mostly in Western business attire for her meetings, but is also likely to don traditional Ghanian clothing when meeting with locals. Schiffer speaks with great enthusiasm and intensity about her work and her personal connections in Africa. Ghanaians have no word for "consequential strangers," she says, but having a broad network of affiliations is crucial for survival. "I expected that it would be all about family, but it was very easy for me as a stranger to develop something similar to family." The man who helped her find a house in Bolgatanga and get a telephone in two months instead of nine became her "uncle." Others are now her "brothers" and "sisters."

A country the size of Oregon with over six times its population, Ghana is plagued by poverty, erratic electric power, and the ever-present threat of famine and disease. Life expectancy is fifty-six. Water shortages and water pollution not only compound these challenges, they put an already vulnerable region at risk of terrorism.[41] In 1998, rebounding from yet another water-related issue—paralyzing drought—the National Water Resources Commission of Ghana decentralized the system by creating a series of basin boards to coordinate policies at the local level. Theoretically at least, the various members of these boards would combine resources and know-how to develop an integrated system of water management that would benefit all parties.

However, when Schiffer began working with the White Volta Basin Board, which was inaugurated in 2006, each member of the group had a different agenda and perspective. They talked about the problem, Schiffer recalls, "as if there were many different waters—irrigation water, drinking water, water as a part of an ecosystem. In the end, though, it's just one water, and by making their decisions without coordination, the agencies just move their problems to the next agency and cannot find holistic and sustainable solutions." The board also lacked enforcement authority. If members agreed, for example, that farming close to the river caused siltation—erosion of the banks which then blocks the flow—they had no way of stopping the practice. "My job was to help them better understand the situation on the ground—who's important, who might be able to police these practices, and who might come up with an alternative," Schiffer explains. "Sometimes you don't need enforcement to solve a problem. You need money or someone who's more influential."

In order to untangle "complexities that are not easily grasped," Schiffer figured out a way to give board members an aerial view of their situation. Adapting principles of social network analysis, she helped them chart what she calls an "influence map." It is built around four basic questions: *Who is involved? How are the players linked? What are their goals?* and *How influential is each one?*

Starting with a large piece of blank poster board—the yet undrawn map—Schiffer represents the participants with Ludo "men" (smooth, two-inch, torso-like wooden figures used in a popular Ghanaian board game; imagine Fisher-Price "little people" without faces or outfits). Using Post-it notes, she identifies each person, or "actor," by name. Such a low-tech and highly visual method is well suited to a region beset by frequent blackouts and to any group in which some participants have weaker language skills than others. Simple graphics represent relationships: Colored lines from one person to another show *links* between actors. An arrow at the end of a line between two people indicates the *flow* of that link. For example, if Sam commands Joe, the arrow points from Sam toward Joe. If there is an exchange *between* parties—say, they regularly trade information—a two-headed arrow is used. Under each name Schiffer designates the person's *goal* regarding water usage by writing "D" for economic development or "P" for protection of the environment. Finally, each Ludo piece is placed on a tower of checkers, or no checkers at all, to indicate the player's respective power—but only in this particular situation, Schiffer stresses. A member might have far-reaching influence in his own village, but very little clout when it comes to changing water-use policies.[42]

Admittedly, a written description of influence-mapping can seem complex, even confusing. But for interviewees who are there *in the moment*, the approach offers amazing clarity and sparks invaluable insights about their own and others' perceptions. A seemingly straightforward question like "Who is involved?" can elicit dissimilar answers. For example, the basin officer—the only full-time employee on the board—cited many people, while a board member who lived in a village came up with far fewer names. Also, as network analysts often lament, memory is fallible.

Even the basin board officer, who was responsible for coordinating all the participants, remarked, "Throughout the discussion I remembered a lot of actors that at first had slipped my mind."

After meeting with basin board members individually, Schiffer continued the process with the group until everyone had seen and discussed each other's maps. Their understanding came not from the finished product, which to an untrained eye looks like a tangle of boxes and arrows and letters adorned with various game pieces. The *process* itself was key. As one of the regional technical officers remarked, "For me the most interesting part was putting everyone on influence towers. It's so easy to get the full picture if you have everything in front of you like this."

How well did it work? The governance process in Ghana is slow; and attitudes take longer to shift when you're dealing with seventeen people. Schiffer doesn't boast radical change, but her mission was a success nonetheless. "The activity of sitting together and trying to grasp what this whole network looked like allowed the board basin members to express their views, to talk about their previous experiences, and to figure out how they can put it all together. They have better relations between them as a result and a common vision."

The lessons of Bolgatanga apply to any gathering of individuals who can't get past their own narrow perspectives—battling factions in a neighborhood association, a PTA, or a small business. "Very often we just assume that people see things the same way as we do," says Schiffer, "and a lot of the frustration of working with people comes from this fact. They do things that we find stupid in one way or the other, but we don't realize that in *their* understanding of the situation, their actions make a lot of sense. This is why drawing an influence map together works so well, especially for consequential strangers who are stuck with each other and a task."

Influence mapping can also help individuals untangle problems by giving them a clearer view of the territory and their place in it. Schiffer guided a friend—we'll call her Pat Jones—through the process. Jones had been assigned by an international aid agency to a school in Ghana but kept meeting resistance whenever she proposed reforms to the system. Until Schiffer helped her graphically lay out the players, their links, their goals, and their spheres of influence, Jones hadn't realized that some people saw her merely as a fund-raiser, not someone sent there to make policy changes. Furthermore, the people on *her* wavelength, who welcomed reform, wielded far less power than those whose goal was money. "She had to change her goal, at least initially," Schiffer explains. As a workable compromise, Jones decided to launch a fund-raising effort. But she also specified that new funds would be used to improve the school.

Facing any "brick wall," as Pat Jones initially described her situation, often feels insurmountable. Influence mapping allows you to perceive ways *around* the wall that aren't apparent when you're looking at it head on. Instead you elevate yourself to view the bigger picture. You can then see what's happening *between* people, and discern how much sway they have over one another. The most influential players typically have a lot of links—a guy like Graham Spanier, for one. Power and control can also come from bridging—joining people or groups who would otherwise not be connected—which is what Karla Lightfoot and Craig Wynett do so well. Movers and shakers also tend to be only a few degrees of separation away from what they need—to get to someone they don't know, they don't have to go through as many people as others might. But even if you don't have power yourself in such situations, being *connected* to someone who has a lot of links is useful, too—as long as you're aware of the flow of information and influence.

Charting her situation with Schiffer, Pat Jones realized that her only link to an important policy maker at the national level was through her biggest enemy, the regional head of the department, who was responsible for the administration of all schools in the area. Armed with this knowledge, she began to cultivate relationships with other powerful people involved with the school who didn't necessarily see reform and money as mutually exclusive goals or were at least open to other ideas. Eventually, those new connections allowed her to bypass her adversary.[43]

The view from above gives us a whole other vocabulary, and an understanding that the potential to solve a problem is not simply located within a single individual. It comes as well from an awareness of your social ties, an appreciation of the wide range of people in your convoy—especially those on the periphery—and an understanding of how various factors converge and affect your everyday life. As we will see in the next chapter, your convoy not only travels *with* you, it propels you. It is an aggregate force of transformation, changing you and moving you forward, often into unknown territory.

3

Beyond the Confines of the Familiar

> It is hardly possible to overrate the value . . . of placing human beings in contact with persons dissimilar to themselves. . . . Such communication has always been, and is peculiarly in the present age, one of the primary sources of progress.
>
> —*John Stuart Mill*

> Oh! The places you'll go!
>
> —*Dr. Seuss*

An Unwitting Social Experiment

On a shopping excursion with her husband, Sue Ellen Cooper bought herself a bright red vintage fedora just for the fun of it. A few months later, Cooper, a mural painter and freelance illustrator from Fullerton, California, started a birthday tradition: She gave a red hat to each friend who turned fifty (or older). Cooper also included a framed copy of "Warning," a poem she had discovered decades earlier in a funky used-book shop. It's about a woman pondering the freedoms she'll allow herself when she is old. She'll wear purple with a red hat, learn to spit, and in other ways make up for the "sobriety" of her youth. "But," the woman muses, "maybe I ought to practice a little now? So people who know me are not too shocked and surprised."[1]

Practicing seemed like a good idea to Cooper and her friends. At one point she convinced the lot of them to go out for lunch in their red hats and purple outfits—an outing that somehow unleashed their most carefree, playful selves. "Something magical happened that afternoon," says Cooper. Dubbing themselves the Red Hat Society, they vowed to plan other adventures. Little more than a decade later, thanks to word-of-mouth (more on that later), the Red Hat Society is everywhere. Although the name might conjure an image of latter-day dowagers, this is no ladies' auxiliary club. Their only rule is that there are no rules. Now with nearly 40,000 chapters throughout the United States and abroad, an estimated million "Red Hatters" have inspired media coverage, conventions, a Broadway musical, and a platinum MasterCard.

A generation largely comprised of wives and mothers who stayed at home, worked, or volunteered, Red Hatters are married, widowed, divorced, and single. They're now at a point in life when some of their old roles have become less relevant or less appealing. It's easy for them to feel invisible. So they relish small acts of rebellion, like eating dessert before the main course, entering a grape-stomping contest (à la Lucy and Ethel), parachuting from a plane to celebrate a sixtieth birthday. Imagine a mother of four, unleashing her inner Rambo, her first time ever at a firing range, or a gaggle of grandmas playing laser tag against local teenagers. One group held a "wallflower prom"—no dates, but heavy on the glitz and glamour. Another chapter marched in a Mardi Gras parade, led by a fiftysomething who brought her baton out of storage and revisited her old role of majorette.

But this is not simply a story about women finding companionship in midlife or allowing their "inner children" to come out and play. The Red Hat Society is a social laboratory of sorts, illustrating one of the key benefits of consequential stranger relationships: Each tie is a potential resource, a spark that ignites our self-awareness and often propels us in an unexpected direction. It is often in throwaway moments and everyday conversation with our acquaintances that we acquire important information, decide whether or not to embrace a new idea or product, or try on a persona that is less likely to be welcomed at home.[2] A story told by former first lady Laura Bush about a visit to her in-laws' house illustrates this point: "George sat on the sofa and put his feet up on the coffee table. And all of a sudden, Barbara Bush hollered, 'Put your feet down.' George's dad said, 'For goodness' sake, Bar, he's the President of the United States.' Without pause, the older Mrs. Bush replied, 'I don't care—I don't want his feet on my coffee table.'" Laura Bush concluded that "even Presidents have to listen to their mother."[3] But the story also shows how intimates tend to freeze-frame us. They see only one facet of our identity, whereas casual relations are more likely to allow us to TiVo different aspects of ourselves.

Together the Red Hatters sustain a culture that encourages them to become *more* than who they are. And yet there are no obligations; the main objective is to have a good time. As Cooper explains it, new members are sometimes "giddy with the sense of freedom. They can express who they are *today.* They don't have to conform to an old image or explain that they are changing certain aspects of themselves."[4] The society offers its members a smorgasbord of relationships that come with no baggage and even less predictability. Many join *because* they want novel experiences and an opportunity to, metaphorically and literally, wear a new outfit. "On one of our bus trips, a woman revealed that she normally dresses very 'corporate' and behaves in a rather circumspect manner at work," Cooper recalls. "She didn't think her coworkers would believe it if they saw her in red and purple, with feathers and rhinestones! In some ways, this is akin to an actress playing a role and really putting herself into it. After all, she's just playing a part!"

That we slip into different roles is not a new idea. In Shakespeare's *As You Like It,* written in the late sixteenth century, the melancholy Jaques declared that all of us are "merely players," and that "one man in his time plays many parts." Some believe the concept was already clichéd by then. The preeminent psychological theorist William James, writing in 1890, put forth the notion that "a man has as many social selves as there are individuals who recognize him and carry an image of him in their mind."[5] This is no less true today. In order to deal with the demands of modern life, we have to inhabit and manage a variety of identities—personas that emerge in different situations. We live *niched lives*, hopscotching from one cluster of our convoy to the next. We reach into our closets and select whatever garb—or self—fits the occasion. We talk the talk and play by the rules of each role. A parent and partner one minute, and the next, a market analyst, a blogger, a wine connoisseur, a tai chi student, an inveterate garage-sale shopper, a fan of Alicia Keys.

As psychologist Kenneth Gergen explains it, our psyches are continually being "populated" by the people we encounter—in large part, our consequential strangers.[6] It's no longer about having "a basic self"—one identity and one set of predominantly close ties, as it was a century ago. Each of us is a conglomerate of identities played out on different stages. We are informed, and continually updated, by the many consequential strangers in our lives. "Now you're traveling from day to day in a multiplicity of relationships," says Gergen. "None are overwhelming, and you can move across one to another with some alacrity."[7]

Many social scientists today look at the self in a more expansive way. It is not solely a "personal" self that strives to be unique. It's also a "social self" that seeks connection and strives to belong. This social self is defined by its consequential strangers—its weak ties and its membership in larger social structures, be they groups (a church committee, a soccer team) or collective identities (Muslim, steelworker).[8]

Having an "extended," or complex, self—shaped by interactions with a mixed array of people—is like knowing a variety of dance steps: Whatever the music, you've got the moves. You're better able to adapt to different situations and settings and more likely to gain access to a wider range of information. Surprisingly, our casual connections not only make it easier to navigate our way through many kinds of social territories—even *up* the class ladder—they can literally change who we are and what we believe in. The fact is, most of what we know about ourselves comes from our relationships. Certainly genes and experience count, too, but others hold up the mirror—we see ourselves through their eyes. That intimates have an impact on our identity is unquestionable. But it is consequential strangers and the routine interactions and everyday conversations with them that take us beyond the familiar and broaden our sense of self so that we better understand the world and our place in it.[9]

Rule of the Roles: Less Is *Not* More

"I wear a lot of hats. The only time that's a problem is when one of them doesn't fit right," jokes Pat Hickok, a wife, mother and stepmother, and grandmother. Now in her early sixties, Hickok has been a joiner all her life and a bundle of energy. A professional nanny by day, she is "queen" of her Red Hat chapter. She communicates (mostly by email) with members throughout the country and is always game for adventure with her cronies. She's considered a "level one." A less active "level four," she clarifies, would have "only two or three outfits and go out once a month at most." Hickok joined in 2003, when she was living in San Diego and happened by the table of a woman selling red hats at a street fair. "I was looking for new friends and for something new to do, so I took a card." When Hickok and her husband of thirty years decided to relocate to Las Vegas, she simply started a new chapter—the Sin City Sweethearts—and welcomed all comers. Her tiny chapter is so diverse it almost sounds like she's making it up: "a lady who works full-time at a church, a Jewish woman on her third marriage, a recent widow, and a black lesbian raising her children and grandchildren." Hickok couldn't be happier. "I'm not interested in a melting pot. I like a buffet. Meeting them opened up a window in my life that once had a shutter on it."

Not to beat a metaphor, but we don't have to join the Red Hat Society to wear different hats. Each person we're connected to gives us an opportunity to step into different roles. The hat we wear depends on whom we're with, what we're doing, and the situation. An acquaintance you play basketball with might bring out the fierce competitor in you as well as your great sense of humor, but when you see him at church, you're not likely to showcase that fun-loving athletic self. We're usually conscious of these multiple selves because we *feel* different enacting each role. In a survey of a university community in Arizona done in 1995, 38 people reported a total of *559 distinct identities.*[10] Some of us long for a *less* complicated life, complain about too many emails, phone calls, and obligations. But there is no going back; the genie is long out of the bottle. Modern life requires multiple roles.

In decades past, some social scientists who studied identity warned that occupying different roles could put people at risk of "role conflict" and "role overload."[11] The concern has some merit: Juggling competing roles such as mother and career woman can be stressful and exhausting. And sometimes a particularly dominant role can seep into other situations.[12] It's like the old joke about the stay-at-home mother who absently turns to her tablemate at a dinner party and begins to cut his meat for him. The "mother" in her is never off duty.

When we experience "mixed feelings," one role theorist speculates, it sometimes may be because a particular situation activates two contradictory roles, even if only in our minds.[13] Let's say you're a corporate lawyer advising the CEO about opening a new factory in a third-world country. Your lawyer self is front and center, outlining the facts of such an expansion. But the discussion also awakens your social-crusader self. Inside your head, the lawyer wants the company to prosper, but the activist asks, *At what cost?*

Such realities aside, however, most of our roles, especially those played out with consequential strangers, are enacted on *separate* stages. Even more important, a rash of new research indicates that the rewards of having a complex self far outweigh the risks. "There's an economy in having a multiplicity of relationships," says Kenneth Gergen. "You come off feeling good about yourself."[14]

Other social scientists agree. We see ourselves in others' eyes. Their responses to our behavior confirm our greatest hopes or our deepest fears. They give us new ideas about what a self can be in different settings. Their reactions let us know whether we're doing what is expected of us. And we are more likely to value ourselves when others do. Sociologist Peggy Thoits sums it up: "Generally, the more role-identities individuals hold, the more purpose, meaning, behavioral guidance, and approving social feedback they have available, and thus, the better should be their mental health or general well-being."[15]

Clearly some of the roles we enact are more important, or "salient," than others, and some have a more beneficial effect on our levels of stress—but the two don't necessarily go together. Comparing and ranking the importance of seventeen different roles, Thoits found that women valued roles based on primary relationships, while men preferred roles based on achievement. No surprise there. However, Thoits also expected that the more salient roles would promote psychological well-being. But that was *not* the case. The easier-to-exit *voluntary* roles such as school crossing guard or member of the Red Hat Society were associated with enhanced well-being—higher self-esteem, mastery, and physical health, as well as lower depression—while *obligatory* roles such as spouse, parent, and worker, which demand concentrated time and energy, sometimes translate into "role strain." You have arguments with a spouse. You put in long hours at work. Your children have tantrums. Handling any of these situations is hardly a walk in the park. Therefore, Thoits concluded, obligatory roles bode well for mental health only when they're *not* fraught with tension.[16]

Complex Selves and "Fancy Minds"

Granted, occupying a role is different from having a relationship, but the two usually go together. We are rarely actors without audiences. And like a tree falling in the forest, we feel most authentic in a role when we have witnesses. Not all roles have built-in "partners," such as parent and child, employer and employee, teacher and student, but many involve consequential strangers. An artist who works alone might have a teacher, a rep, customers, and vendors from whom he usually buys supplies. He plays a slightly different role with each one. This juggling of the different selves that are enacted in each situation is what sociologists call a "complex role set."

The late Rose Coser, a sociologist, reasoned that a simple, or restricted, role set can cause a person to feel isolated and bored. If everyone and everything is familiar, there's not much novelty in your life and you don't have to stretch yourself, whereas a complex role set constantly challenges your intellect and problem-solving ability. The role of "physician," for example, involves interaction with patients, hospital administrators, representatives from drug companies, and medical students. He or she has to interact differently with each of the people in that "set." The mere act of moving from one person to another is stimulating. It causes us to "make mental adjustments to the new role partners," Coser observed, and "to negotiate, exercise judgment, reconcile, compromise, and take account of the intentions, purposes, motivations, and perspective."[17] Whereas we tend to put our minds on auto pilot with intimates, verbal shorthand usually doesn't suffice with an acquaintance. Instead we are forced to use what Coser called "elaborated" speech, which can be "understood by everybody."[18]

Coser's theory helps explain why history professor Henry Graff relishes meeting academics from other disciplines. As he puts it, "it gives me a fancy mind." Graff is one of the country's foremost experts on the presidency—the late Harry Truman and Gerald

Ford each attended his lectures. He speaks with the confidence and authority of a man who has been a frequent guest at the White House and has mentored many great minds. Now in his eighties, he is mentally sharp and physically active. When he retired a few years ago, he had no intention of becoming irrelevant. But there seemed to be no place for him at Columbia University, where he'd spent a good part of the last sixty years. He felt his life getting smaller, opportunities for mental stimulation less frequent. Gone were the students he advised, the fellow professors with whom he collaborated.

"When you're emeritus, you ought to be given invitations, be on mailing lists, be in touch with what's going on." To remedy the situation, Graff became one of the founders of EPIC—Emeritus Professors in Columbia. Through EPIC, Graff has gotten to know professionals in different fields—doctors, physicists, art professors, and others for whom he didn't have time earlier in his career or might never have encountered. He enjoys the outside speakers who are invited to the monthly EPIC lunches because they tend to address controversial subjects. It makes him think and leads to lively conversation afterward with a variety of consequential strangers. Being an active member of EPIC forces Graff to venture beyond his own area of expertise and engage in elaborated speech. It hones his fancy mind.

Graff's story illustrates another important point: Having a broad pallet of relationships is especially important when we have to add, modify, or exit a role, as we invariably do throughout life. We're most likely to audition for a new role, experts say, when an old one no longer feels comfortable, as might be the case with an untenable job situation or a rocky relationship, or when we move into a different "season" of life. For Graff, it was retirement. Loss of the "worker" role is particularly difficult in a world where money is equated with value.[19] For some of the women in the Red Hat society, it was the empty nest. And for Fingerman, as you may recall from the Introduction, it was the transition to motherhood.

To shift gears, we have to *believe* that it's possible to change, and we need others around us who provide support in order to make that change.[20] Those "others" might be people close to us, but—at the risk of saying this too many times—consequential strangers are *most likely* to show us a way we'd never thought of and, as we pointed out earlier, to accept us in a new role. They coax us into unknown territory. We gain a greater sense of control—mastery—over our lives and can plow ahead, no matter what.[21]

It's Not What Happens to You in Life . . .

On a Monday afternoon more than a decade ago, Doug Davis, a decent, hardworking, and by his own description, a "big jokester" of a guy, had just finished building a deck. Stocky but well-toned, standing six feet two with blond hair, he was the picture of health. His new business was just starting to take off, and despite some achiness, Davis thought little of it. He had good reason to assume the worst was behind him. Five years earlier, only three months into his marriage, he had fought his way into remission from chronic mylosis leukemia, the so-called "lesser" of the leukemias, enduring a debilitating bone marrow transplant that left him sterile. Fortunately, his doctors had advised him to freeze sperm prior to the treatment. Now, he and his wife had a three-year-old son and a daughter a few months old, and his new deck-building business was thriving.

By Tuesday, Davis felt worse. He thought it was the flu. "I didn't know it then but my body had started eating my red blood cells. I don't remember anything except them rushing me into surgery."[22] Doctors first removed his spleen. But that left him vulnerable to a staph infection which then mutated into a condition that caused blood to clot instead of flowing throughout his body. The clinical term, "disseminated intravascular coagulation," is usually shortened by medical personnel to "DIC," as in "death is coming."[23]

Davis didn't die, but his limbs turned black. When he could

no longer move his fingers, his left arm was removed five inches below his elbow, his right hand a week later. In an effort to save his legs, he was put into a hyperbaric chamber to inject oxygen into his system, but that only delayed the inevitable. A few weeks later, both legs were amputated. He was twenty-five years old.

Doug Davis had always thought of himself as a "hands-on kind of guy." He loved to hike and run. As a kid, he had spent hours building LEGO creations. A reluctant student who lived for shop and computer classes, he was still an inveterate tinkerer, a carpenter whose services were in demand. Now, Davis lay in the hospital, shocked and depressed. His limbs were central to his identity. Who was he? What kind of life could he expect? His wife and family were there for him and would continue to cheer him on, but they couldn't *know* the anguish he felt. Fortunately, he went straight from the hospital in his hometown of Fredonia, Wisconsin, to the Spinal Cord Injury Center of Froedtert Hospital in Milwaukee, where he met a stream of consequential strangers.

There was the prosthetist who made his first set of artificial arms, and later his legs. There was the young male therapist who helped him understand the emotional trauma, a guy he's still in touch with. And there was the cute young occupational therapist who "kept trying to find things I couldn't do." She'd give him a milk carton and say, "Open that." She'd challenge him to the travel-sized version of Connect Four in which players take turns dropping thin checker-like pieces ("smaller than a nickel") into narrow slots at the top of a plastic grid. "I kept joking with her that she'd never stump me—and she never did."

Equally important were his peers on the spinal cord unit. "I'd eat dinner with all the guys. Some of them were paralyzed below the waist. Others could barely move their heads." Davis felt "lucky" because the surgeons had been able to save his elbows and knees, making it easier for the prosthetist to fit him with artificial limbs. "I started using my new arms right away to feed myself. He said he'd get me up and walking again, too. It might not be tomorrow but in a year. Compared to the other guys, my situation wasn't so bad."

Davis indulged in something we all do, especially with consequential strangers. Psychologists call it "social comparison." When we see someone who is worse off—say, not as good-looking, smart, or skilled, or in less desirable circumstances—we compare "downward," which makes us feel better about our own situation. Oddly enough, we do this even when we feel good about ourselves. In contrast, when our self-esteem is low, we're more likely to make "upward" comparisons—we covet another's traits or possessions—which makes us feel significantly worse. Most downward and upward comparisons are targeted at acquaintances. We understandably reserve same-level comparisons (which also make us feel good) for people in our inner circles.[24] After all, it would threaten a close relationship if one person felt superior (or inferior), whereas no such danger exists with a consequential stranger.

Sociologist Arlie Hochschild calls it the "poor dear" hierarchy. Studying a vibrant and diverse community of older people who resided in a low-income public housing project in the San Francisco Bay Area, Hochschild found that residents compared downward when the other person was in deteriorating health, had children who rarely or never came to visit, or had the misfortune of aging more rapidly. To a resident who continued to be politically active, a person who spent the day playing cards was a "poor dear." To a tenant whose health was failing but who was still managing to live on her own, anyone who lived in a nursing home was a "poor dear." Hochschild concluded, "Almost everyone, it seems, had a 'poor dear.' "[25]

You might think of Doug Davis, who stands on bionic legs and sports a metal hook on one arm and a more handlike plastic mechanism on the other, as a "poor dear." But not if you got to know him. Now in his late thirties, he is a husband and father to two active teenagers, works at a nine-to-five job as a tool-and-die designer, and has a rich social life. If you drive by his house on a Saturday afternoon, you're likely to see him mowing his lawn, throwing a ball for the dog, playing soccer, or racing remote-control cars with his kids. Talk to him for a few minutes, and you'll forget about his limbs.

Initially he was concerned about how his family, old friends, and other able-bodied people might react to him, and he chose his prosthetics accordingly. Today, though, practicality trumps presentation—covered legs are heavier, "pinkish" arms get dirty easily. He doesn't worry about the reaction of new acquaintances. "We're big campers, and we've met a lot of people who go camping. Some are uneasy at first, but then I'll crack a joke, like I might boast that *my* feet aren't cold. Or when we're barbecuing, I'll just turn the brat with my hook instead of using the flipper. As they get to know me, *they* start cracking jokes, and that's when I know they're fine."

Davis's social convoy also includes people he has met through the annual One-Arm Dove Hunt in Olney, Texas, a sporting event that attracts upper-body amputees from all over the country. "Back home, I can go months, even a year, without seeing another amputee," he says. "They all have different ways of doing things and you learn a lot." At one end of the spectrum are attendees who have round-the-clock caretakers and can do very little on their own; at the other are people like Davis. He shines in this setting. By being part of this large, diverse collective, he nurtures what psychologist Marilynn Brewer calls his "extended self"—a self that is shaped by weak ties. Being a member of a larger social entity encourages a person to behave in a way that makes him or her a "good" representative of that group—a good Catholic, a good cop. Although Davis doesn't think of himself as "disabled," at the dove hunt he can't help but identify with fellow amputees, recall his own early struggles, and, most important, see how far he has come.[26]

Doug Davis is a testament to the fact that when we expand ourselves and traffic with different kinds of people, we broaden our repertoire of responses. As we noted in Chapter 2, "diversity" is a way of infusing an ailing institution with new life. Contemporary research suggests that a similar proposition might be applied to any challenge. Scott Page, a professor of complex systems, cites the example of InnoCentive.com, a website created by Eli Lilly where members of the scientific community ("seekers") can post complex problems. Anyone willing to register on the site can take a shot at solving them. In its first four years, InnoCentive attracted more than eighty thousand "solvers" from all over the world. A study of the site found that when solvers from *multiple* scientific disciplines tackled a problem, they were more likely to come up with an answer. In other words, bringing people together from different perspectives was more effective than, say, relying on a more homogeneous group comprised only of chemists.[27]

As individuals, says Page, we also do better when we recruit members of our convoys who come from diverse backgrounds and orientations. It makes us question old assumptions. "People will say it's about exposure to new information, but it's more than that. A consequential stranger can give you a different way of seeing a problem, which exponentially increases your chances of solving it." If we think of our ideas and abilities as a set of tools, Page points out, other people are bound to have tools we don't know about. And for each new technique, idea, or bit of information that comes your way via consequential strangers, the "set of possibilities" increases exponentially.[28]

And it's the gift that keeps giving.

The Loop of Loose Ties

Shortly before Christmas a few years ago, an elderly black woman who boarded the Fifth Avenue bus in Harlem walked up and down the aisle, seeming to "extort" money from the other riders. She hit up the "regulars," predominantly black and Hispanic housecleaners and handymen who worked in the luxury high-rise buildings, hotels, and restaurants that characterize the string of pricey neighborhoods the avenue intersects. "I saw her in the rearview mirror," recalls the driver, Barbara Green, a stocky woman with a strong voice and a smile as bright as her short-cropped blond hair.[29]

As the old woman was about to get off at her stop, she handed Green a worn white envelope. Inside was more than two hundred dollars in small bills. Green, who had driven this same route for eight of her thirty years as a New York City bus driver, had come to know many of those daily riders, if not by name, then as "mami" or "papi," Spanish terms of endearment and respect. "I knew where they lived. And when I dropped them off at night, I'd give an extra look down the block to see that they'd be okay." Growing up as the daughter of "the maintenance guy" in a low-income housing development, Green knew how much those extra ones, fives, and tens meant to her benefactors.

Now in her early fifties, Green has never forgotten her roots, perhaps because she's come so far from them. After graduating from high school, she worked as a bank teller. Five years later, lured by a twice-as-large paycheck, a hefty pension, and generous medical benefits, she switched to an occupation that has given her a "window on the world." Every day, there's an array of people to watch and deal with: the Asian woman who sells her tea every morning, other drivers and dispatchers (mostly male and nonwhite), and a multihued collection of commuters from all parts of this diverse city. Some passengers are more likeable than others, but Green connects with most of them, even some of the wealthy matrons with their glossy designer shopping bags. She is constantly *learning.* It's a talent she honed as the only child of much older parents whose hardscrabble existence didn't allow money for babysitters. "I went everywhere with them—restaurants, bars. My first wake was at seven. I had to be a good little kid, act like an adult. You learn social skills that way. I don't do well at paperwork, but I can talk my way through anything."

That Barbara Green has spent her life in New York City is obvious from the way she says "cawfee" and "tawk." It's clear, too, that this is a capable woman who looks you in the eye and shoots straight from the hip. Less apparent, however, is that in addition to her socializing with other city workers and union members, Green's convoy also includes doctors, lawyers, and executives who "fly all over the world, just to go to a meeting." She eats at trendy restaurants, takes in Broadway shows, and owns a summer house on Fire Island, an upscale strip of land nestled between Long Island and the Atlantic Ocean. A few years ago, to celebrate her fiftieth birthday, she "splurged" on a one-week trip to a posh dude ranch in Arizona and has returned annually ever since. And when she retires a few years from now with that hefty pension, she'll winter in her Florida condo.

Sometimes she pinches herself. "I definitely hang out with people who are out of my class." Recently, in fact, she discovered that a repeat guest at the dude ranch—one of the "horse people," as she calls them—grew up on the tony Upper East Side of Manhattan. "I joked with her, 'Oh, in the eighties you were one of those rich kids I used to pick up.' And here I am, twenty years later, sitting at the same dinner table with her."

Barbara Green, a kid from the projects, beat the odds. Although we'd like to think that class restrictions ended in the Victorian era, it's still difficult to scramble up the social ladder and maintain relationships outside your class.[30] Education is one route. But surprising research by sociologist Bonnie Erickson indicates that when a person like Barbara Green manages to challenge the class trajectory, it also could be because she has acquired what we call "culture smarts"—knowledge of art, music, books, sports, restaurants, business trends, theater, movies, fashion.[31] Culture smarts is the stuff of cocktail-party chatter. It greases the conversational wheels, enabling you to mix it up in any kind of crowd.

We acquire culture smarts mostly through consequential strangers—individuals in our convoys who are different from us. It starts at home and in school. But Erickson's research shows that family is not destiny. As we move through life, we continue to learn different cultural "genres." We might discover useful business magazines through a coworker, learn about art from the owner of an antiques shop, are clued in about the latest fashion by our hairdresser, and discuss who's slated to win a Grammy with the twentysomething IT guy at the office. As Erickson puts it, "The single most powerful teacher of cultural variety is contact with people in many locations."[32]

To test this theory, Erickson uses an "occupation test"—a list of jobs ranging up and down the socioeconomic ladder. She asks participants to put a checkmark next to job categories in which they know someone "well enough to talk to." They then indicate whether the contact is a relative, friend, or just someone they know. (We provide a similar test in Appendix II.) Erickson's findings have been consistent over nearly two decades: "If you know people in lots of different occupations, you have access to information and resources all over the place." It's like enrolling in a liberal arts program, says the sociologist, and getting a degree in "a little of almost everything." Typically, the shortest list of contacts is relatives, friends next. The longest list, our "teachers" of culture, are *weak* ties—consequential strangers.

Erickson is sometimes asked the "point" of including low-prestige occupations in her studies: "The implication is that high-status groups don't need them. I totally disagree. We need a lot of different resources. Variety enriches your mind, your awareness. Having only a whole bunch of snotty professional friends can be limiting."[33] Erickson grants that advantaged individuals generally know more than others about culture. However, the *reason* for this, she maintains, is that the elite typically have more diverse convoys, *not* that they're privileged.

Theoretically, then, anyone can *acquire* culture smarts by knowing consequential strangers from a variety of worlds. On our occupation test, Barbara Green scored well above average. In one national survey listing twenty-two occupations the high was nineteen.[34] Given the same test, Green knew people in all twenty-two.

Erickson also points out that having culture smarts isn't a matter of cultivating *refined* taste. It's better to be a "cultural carnivore." Soap operas can get you just as far as classical opera—probably farther. People in higher socioeconomic groups may be more likely to indulge in highbrow offerings, but only a minority actually *do.* Indeed, a consul general in New York City from a high-status Latin American family, who has a master's in literature, a law degree, and is well versed in the classics, admits that television shows like *Entertainment Tonight* provide the best conversational fodder for the endless stream of obligatory dinners, parties, and diplomatic meetings she must attend.[35] In a similar vein, Green doesn't need to have esoteric knowledge of equestrian history to carry on conversations with her "horse people."

The "culturally adroit" know how to tailor their patter to particular situations, and the more they know *across* genres, the greater the probability that they will find common ground with almost anyone. It becomes an unending and self-perpetuating process—"a lifelong set of feedbacks," as Erickson describes it—a loop. "Diverse networks build culture, both help people to get better jobs, better jobs add richness to network and culture, and so on."

Think of it as "the loop of loose ties."[36]

Mark Granovetter exemplifies how the loop works with careers by imagining an urn filled with red and white balls. The red balls represent useful contacts—in this case, people with good job information—typically, our weak ties. The white balls are everyone else. An urn belonging to a better-connected individual would naturally contain more red balls. Each time she takes advantage of a new opportunity such as switching to a better job, she makes new connections, thereby upping her red-ball total and making it possible for her to continue her upward climb.[37] This is not just theory. A recent study by a Harvard Business School professor, Boris Groysberg, found that female analysts on Wall Street are more likely than men to retain their "star status" when they switch jobs. Whereas men rely on internal networks within their companies, women build their success on relationships with clients and colleagues who work elsewhere—red balls *outside* the firm.[38]

The urn analogy can be applied to any number of life's challenges, not just career mobility. Let's say that the red balls stand for consequential strangers who can potentially add new "tools" to our repertoire, not just career leads. Consider the people you've met in this chapter: Barbara Green has an array of passengers in her urn, Pat Hickok, four utterly different women in her Red Hat chapter, and Doug Davis, his fellow "dove-shooters." Each "red ball" in their respective urns has the potential of offering a different way of perceiving, talking, and doing. Each inspires them to express a slightly different persona, not in a duplicitous or pathological sense, but in service of developing a more complex self. And each contact is a potential link—a bridge—to new connections, which in turn increases the number of red balls in their urns.

The loop of loose ties is constantly in motion. Granovetter also points out that some white balls can morph into red over time. People get married, move, or take different jobs. By dint of their new circumstances, they can become a more valuable resource. For example, early in Blau's career as an editor in educational publishing, she met Suzanne Slesin, who was around the same age and fresh out of graduate school. Through a connection of her own, Slesin had been hired by the editor-in-chief of the division and was "given" to Blau as an assistant. A few years later, when Slesin was working at *New York*, she introduced Blau to Joan Kron, an editor there who then commissioned Blau to write for the magazine. In essence, Slesin "brokered" a connection that enabled Blau's switch to journalism. Slesin, who then became a *New York Times* editor and reporter and has since written many books of her own, is still one of the brighter red balls in Blau's urn.

"What makes balls red," Granovetter clarifies, "is not only their own qualities, but where they sit in the social structure, and this changes over time. Conversely, your red balls may move to places where they become less relevant [for example, a former professor retires], and they may then turn white."[39]

Freedom Summer: We Become Who We're With

Granovetter's urn brings home the point that although we are each unique beings with our own tastes, preferences, and desires, we don't exist in a vacuum. For example, after giving a speech at a music industry meeting about his book *The Tipping Point*, journalist Malcolm Gladwell attended a cocktail party where he was cornered by an executive who claimed that "pop music was being ruined by radio's adherence to market research." At the time, Gladwell was already working on his next book, *Blink: The Power of Thinking Without Thinking.* The executive's comment got Gladwell thinking, and he eventually turned those ideas into a chapter about the limitations of focus-group feedback in certain industries. "Would I have developed that view of market research had I never gone to that conference?" Gladwell muses on his website. "I don't know. But probably not." The industry executive was undoubtedly one of many professionals Gladwell met that day, a guy who had something on his mind and was thrilled to pontificate to a journalist. It was just an ordinary moment between two people. But Gladwell recognizes that such encounters change him, even in small ways: "When you give a speech to a particular group, you expose yourself to the opinions of that group, and that exposure cannot help but affect the way you think."[40]

The extended self, the part of our identity that is tied to another person or social group, is continually affected by consequential strangers. In the course of any given day, each encounter leaves us with impressions—images and ideas that in turn color our perception and influence our behavior. We then bring that newly informed self into our next encounter, where we exchange more impressions.[41]

This constant and dynamic process helps explain why close to a thousand young Americans from cushy middle- and upper-class homes put themselves in harm's way in the summer of 1964. Jim Kates was one of them, a senior in high school in White Plains, New York. His parents were divorced, his father living in Manhattan. Mom and Dad were "friends with people on the Left" but not activists themselves. A freshman at Brandeis whom Kates met through an old school chum asked if the two of them would help with a food and clothing drive on behalf of Greenwood, Mississippi, where civil rights organizations were about to launch a voter registration campaign. The boys were reluctant at first. They were already involved in a local "poverty drive" at their own school. However, when they read the pamphlets and campus newspaper the Brandeis student had left them, it opened their eyes to a reality that was far from their privileged universe. Within a week they had written and printed a flyer, invited ten classmates to get involved, and mobilized more than two hundred students to canvas Westchester County. Ironically, when Kates heard about the near-murder of one of the SNCC volunteers in Mississippi, he told his friend, "I'll do everything I can up here, but I'll be goddamned if you catch me going down there!"[42]

A year later, he was in Oxford, Ohio, at a Freedom Summer orientation meeting where college students from all over the country were given a crash course in activism. One of the bits of news they heard that week was that three of the other volunteers who had preceded them, James Chaney, Andrew Goodman, and Michael Schwerner, were missing. And although no one said so above a whisper at first, the three were presumed dead.

This was their welcome to Mississippi, a state mortally committed to preserving the "Southern way of life" even as the rest of the region was grudgingly beginning to change. Since the early fifties, the NAACP and other predominantly black organizations had successfully challenged Jim Crow laws, resulting in the 1954 Supreme Court decision that declared segregation in public schools illegal. The success of bus boycotts, sit-ins, and freedom rides further buoyed the hopes of black activists, but change was slow, especially in Mississippi. Most white citizens there were as virulently opposed to integration as they were to modernization—for generations, the "planter elite" had relied on cheap agricultural labor. Mississippi had the lowest rates of high school completion and the highest rates of poverty, the lowest rates of black voter registration and the highest rates of lynching.[43] Although white civil rights workers, led in large part by the Student Non-Violent Coordinating Committee, or SNCC (pronounced "snick"), knew the extent to which the most bigoted would go to thwart their efforts, the rest of the country was mostly unaware of the violence at that point. Freedom Summer, a project that lasted for a mere three months, would not only make visible the horrors of Mississippi, it would transform the consciousness of America and mark the true beginning of what we now think of as "the sixties."[44]

What made Freedom Summer volunteers like Jim Kates willing to leave the comfort of home to risk their lives? Doug McAdam, a sociologist who has spent most of his career studying the link between social movements and networks, wanted to find out. Looking for a list of the participants so that he could interview them retrospectively, McAdam happened on a box of materials at the King Center in Atlanta. Inside were the original five-page questionnaires the 959 applicants had filled out prior to that eventful summer. He could barely still his researcher's heart as he realized that before him were not only the responses of the 720 students who actually went to Mississippi that summer, but also those of the 239 no-shows—a natural control group. By comparing the two groups of applicants, McAdam might discover what set the no-shows apart from those who actually made it to the front lines.

The applicants, who were of different religions and from all parts of the country, were indistinguishable in terms of attitude. Most had grown up as the protected, if not pampered, offspring of parents who had lived through the Depression and World War II and believed wholeheartedly in the postwar promises of America. Thanks to their prosperity, their children also had the time and money to get involved. *Ninety percent* of the applicants belonged to some type of organization—62% listed two or more. Nearly half (48%) were members of civil rights organizations, which meant that most already had a taste of what it meant to be part of something bigger. "Playing at being an activist," McAdam explains, "is usually the first step in becoming one."[45] Their motives were a mixed bag, but youthful idealism was evident in their responses to questions on the applications. Contrary to popular belief, they did not enlist as an act of rebellion; most of their parents sympathized with the movement. Many mentioned the late President Kennedy's call to "do" for their country. Being young, some were also in it for the adventure. Jim Kates, for one, finally decided to go because his original summer plans—to work in a theater in Nantucket—fell through.

Gung-ho as they all might have been when they applied in February or March, waiting until June gave them ample opportunity to have second thoughts. Beatings and burnings, even murder, were commonplace in Mississippi, but now the violence was escalating, largely in anticipation of the "army from the North." The news was enough to convince some to watch from the sidelines. Others, especially women and applicants under twenty-one, were held back by apprehensive parents who refused to sign permission forms.

But the single factor that distinguished the participants from the no-shows, McAdam found, was "social proximity." When they were asked to name ten or more people who "would be interested in receiving information about your [summer] activities," around a quarter of all applicants listed other project participants. But the volunteers listed more than *twice as many* as the no-shows. Backing out meant disappointing, or risking the disapproval of, people they knew.[46] Volunteers also belonged to more organizations than the no-shows, particularly civil rights groups, and they were more deeply immersed in the cause. This not only gave them the opportunity to "play" the activist role, it put them in groups of like-minded people.

It's impossible to discern from the applications whether these connections were best friends or casual acquaintances. However, as McAdam explains, "a movement can't spread without the influence of weak, bridging ties." This is certainly evident in interviews with Freedom Summer veterans. Asked what motivated them, most begin by talking about a person or group that piqued their awareness. Sometimes it was a close friend, sometimes not. The student from Brandeis who whetted Jim Kates's appetite was a friend of a friend. Others were influenced by teachers or local organizers. And when they talk about their experiences *in* Mississippi, they speak mostly of the bonds they formed with volunteers from other parts of the country, townspeople and teachers they worked with, and families that housed them. For many, this was their first time living in a rural, impoverished setting, no less in the black community. Interacting with such a variety of people—by definition, consequential strangers—expanded their consciousness, gave them a different sense of themselves in the world.

"I was on a project with forty people. You had friends, but mostly not," offers Chude Allen, a self-described "goody-goody" from the Midwest, the daughter of God-fearing Eisenhower Republicans.[47] That a young woman could be "sexually active and mellow about it," for example, was something that had never occurred to Allen, who was "saving it for marriage," as good girls then did. "It opened a door for me."

Volunteers always traveled in twos. They didn't choose their partners; it depended on what they were assigned to do on a given day. Jim Kates recalls a time when he and Willie Curtis Johnson, a local high school boy, were returning from a voter registration drive. Seeing an ominous group of good ol' boys ahead of them, Johnson, having learned early in life to dodge angry white men, crossed the street to avoid trouble. Kates, accustomed to white privilege, kept going until one of the men blocked his path: "Boy, you better be out of town by sunset if you don't want to end up like those three." Kates knew he meant Chaney, Goodman, and Schwerner. Only days before, he had written in his journal, "How the ghosts of those three shadow all our work!" Seeing the standoff, Johnson suddenly called out to Kates, beckoning him toward his stepfather's barbershop across the street. Petrified, Kates turned his back on the three white men and started walking. He got lucky that day, thanks to the quick thinking of a young black man he hardly knew.

Allen, Kates, and other volunteers say they were "forever changed" after that summer. They met people they would never have known, heard stories they would never have heard. As in the case of Doug Davis, the experience activated their extended selves. Psychologist Marilynn Brewer notes that when "the boundaries of the self are redrawn" in this more expansive way and particular roles are "activated" by being a member of a group or collective, those roles in turn become more important to us. We want to behave in a way that reflects well on the group.[48] In all likelihood, Kates had the courage to turn his back on the men who threatened him, because at that moment he was not acting out of self-interest. He was on a mission. This also might explain why he and his fellow volunteers didn't boast of their personal exploits when they returned to their respective campuses. "Other people recognized our experience, but we could not trade on it. We had been foot soldiers." The cause was greater than any one of their individual selves.

After they left Mississippi, Freedom Summer veterans insinuated themselves in the various other liberation movements that characterized the decade. Liberalism and social justice became central to their identities. Their lives were filled with consequential strangers who were very different from them (and from one another) but equally committed to changing the system. Asked to define their political leanings, with "1" indicating the far left and "10" the radical right, both groups of applicants started out in the 3.5 range. After the experience, however, nearly two-thirds felt they had moved "further to the left," while the no-shows exhibited only a slight change. But a numerical comparison doesn't begin to capture the true impact of Freedom Summer, says McAdam: "For it wasn't anything as narrow as their attitudes that changed, as much as it was the way they saw and interpreted the world."

Six Degrees Beyond the Influentials

Some ideas are either so seductive or intuitive, we accept them without question. For example, the notion that we're only six people—degrees—away from each other has inspired a parlor game, a play, and numerous film and television shows. That the idea was so readily adopted owes in part to the fact that all of us have had six-degree experiences, most of which involve tales of consequential strangers: Someone you meet by chance at a ball game just happens to be an alumna of your college. From her you learn that a fellow dorm mate is now engaged to Marty Molar, who just happens to be your mother's dentist! It's reassuring to think that "science" can explain such moments. However, the reason we believe they occur with "regularity," says sociologist Duncan Watts, author of *Six Degrees: Science in a Connected Age*, is that we pay closer attention when we're surprised by events and therefore misjudge their frequency.[49] In fact, Stanley Milgram's 1967 "small world" experiment, in which volunteers were instructed to deliver an envelope to a stranger by giving it to someone in their own social network, had a very low completion rate—5% in the original study, 29% in a follow-up.[50] And in Watts's 2003 version, conducted via email, only 384 of 24,163 chains reached their targets.[51]

Another notion that has been widely embraced is that if you want to spread word or promote a new idea, find yourself an "influential"—a voice of knowledge, a person others respect, a trendsetter or "early adopter" who's game to try a new idea or product and then likes to talk about it—in short, someone who's well connected. Marketing texts are filled with anecdotes about the importance of reaching a "network hub." Certainly a star spokesperson may be effective in some cases, but more often you don't necessarily need one. As the case of Freedom Summer exemplifies, messages spread and movements grow out of everyday relationships. The same was true for the Red Hat Society. After Sue Ellen Cooper's first outing with her flagship group, friends of friends told their acquaintances, and chapters began to spring up. An amazed Cooper likened herself to the fictional Forrest Gump, running for no particular reason when all of a sudden "a few people start to jog along behind him, and then a few more, and then a huge crowd!"[52]

A crowd of consequential strangers.

Experts' opinions are not necessarily better than laypeople's. In 2003, researchers at Elon University and the Pew Internet & American Life Project surveyed longtime Internet experts for their predictions about how increasing use of digital technology might affect our habits and society as a whole. They repeated the survey three years later, sending it to the original participants and their colleagues. But the researchers also contacted people on their email list, some of whom were "working in the trenches of building the Web." Comparing the responses of "Internet pioneers" who'd been online before 1993 with people who were "not necessarily opinion leaders for their industries or well-known futurists," the second report noted that "it is striking how much their views were distributed in ways that paralleled those who are celebrated in the technology field."[53]

Recent research also points to the importance of routine conversations between ordinary people. In a study that analyzed a three-month word-of-mouth advertising campaign for Rock Bottom Brewery, a national chain of brew pubs, professors of marketing David Godes and Dina Mayzlin were interested in "incremental" word-of-mouth—recommendations that had not already been shared within a person's social network. They compared "loyals," frequent diners who were experts on Rock Bottom, and "agents," average Joes unfamiliar with the restaurant who had volunteered to eat there. As it turned out, the nonloyal agents were far more effective at singing the restaurant's praises than repeat customers. The researchers concluded that "opinion leaders" couldn't be counted on to keep spreading the word. Once they tell people in their convoys about Rock Bottom, they don't feel the need to continue talking about the restaurant. To generate further word-of-mouth, then, management might better target people on the periphery who were less loyal but in a better position to bridge into other networks.[54]

Rethinking these two seemingly immutable principles—small world and the preeminence of key individuals—has significant implications for social movements, marketing, and the mundane moments of connection that occur when we converse with others. Undeniably, our multilayered lives allow us to build bridges to a variety of consequential strangers in other networks, as well as those in our own convoys. Given digital technology, the task becomes even easier. In some cases, it *is* possible to reach someone in six degrees, sometimes even fewer. But Watts and his colleagues asked senders *why* they chose a particular person to carry out the link in his small-world study. As earlier network analysts found, targets—usually acquaintances—are often selected because of the kind of work they do or where they live, but having many social connections was *rarely* cited as a factor. This led the authors to conclude that "social search" appears to be more egalitarian than dependent on "a small minority of exceptional individuals." The devil is in the details. The transfer of information isn't quite like the spread of a virus, Watts stresses; the next person is *not* automatically infected. When ideas or information are involved, each link in a chain depends—among other factors—on whether the recipient is *motivated* to make the next connection.[55]

Sociologist Alexandra Marin found a similar phenomenon when

she looked at how people make decisions to share or withhold job information. For the most part, people who knew of openings at their company were more likely to tell prospective job-seekers about an opportunity *when they knew the person was in the market for it.* "It acknowledges that the people in networks are actually making choices. They're not just 'pipes'—the term sociologists use. They're human beings who make choices about telling you or not telling you. And they make those choices based on their own thoughts and perceptions." In another study, when people were asked to recall *why* they shared either negative or positive recommendations for services over the previous six months, the number one reason was the other person's "felt need." That is to say, they suggested an accountant around tax time, a travel website when they knew the other person was planning a trip.[56] The lesson here? Let your consequential strangers know what you need.

Ultimately, a complex array of factors determines who we tell and whether that information or idea will continue to travel. However, one thing is certain: As consumers of information, we've become more savvy about filtering out the truth. Because of this, says Dave Balter, founder of BzzAgent, a word-of-mouth ad agency, the consumer landscape has changed from "at" marketing to "with" marketing. We no longer buy products simply because of catchy slogans, compelling visuals, or great stories flung in our direction by a handful of journalists or experts. Instead we read blogs, visit websites to compare products, and—mostly—we talk to each other.[57]

Arguably, discussing products and services is an inescapable necessity of modern life, since so much of our time is spent making consumer decisions. In the age of "with" marketing, we feel our power and want to be part of the process, which is why companies have invested huge sums in websites that allow them to hear from and talk directly to people that buy and use their products. A study in 2000 suggested that approximately two-thirds of the U.S. economy is at least partially influenced by word-of-mouth.[58]

Is it any wonder, then, that word-of-mouth, a strategy that dates back to biblical times, has seen a resurgence in the twenty-first century? Its growth is a natural by-product of networked individualism: Marketing mavens want to tap into our personal convoys. They know we're skeptical about grandiose advertising claims and that we compare notes with one another—a process that has been abetted and accelerated by the Internet. Approximately 30% of web users rate or review products and services online, and 81% read online comments before they buy.[59] However, 80 to 90% of word-of-mouth takes place in the *real* world.[60]

Dave Balter oversees an unpaid army of "BzzAgents"—some 400,000 people who are willing to spread information about new products and write reports about their conversations. They are neither shills nor stealth marketers. On the contrary, they are honor-bound to tell people that they're part of a word-of-mouth campaign. Their "reward" is points, redeemable for unimpressive prizes that 87% of agents don't even bother to collect. So why would anyone do it? Balter chalks it up to a desire to help, to educate, to validate their own opinions, and to show others that they're in the know. Talking about products is also a means of telling other people about yourself.[61] Owning a Viking stove or installing solar panels furnishes clues to your identity. We are what we buy.

Perhaps most important, conversing about products and services enables us to connect with others and to stand on common ground. *Which large-screen TV do you think is best? You've got to try their osso buco. I found this great free music site. Who cuts your hair? I found something new for my allergies. Any ideas where I can get a new couch?* In a consumer-oriented society, such exchanges are a form of culture smarts. Just think back to the last social gathering you went to; chances are someone whipped out a new electronic gadget, touted a recent adventure trip, or warned not to call an electrician they'd used. You don't have to be a BzzAgent to engage in "brand-related discussions," says Walter J. Carl, an assistant professor in the Department of Communications Studies at Northeastern University. He found that BzzAgents referenced products, services, or companies in 29% of their daily interactions—not surprising, as that's their job. But "everyday people"—students recruited from communications classes and business studies—have such discussions 14% of the time. In both cases, the majority of conversations were unplanned.[62]

Erin Childs is a typical BzzAgent. The 35-year-old mother of two is a part-time lawyer who looks very much like the girl next door. She heard about the agency while "lurking" in a chat room discussion of new baby products. Initially lured by the promise of a free seventy-dollar toothbrush, Childs, who "loves to try new products," jumped at the opportunity to become an agent. In a sense, it's what she does anyway. As a BzzAgent, most of her initial targets were consequential strangers. She hung up Raid bee traps at the local park and talked to other mothers about it. During a plane trip to a business conference, she touted Listerine Whitening Strips to a colleague. She put out a platter of pretzels, cheese, and crackers accompanied by a selection of Grey Poupon mustards as a "quick appetizer" when neighbors stopped by. She suggested Eucerin Daily Replenishing Lotion to women in her playgroup who were worried about their babies' dry skin. And when she gave Pledge dusters and multisurface wipes to her cleaning woman to use and recommend to other clients, she felt like she was returning the favor. "In the past, she's turned me on to cleaning products that I'd never have known about if it weren't for her. That's what often happens. From people you wouldn't think of that way, you find out amazing things."

Interestingly, Walter Carl found no significant differences between agents and nonagents. Gender, income, and other demographic variables don't play a role in their success. *Relationships* do. We are all potential word-of-mouth agents, not just the mavens and magic people. Sometimes valuable tidbits travel via consequential strangers by accident, sometimes, as in institutionalized word-of-mouth campaigns, by design. But even then it's about common ground. Erin Childs oozes enthusiasm and sincerity—not because she's putting on an act but because she's displaying an aspect of her "self" that fits the situation. There is nothing heavy-handed about her delivery; it's just part of everyday conversation. People see that she's genuinely impressed with a particular product, so they're willing to try it themselves.

And it's not always about products. Doka Gurung, who lives in Lo Manthang, Nepal, is part of a volunteer force described as "one of the great unfolding public health triumphs of modern times."[63] In 2006, Nepal saw a *90% decline* in measles-related fatalities, while in neighboring India, complications of the disease continued to claim close to 100,000 young victims a year. Nepal's secret weapon was 50,000 mothers like Gurung, most of them illiterate, who explained the dangers of measles and the benefits of vaccination. The night before the vaccine and other medicines are trekked thousands of feet up the steep and winding mountains, Gurung acts like a town crier, reminding her fellow villagers, "Come for the measles vaccination tomorrow!" The Nepalese mothers also dole out lifesaving doses of vitamin A, deworming tablets, and packets of oral rehydration salts. The job pays no salary but is "a way to contribute and win respect." Now in her early thirties, Gurung has been part of this unusual "army" for nearly a decade: "If I didn't tell them about vaccination programs or medicines, they wouldn't know."

Doka Gurung's influence lies in the relationships she's forged with consequential strangers in her village, and her identity is further shaped by those interactions. Her trustworthiness and reliability—qualities that render her an "expert" in her compatriots' eyes—are more important than any particular asset that she, as "teller," possesses. A resident of Lo Manthang and mother of four herself, she has what inner-city kids would call "street cred." Similarly, recall the record industry executive who cornered Malcolm Gladwell at a cocktail party. He was a reliable source in the journalist's eyes because he knew the industry and felt passionate about his opinions. The exec wasn't a luminary in the field, but he managed to plant a new idea in a very fertile mind.

In the final analysis, the consequential strangers in our convoys, and every conversational exchange we have with them, take us beyond the familiar. They enable us to develop a more complex self that, in turn, helps us make sense of the world and our place in it.[64] And as we will see in the next chapter, such connections are also vital to our well-being.

4

Good for What Ails Us

> Everyone who is born holds dual citizenship, in the kingdom of the well and in the kingdom of the sick. Although we all prefer to use only the good passport, sooner or later each of us is obliged, at least for a spell, to identify ourselves as citizens of that other place.
>
> —*Susan Sontag,* Illness as Metaphor *(1990)*

The Man Who Would Not Die

Art Buchwald insisted on living while he was supposed to be busy dying. In his early fifties, sharing his "death fantasy" with fellow journalist George Plimpton, he imagined himself at the age of ninety-three, dropping dead on the center court at Wimbledon during the men's finals.[1] Thirty years later, the dry-witted raconteur had to revise his plan. At eighty, he had already lost a leg to diabetes, and his kidneys had shut down. To prepare for the surgery, he had reluctantly agreed to several sessions of dialysis—three times a week, five hours per session—to rid his body of toxins his kidneys could no longer filter. But after the operation, the indomitable eighty-year-old declared, "That's it. I don't see a future in this, and I don't want to do it anymore!"[2] As far as Buchwald was concerned, the procedure was "like being connected to a washing machine." His doctors warned him that he would die within weeks. Family and close friends were understandably distraught over his decision. But if he couldn't control his life, Buchwald at least wanted some say in his death. Resolute, he moved to the hospice wing of the hospital.

Word got out. Diane Rehm, the popular public radio talk show host in Washington, D.C., invited Buchwald to be on her midday program. Buchwald didn't think twice. "I figured, what the heck. I had nothing else to do." Broadcasting from the hospice, he talked about his decision, about dying, about his children's reactions—things most of us ponder but are reluctant to discuss. Letters and emails poured in. Every major media outlet wanted him. "I enjoyed the interviews because it gave me something to do besides watch *Wheel of Fortune.*"

The unexpected publicity blitz inspired members of Buchwald's convoy, intimates and consequential strangers alike, to converge at his bedside. "So far, I've heard from everybody in my life—from my public school days, the University of California, the Marine Corps, my Paris pals, and all the people I knew or who claimed they knew me in Washington," Buchwald mused. "I received nearly three thousand letters, many of them from people who were connected to me (or thought they were) in some way. I had met them in Paris, or I'd spoken at their graduation. Then the visitors started to arrive. Every letter, phone call, and visit made me remember an incident or a little gift from the past."

The sitting area down the hall from his room became Buchwald's "salon," and well-wishers brought him what he loved most: lavish amounts of food and good conversation. "People couldn't believe I was having so much fun. The word spread that if you want a good time, go to Washington Hospice." Shortly thereafter, his kidneys started working again. He became known among the staff as the Man Who Would Not Die.

Positive emotions and laughter are good medicine.[3] Even better when the joke is shared. Buchwald used his razor-sharp wit to cut through questions of death, the afterlife, and the meaning of it all. He planned his own memorial service. He also resumed writing his longtime *Washington Post* column and started a new book as well. Only one in ten patients leave hospice alive. Buchwald not only joined their ranks, he survived long enough to see the publication of his aptly titled memoir, *Too Soon to Say Goodbye*.

The story captured our hearts and imagination for several reasons, not the least of which was that he decided to die *his way*. But Art Buchwald's struggle also resonated because we ourselves are often faced with such quality-of-life-and-death decisions—if not our own, then our loved ones'. No one knows why his kidneys miraculously started working again, or why he lived more than seven months longer than his doctors had predicted. But perhaps research on "social integration" and a related idea, "social support," offers a different way of looking at Buchwald's situation. When you're ailing or have an unexpected change of course in life, having loved ones in your corner is both comforting and beneficial. However, you also need consequential strangers to sustain you. Buchwald had an array of visitors to talk with and get advice from—a variety of close *and* casual relationships. He may have lost the war against his disease, but he seemed to die a happy man, and who can ask for more at any age?

Looking for a Different Story

The state of health in America today is complicated, with far more nuances and uncertainties than a sound bite on the evening news can capture. While some groups of people are at greater risk of sickness than others, "fit" Americans, largely middle-class and college-educated—are healthier and more health-conscious than at any point in human history. Even centenarians are often in surprisingly good condition.[4] People still get sick, of course, but because many infectious diseases are today either treatable or preventable, chronic illness is now the leading cause of death throughout the world.[5] According to the Centers for Disease Control and Prevention, at least ninety million Americans—*25% of the population*—have one or more chronic conditions; nearly half have multiple chronic conditions, some more life-threatening and debilitating than others.[6] The irony is that although as a nation we're healthier than ever, millions of us nevertheless travel to "the kingdom of the sick," sometimes for extended stays. Maladies such as cancer, heart disease, diabetes, kidney disease, AIDS, arthritis, and respiratory problems can persist for decades. And it can be a very lonely experience.

The shift to chronic suffering calls into question one of our basic "stories" about modern medicine—the notion that once doctors discover the physical reason for our physical or mental distress, they can "fix" us. The problem is, despite the wonders of technology and pharmacology, physicians can't always find the cause nor cure the illness. As in Art Buchwald's case, the best they can do is suggest drugs or therapies that are sometimes as taxing as the disease. But we want more. So we turn to alternate cultural narratives about healing—stories that put our minds, our personalities, and, most important, our social lives into the medical equation, stories that give us some degree of hope, even in situations that appear hopeless.[7]

The concern goes beyond chronic disease. Almost everyone has had to deal with a violent or life-threatening situation, as well as the death of a loved one.[8] So we soak up other people's journeys, and there are plenty to chose from. A quick, admittedly nonscientific search of memoirs available at Amazon.com on a random day in 2008 yielded 66 titles under the heading of "coping with disease," 80 about "mental health," and 210 on "illness." Another 896 titles came up for "coping with trauma." Memoirs of adversity and triumph show us how other people make sense of difficult chapters in their life stories—and we're drawn to them because we are constantly in the process of rewriting and reassessing our own autobiographies.[9]

When Robin Roberts, a TV newscaster on the *Good Morning America* team, learned she had breast cancer in 2007, she invited millions of viewers into the experience. She brought a video camera to doctors' appointments. Chemotherapy, radiation, shopping for wigs—nothing was off-limits. She laughed and cried, and we rooted for her just as we cheered on Lance Armstrong, Christopher Reeve, Magic Johnson, and Melissa Etheridge, just as we wished that Buchwald would live forever. We don't know these people, but we certainly know a lot *about* them, and being privy to the details of their lives almost makes them *feel* like consequential strangers. They *could* be people we know; in fact, they could be us. Their individual experiences, especially in light of research that links social connections and health, comprise a cultural fable about the power of relationships. This "healthy ties" narrative, as health historian Anne Harrington calls it, reassures us that human connection is just what the doctor ordered.[10]

To Catch a Cold

In the mid-nineties, an intriguing advertisement appeared in the classified section of several Pittsburgh newspapers:

> ATTENTION! PITT/CMU COLD STUDY
>
> Participants in this research study will be exposed to a common cold virus & isolated in a local hotel. Qualified volunteers (ages 18–55) may receive up to $800 upon completion of the study.

Hundreds responded to the ad, but only 125 men and 151 women were deemed healthy enough to make the cut. They were put through a battery of physical tests, given a personalty profile, and interviewed about their health histories and habits. Did they smoke? drink? exercise? sleep well? take vitamin C and zinc? The volunteers' level of "social integration" was assessed by asking them to think about their close and casual relations. Who did they see or speak with at least once every two weeks (email was not yet a factor in most people's lives)? The goal was to determine how *diverse* their convoys were, not how large. They were therefore given one point for each *type* of relation: spouse; parents; in-laws; children; other close family members; friends; coworkers; neighbors; schoolmates; fellow volunteers (charity or community work); members of religious groups; and members of nonreligious groups (a catchall category described as "social, recreational, or professional," which could include anyone from a bowling-team buddy to a fellow PTA parent).

For six days the human guinea pigs were quarantined on a private floor in a hotel not far from downtown Pittsburgh where they were given carefully calibrated nose drops containing a cold virus.[11] Each person was assigned a standard room with a TV. A large lounge area was equipped with chairs, couches, a pool table, and a TV/VCR. The volunteers could also read books or magazines they had brought with them, work on laptops—anything that would help pass the time. Other participants' quarters were strictly off-limits. Socializing in the hallway or lounge was okay, but the volunteers were cautioned to stay at least three feet apart lest they get an even bigger dose of cold virus from another person's cough or sneeze. They were also given personalized plastic bags—for used tissues—that were turned over at the end of each day and weighed to assess "mucus production." A person was said to have a cold if his or her body showed an increase in viral antibodies and displayed objective signs of the illness such as heavy mucus and congestion.

Not everyone got sick. Even though each volunteer was given a cold virus, those who had a rich web of relationships were far less likely to come down with a cold.[12] People who interacted with only one to three different types of relationships in a two-week period had *more than four times the risk* of developing a cold than those who interacted with six or more types. In other words, having a diverse convoy acted like a dose of medicine for the immune system—the cells, proteins, tissue, and organs that work together to keep viruses and other foreign invaders at bay. In fact, Sheldon Cohen, the psychologist who has been conducting these "viral-challenge" studies for the past two decades, maintains that when it comes to risk factors, "lower levels of social integration" are right up there with cigarette smoking.[13]

Although the idea that social networks affect well-being goes back more than a century, the concept was reinvigorated in the seventies when Lisa Berkman, then a graduate student in public health, discovered a strong correlation between social ties and mortality. Berkman decided to look at the data collected from nearly 7,000 people who had taken part in a 1965 public health survey in Alameda County, California. Because the questionnaire included items about marital status, number of friends, and membership in religious and voluntary organizations, Berkman was able to piece together the composition of the respondents' networks. The evidence was compelling: People who lacked close and community ties, including consequential strangers, were more likely to die nine years earlier than those with more extensive social connections—women 2.8 times more likely and men 2.3.[14]

Since Berkman's discovery, a host of community-based studies, here and abroad, have linked other benefits to social integration. People with diverse ties report better mental and physical health and engage in fewer risky healthy practices, like drinking and smoking, than people who are socially isolated.[15] The socially integrated are not only less susceptible to infectious illness, as Sheldon Cohen's work has consistently shown, they are also more likely than their more isolated counterparts to survive heart attacks or cancer, less likely to suffer from depression or anxiety.[16] Of course, the evidence is indirect—we're talking about correlations, not cause. Although investigators attempt to take prior health status into consideration, it is also possible that people who are sick withdraw from the social world *because* they are ill, and not the other way around. Nonetheless, cumulative data strongly suggests that being more socially involved confers multiple health benefits.

Even a recent analysis of autobiographies written by 96 psychologists and 220 contemporary authors yielded surprisingly similar results.[17] Using the first ten pages of each book, the researchers counted the number of times the author referred to social roles such as mother, brother, cousin, friend, coworker, roommate. Even though the writers weren't purposely describing their personal networks, they were presenting their overall sense of themselves in the world. Authors who fell in the top third, listing the most social-role terms, lived more than six years longer than those who fell in the bottom third. (Again, this research does not disentangle *why* mentioning social roles was associated with living longer.)

That we highlight these various findings about the role of peripheral ties is not to understate the significance of the people closest to us. Almost all of the studies also stress the importance of intimates, especially when it comes to older people. However, investigators who have considered *both* kind of ties find that having a mixed network gives you more options.[18] In short, although loved ones are universally important, *all* relationships influence our physiology and psychology. We don't necessarily need a lot of relationships; it's *variety* that affects our well-being.

Having a "tribe," agrees social neuroscientist John Cacioppo, who has spent the last twenty years parsing loneliness, is the flip side of social isolation, which puts people at risk for mental and physical illness.[19] However, social integration is not a one-size-fits-all prescription. Just as we inherit a particular body type or eye color, Cacioppo points out, we are each born with "a certain level of need for social inclusion (also expressed as a sensitivity to the pain of social exclusion)."[20] So what feels like "connection" to one person might be too little or too much for another.

An Unexpectedly Healthy Man

Though he's pushing seventy, Henry Perlman* doesn't advertise it. He's youthful, trim, stylish, and in the summer, deeply tanned.

Considering the fact that he declared himself an alcoholic a few years ago, he is in surprisingly good health. At his first Alcoholics Anonymous meeting, he announced that he intended to drink again when he got home that night. Afterward, a man came up to him and handed him a white scrap of paper saying, "Call me, and I'll talk you out of it." Miraculously, Perlman called and hasn't taken a drink since.

Perlman is not the kind of guy who surrounds himself with intimates. He has never been in a long-term relationship, but he has one close friend who is "like a brother." He prefers to keep others at a comfortable emotional distance, and his former job as a customer relations manager at a busy midtown bank in Manhattan gave him exactly the kind of social contact he prefers: a steady stream of recurring and familiar faces, no strings attached.[21]

Looking from the outside, we might assume that, given the paucity of strong ties, Perlman is lonely and therefore at risk. Certainly a man who has been drinking for fifty years could be in poor health. However, no one knows exactly how connection "gets under our skin"—that is, how social ties protect us against illness or help us heal. The process is a complex amalgam of environmental and social factors, as well as our individual histories, traits, and the genes we inherit.

Perlman's convoy has always been comprised mostly of consequential strangers. Being the only child of two handicapped parents, he learned early not to ask any one person to bear the brunt of his needs. Depending on the time, place, and his mood, he gives each person in his life a small piece of himself and asks little in return. Still, he gets what he needs. When he worked at the bank, he could predict who would show up on which day and knew how much the person earned. For the special few, he'd stretch the rules if necessary—say, cashing a paycheck without proper ID. He knew them only fleetingly, but that was good enough. "I looked forward to seeing certain people," he offers, "because I could tell them the horror stories." When another customer gave him a hard time, Perlman would scan the faces of people waiting in line, looking for one of his favorites. Making eye contact with Perlman, the familiar customer might then roll her eyes or, when it was her turn at his desk, whisper a conspiratorial comment like, "I can't believe you have to put up with *that*." Those momentary interactions made Perlman feel valued and supported. "It was a great source of comfort," he says, "and I guess it was a mutual feeling, because even when there were long lines, many of them would tell me, 'I waited just for you.'"

Scientists suspect that social integration "works" through social norms—generally accepted standards of behavior. That is, people with more varied convoys may feel greater social pressure to stay healthy (assuming that their associates are) and to adopt healthful behaviors, such as eating well, taking vitamins, and exercising regularly. The diversely connected also seem to be less susceptible to social pressures to smoke and drink excessively than isolates who don't have this protective mantle.[22] In Henry Perlman's case, the social norms imposed by his work role kept his drinking in check. He drank almost every day of the forty years he worked at the bank, but he had to show up the next day and be a dutiful and conscientious employee. The job itself provided structure and rules. When he retired, those controls fell away.

"Instead of going to museums and appreciating the city now that I had all this free time," he admits, "I drank my nights away and slept my days away." Just as important, Perlman lost the security of being part of a diverse "community" of customers and coworkers. The bank provided him with contacts that ranged from construction workers to CEOs. In contrast, his social universe in retirement was almost entirely populated by other drinkers. The guys at the trendy uptown bar where he spent his nights didn't question the fact that he got sloshed every night—they did, too—and this made it easier for *him* to indulge.

When Perlman started going to AA meetings, members warned him to avoid "people, places, and things" associated with drinking—a timeworn AA aphorism that reflects the importance of social norms: seeking people and situations that will inspire a healthier self. Although believing in a "higher power" is also part of the program, atheists and agnostics who resist this notion are told to think of G-O-D as a "group of drunks." Perlman obeyed and has stayed sober in part because he replaced his drinking buddies with a more diverse crew of consequential strangers—fellow recovering alcoholics whose social lives no longer revolved around drinking. "I can't say they're my friends, but I see those people almost on a daily basis. If I don't see certain people, I get concerned. Are they okay? Did they have a drink? Are they sick? If they drop out, I worry." He also believes that they worry about him.

Even when everyday interactions with others don't explicitly involve support with a capital S, social integration gives us options. Having a variety of people to turn to, be they colleagues, club members, clients, or a group of drunks, gives us a sense of control and buoys our mood, which is even better than an apple a day.[23] And when something goes wrong in one setting, it might not feel as overwhelming if you can process it elsewhere or retreat to a realm that brings out a different one of those multiple selves we discussed earlier.

John Cacioppo incorporates this idea in his exploration of loneliness. He not only asks participants to rate the extent to which they agree or disagree with statements about themselves as *individuals* ("I lack companionship," "I feel left out"), but also statements about their *relationships* ("people understand me," "I have people I can talk with") and their *group affiliations* ("I am part of a clique," "I am a member of an organization"). Feeling lonely, he says, is a function of all *three* types of connection. This is good news for the 43% of Americans who are single, many of whom complain that they've been painted with too broad a brush.[24] Being unmarried in and of itself, Cacioppo found, is not necessarily equated with isolation: "Marriage does predict lower loneliness. However, marriage does not *ensure* lower loneliness. Single people with great friends and family can be nonlonely, and estranged married couples can feel highly lonely," Cacioppo points out. "That is not to say that different social inputs are completely fungible, but when it comes to loneliness they aren't entirely distinct, either."[25]

Social integration is a boon to well-being regardless of what else is going on in our lives. However, a diverse convoy can also confer a slightly different kind of health benefit, *social support*: the giving *or* receiving of advice, information, financial aid, emotional succor (comfort, ego-boosting), or material assistance, such as help with chores and errands. We rarely rely on one person for all the different types of support.[26]

Getting appropriate social support can protect us from stress—a word that comes into virtually every conversation about well-being. A frequently cited example of this "stress-buffering" effect occurred when expectant mothers were admitted to a hospital in Guatemala for their first delivery—an anxiety-provoking situation for most women. Some were randomly assigned to go through the process on their own, while others were paired with a *doula*, a trained birthing companion (not a husband or a close friend) whom they had gotten to know before they went into labor. The women who had *doulas* not only had fewer complications during childbirth, they also were more responsive to their new babies after delivery.[27]

Sometimes, the other person need only listen: The mere act of *describing* a difficult event in detail can ease stress over time.[28] And consider this recent experiment: A group of "subject" rats in Tokyo were put into a specially wired box that allowed the researchers to give random, half-second electric shocks to their feet. On the following day, they were placed in the shock box again, but under three different conditions: with a partner rat who had also been zapped, with an unshocked partner rat, or alone. The shocked rats naturally showed fear responses when they were returned to the shock box under any of these conditions. They "froze"—didn't move except to breathe—and their body temperatures rose. However, such fear responses were not as strong when another rat was present, particularly if that other rat had never been shocked. These findings support the importance of recruiting other people outside our own situation when we are in crisis.[29]

In 2007, H&R Block adopted a new slogan, "You got people," to let customers know that even if they did their taxes at home using the company's computer software, live human beings were only a click or call away. That's not only good business, it's sound psychology. Perception is a key aspect of stress-buffering. We do better even if we just *think* we have "people." When two groups of healthy volunteers were asked to speak publicly—for many a heart-pounding proposition—those who were told that someone was waiting in the wings to cue them in case they faltered (even though no one actually was) had lower heart rates and blood pressure than the group who received no offers of support.[30] In a similar vein, parents of children with cancer who reported that they had people who helped them were not as physiologically affected by the stress of their situations as those who said they didn't have support.[31] The converse may be true as well: Thinking that you have no support can *add* stress. Among breast cancer patients, social isolation prior to diagnosis accounted more for health-related quality-of-life issues than either the kind of tumor a woman had or the effects of her treatment.[32]

Thus, it's no accident that Henry Perlman thought of customers who acknowledged him as "a great source of comfort." They didn't actually *do* anything to change his situation—being the front man at a busy bank meant he had to deal with disgruntled patrons every day. But in those few moments of connection, he felt as if "his people" were letting him know he was doing a good job. We have no way of knowing whether those brief interactions could actually affect his body's *physiological* responses to stress (as the sense of having supportive others around seemed to do for speech-givers and parents of children with cancer). But at the very least, the social support allowed him to move past the unpleasant encounter and conclude that maybe it wasn't a completely bad day after all.

"Seeking Ways to Find People"

At one of the many Super Bowl receptions in Miami in January 2007, adoring fans gathered around former Colts tight end John Mackey hoping to snag an autograph.[33] His wife, Sylvia, a former model, five-nine and stunning by anyone's standards, stood by his side. She somehow managed a smile each time her husband greeted an unsuspecting fan by thrusting both fists forward to show off his Super Bowl and All-Star rings. He'd point to the Super Bowl ring and in a dull monotone explain, "They gave me this one because I scored the seventy-five-yard touchdown that beat the Dallas Cowboys." She knew John wasn't bragging; he was simply repeating one of the few things he still remembers. He would parrot the same line ten, twenty, maybe even a hundred times a day to anyone who'd listen and often to the same person.

Ten or so years ago, Sylvia Mackey learned that her husband's inappropriate, repetitive, and compulsive behavior are symptoms of Pick's disease, a rare form of dementia. At first John seemed a little forgetful; then it got worse. He forgot he had a sister. He sang karaoke with a stranger at a bar—something he'd never done—and afterward informed his wife, in all seriousness, that he was taking their act to Las Vegas. Once a successful sports agent in Los Angeles, handsome, congenial, and loved by all, he started to make a series of bad business calls. By the time she realized what was happening, it was too late. The man she had loved since college had unknowingly torn down everything they had built. Then in her mid-fifties, Mackey signed up for flight attendant training and proceeded to launch a new career that would pay the bills and provide health coverage.

Illness is a family affair, and the physical, mental, emotional, and financial toll gets worse over time. The sheer stress of dealing with chronic disease can make the patient sicker and the rest of the family more vulnerable. A hint about how this works can be seen in one of Sheldon Cohen's viral-challenge studies, in which he found that people who experienced a lot of stress were more vulnerable to cold viruses. Cohen used three indicators to gauge levels of stress: negative emotions, the number of stressful situations subjects cited, and their *belief* that their lives were in turmoil.[34]

Although Cohen didn't examine caregivers per se, most would probably score at the higher end of each of those measures. Other researchers have found that caregivers—66% of whom are female—are at risk for physical and psychological health problems such as anxiety and depression.[35] As with most medical issues, though, it's not a simple association, among other reasons because people have different thresholds for stress. Some caregivers also have better coping skills to begin with and more people to help out. Of those who experience strain in the caregiving role, though, the downside is considerable: a 63% increase in mortality over four years.[36]

Dementia presents its own challenges. Nearly a third of these caretakers report symptoms of depression during a one-year period.[37] It makes sense: It's a 24/7 job, more demanding than infant care, especially when the "baby" is a strapping six-foot-two-inch, 235-pound man, as in the Mackeys' case. It's one reason Sylvia sold their home in California and returned to Baltimore, where John was something of a celebrity. "I thought it would help him hang on to his memory longer. He was still familiar with the Colts. I also know that when he got to the wandering stage, they'd know who he was."

He has since reached that stage. At restaurants, if she doesn't stop him, John will make off with an entire tray of pastries; in supermarkets, it's candy bars. "If we're at a dinner party, I know he's going to eat his dessert and everybody else's!" She laughs—her sense of humor has kept her sane. But some incidents she can't joke about. At the airport a few years ago, when John walked through the metal detector, his rings set off the alarm. "He had to be wanded but he refused to stand still. Instead," she recalls in a voice still shaken by the memory, "he walked right through and kept going, like he was running through a hole in the line on the football field." Sylvia, who by then had been a flight attendant for several years, feared that in a post-9/11 world, police might be inclined to shoot and ask questions later. With officers in hot pursuit of her husband, she ran after the lot of them, screaming, "Please don't shoot him. He doesn't understand." Since then, the Mackeys have traveled only by car or train.

Still, the challenges never cease. Mackey reads voraciously about her husband's condition so she can gauge what's on the horizon. She knew, for instance, that the day would come when John had to use Depends. "I didn't wait. I did it when he was still in a state where he would accept it." To get him to comply, she told him that the NFL had sent "special underwear." She also refers to his daily medication as "NFL vitamins," because "anything that's NFL-mandated gets obeyed!" But for all her personal strength, resourcefulness, and acceptance, she knows she can't do it alone. "You start seeking ways to find *people*." Research confirms this wisdom: Caregivers who have lots of social ties are at less risk for mental health problems.[38]

Mackey's youngest daughter has been a great help, but others in their inner circle now feel uncomfortable around John or don't know how to react to his mental decline. Some of the couple's old friends limit their visits, and social invitations are rare. Thus, Mackey has come to rely on consequential strangers: the daily home aide, the retired police officer who stops by to "sit with John," the staff at the senior care center, members of the various Alzheimer's support groups she has attended, and wives of other NFL players who share stories about their own husbands' mental decline. A select group of airline colleagues also know about her situation. But of all the wonderful people who've kept her going, it's the gang at the Mount Washington Tavern in downtown Baltimore who allow Sylvia Mackey to regain a momentary sense of normalcy. They remember John as the football hero he once was but also accept him as the genial, simple man he has become. "The place is just like *Cheers*," she quips. The owner started carrying nonalcoholic wine for her, so she can now let John belly up to the bar with a twenty-dollar bill in hand. "He can order his own glass of wine, like a man, so he can preserve his dignity. And if he wanders off, someone always keeps an eye on him." She quickly adds, "It's such a relief not to have to be in charge every minute."

Reaching Outside the (Shock) Box

John Mackey is blissfully unaware, unable to comprehend the drama that swirls around his family. But many who suffer from chronic conditions are all too cognizant of their need for support and the price their loved ones pay.[39] Richard M. Cohen (no relation to Sheldon), a former TV producer and journalist who was diagnosed with multiple sclerosis in his mid-twenties and colon cancer in his fifties, is legally blind and grows increasingly weak and unstable on his feet. His illness colors his relationship with his wife, Meredith Viera, cohost of the *Today* show, and restricts the kinds of activities he can do with their three teenage children. "They, too, are victims. We wear the same clothes and eat the same food. In many ways, we are the same person. My family's burden is equal to mine. For Meredith that is especially true. Cancer and multiple sclerosis have pulled the rug from under me, but she knows she is the one who must remain standing."[40]

Given such strains on our intimates, is it any wonder, then, that Cohen and others with chronic conditions might have to cast a wider net for support? The hardest situations are those that seem to have no end in sight. Illness and other life-stopping crises can feel like a time "out of time" when nothing moves forward.[41] "This is not the sporadic choreography of the occasional bad weekend, a one-time twisted ankle or sore knee," writes Richard Cohen. "Standing on the sidelines is a way of life. The psychological fallout only adds up and multiplies, weighing heavy."[42]

When help is offered by someone *outside* the patient's intimate circle, it's like bringing an unshocked rat buddy into the shock box to lessen the impact. After all, your loved ones are in there with you; they, too, have been shocked. They can be helpful, but not as much as someone outside the box. "Sometimes the very closeness of significant others makes it difficult for them to maintain their support," observed psychologist Niall Bolger after surveying breast cancer patients and their families. Questioning them four months after diagnosis and then six months later, he found that partner support had dropped off dramatically.[43] It's not because family members didn't care. They were burned out and traumatized themselves.

Turning to outsiders lessens the burden on both parties—the constant caretaker who needs a break, and the designated invalid, who feels as if he's a burden. "Can you imagine living with someone who comes home every day and kvetches?" asks Richard Cohen. It's difficult for him to ask for help in any case, but he finds it easier with consequential strangers. "You don't have to draw lines, because you're not that close to begin with. There are almost natural barriers because they have a particular place in your life. There's a built-in distance so it doesn't seem threatening. You walk away from that person—and that person vanishes."[44]

Because we tend to have limited encounters with consequential strangers, their gestures of support are often both unexpected and usually free of emotional baggage. The next-door neighbor offers to water the plants. The guy from accounting stops by after work with several funny DVDs. A bridge partner drops off a lasagna from Costco. It feels especially good to be remembered by someone who doesn't have to. We are also less inclined to bark at casual relations or subject them to our darkest moods, as we might with our intimates, especially on the worst days. Richard Cohen admits he's sometimes unable to prevent his negativity from spewing out onto his family. Afterward, he feels remorseful, guilty, and worried about the toll their caring exacts. His bout with colon cancer, which involved multiple operations and complications, was particularly difficult. Viera, he notes, later admitted, "I felt great distance from you after you came home from all that surgery. I would be lying if I told you I didn't feel put off. Your anger drove us all away."[45]

Sometimes, too, people close to us *can't* be there, and we have no choice but to depend on consequential strangers. Dr. Jerri Nelson had volunteered to spend a year as staff physician at the Amundsen-Scott South Pole Station. Her nearest relatives were 11,200 miles away when she found a lump in her breast. Marooned at the edge of the world where temperatures reach as low as 100 below and residents are plunged in complete darkness for half the year, Nelson found herself in the "unique situation of being the most sick and the only healer." She *had* to rely on other "Polies" whom she had known for only a few months. In *Ice Bound,* her memoir of the experience, she refers to this diverse and caring group as the "community of friends and strangers who rescued me."[46]

Nelson had no choice. But even when intimates are in the picture, consequential strangers play a special role. They can take up the slack, giving your loved ones breathing room and helping with the details and disruptions. They also can provide emotional succor, and encourage you to express feelings that might worry your intimates. Anyone who has spilled his or her guts to a hairdresser or a bartender won't have trouble believing that those two groups have proven to be effective ad hoc mental health counselors.[47] Outsiders tend to let you talk but rarely try to push you into a particular direction, which is harder for family and good friends. They also bring a fresh perspective to the situation, which can change your attitude, open you to a new approach, or distract you in ways your intimates can't. And, especially if they've been there themselves, they have insights and information that a loved one simply *can't* know.

Outsiders Are the Real Insiders

Every year, shortly after the start of Daylight Savings Time, twenty-two women show up for their first paddle of the season. Among them is Gail Miles, an athletic-looking woman with a chiseled face and fierce blue eyes—"Annie Hall" with short-cropped gray hair.

She and her teammates climb into a "dragon boat"—a narrow, forty-foot-long paddle craft with a brightly painted dragonhead at its bow. The breathtaking setting—a fjord surrounded by mountains that drop steeply into the sea, ravens and bald eagles soaring overhead, the occasional otter or harbor seal—is reason enough to take to the water, says Miles. But it is the camaraderie that draws her back each year. She has survived a lumpectomy, two mastectomies, three reconstructive surgeries, chemotherapy, radiation, her husband's death, and at this writing, news that the cancer had metastasized to her liver. Her children, longtime friends, and other close relations have been supportive. But here, on the water with her, are women younger and older than she, a bevy of different body types from all walks of life, newbies and veterans alike. No one cares whether the woman next to her is a jock or a recovering couch potato. The only requirement for membership is breast cancer.

Miles and nineteen other paddlers form two columns on either side of the boat. The "caller"—their coach—sits in the prow, drumming or shouting directions to synchronize their strokes. The "steer person" maneuvers the craft with a twelve-foot oar mounted at the stern. Thump, thump, paddle. Reach and rotate. Paddles overhead. Recover. The caller puts them through their paces, alternating between gentle pulls and hard strokes. At first they knock paddles, splash each other. From a distance, their boat looks like a caterpillar, each of its many legs a second out of sync. But when the teammates concentrate and finally feel the rhythm, their paddles slice through the water almost soundlessly. They move as one.

They thank "Dr. Don" McKensie, a physician and exercise kinesthesiologist at the University of British Columbia, for the experience. Postsurgery breast cancer patients were once cautioned not to tax their arm muscles. Upper-body exercise, it was commonly held, made them more vulnerable to lymphedemia, an incurable buildup of lymphatic fluid that causes chronic swelling and can occur even years after surgery. McKensie, an avid kayaker himself, believed that exercise would *lessen* a woman's chances of developing the condition. In 1996, he recruited twenty-four breast cancer survivors, ages thirty-one to sixty-two, to test his contrarian theory. He chose the two-thousand-year-old Chinese sport of dragon boating because it is strenuous, repetitive, and non-weight-bearing. Only two of his recruits had paddled before. After three months of rigorous training, no new cases of lymphedemia developed, and the women became stronger in every way. McKensie would later report, "The impact of this experience on these women has been overwhelming, the physical changes barely keeping pace with changes in the psyche."[48]

Gail Miles first heard about dragon boating over a game of bridge; a friend's sister-in-law had been part of Dr. Don's first team. Miles, a natural athlete, was eager to regain her strength and stamina. "I wasn't interested in the usual kind of support group where they talk about the downside of cancer and what a bad time they are having." Because it was a sport and not a place where anyone would feel sorry for her, the intensely independent Miles decided to give it a try: "The synergy of the group, the power of that connectedness—it was a real surprise to me that I could work and play on a team."

That Miles and her fellow dragon boaters are not like other sports teams isn't apparent when they are on the river. But later, drenched and exhausted in the locker room, one woman shows off artfully tattooed nipples, another complains about the dimple in her saline implant, and a third discusses what it was like to have a TRAM flap (a reconstruction technique in which abdominal skin and tissue are used to re-create a breast). But, Miles explains, they also don't *need* to compare war stories. "You're disfigured, you've gone through this life-threatening experience—you're still experiencing it. And this group of women shares that, whether we talk about it or not."

Catherine Sabiston and Meghan McDonough, colleagues at

McGill University, tracked a group of breast cancer survivors through their first dragon-boating season. The majority had joined the team mostly to get into better physical shape. And they went into the experience believing they had all the support they needed from their loved ones. But three months later, the neophytes realized that their teammates had given them a kind of emotional sustenance and confidence-building they didn't even know they lacked. "It's something their families *can't* provide," insists Sabiston, "because they haven't been through it."[49]

It's no surprise, then, that when Gail Miles learned that her cancer was back, she told her fellow dragon boaters *first*: "They take it all in, like it's just another part of our experience, whereas my family gets very dramatic." Being part of this group of consequential strangers may not extend Miles's life—despite early claims to the contrary, recent large-scale clinical trials have found that support group attendance has little effect on recurrence or mortality.[50] But being invested in the team certainly affects *how* she lives.

Two of her teammates have died. "There's a sense of 'there but for the grace of God,' when we all go to a funeral," she admits. "But one of the things I didn't realize in the beginning is if I die, I want all of them to know, because they know something about me that no one else can."

Something Old, Something New

Joining with others who are, metaphorically, in the same boat is an idea that has been around since the mid-nineteenth century, when temperance societies and "drunkard clubs" began to employ recovering alcoholics as "counselors."[51] Alcoholics Anonymous, the model for many self-help groups, was founded in 1935 by two consequential strangers who stayed sober by talking to each other about their drinking. The truth is, fellow sufferers have a map of the territory. They are the real insiders because they've been there. They know the pitfalls and the shortcuts to recovery.

Today, every life situation and crisis, every disease, every family configuration has spawned some type of self-help group.[52] But as much as these various groups owe to earlier incarnations, they have also changed with the times. "What we're finding lately," offers Michelle Visca, who runs a series of programs for cancer survivors in Summit, New Jersey, "is that many people don't want traditional groups with a lot of talk. They want to connect on another level that is not about cancer." Visca speculates that the Internet is part of the reason: "Online support is a little safer, a little more comfortable for some people."[53]

We no longer have to leave home to gather information about a disease or talk with fellow sufferers. A Harris Poll upped the number of "cyberchondriacs"—adults who have gone online for health information—to 160 million in 2007, a 37% increase from two years earlier.[54] Tens of thousands participate in online communities. Sometimes virtual support is a matter of practicality: Cancer support groups, for example, are everywhere, because the disease is so prevalent, but if you have hepatitis C and happen to live in a small town in South Dakota, you might be out of luck.

Some medical professionals also see online venues as a way to provide support to their patients. "They're there anyway," says Heidi Donovan, referring to the Internet. An assistant professor at the University of Pittsburgh School of Nursing, Donovan designed an interactive online program for ovarian cancer survivors which allowed patients to post questions about their disease and express feelings they had been afraid to say out loud. Each woman was assigned a particular nurse practitioner, who would respond within twenty-four hours. A consequential stranger relationship developed, giving the patient a dependable connection to someone who knew about her disease but also knew about *her.* Especially with diseases that have many symptoms, Donovan says, patients often feel a need to "protect intimates from what they're going through—what's making them suffer, what they fear. It's hard to share with loved ones on a regular basis." Although it's impossible to say whether this technique will help ovarian cancer patients on a larger scale, Donovan has certainly seen benefits to the small number of patients she's served to date.[55]

If patients are now going online to meet their need for information and emotional support, anecdotal evidence suggests that combining physical activity with peer support might be another idea whose time has come. Why not? You exercise *and* socialize in the company of new people who share your passion. Michelle Visca is currently putting together a new dragon-boating team (there are now over a hundred in the United States and Canada). She also offers a yoga-for-survivors group and a "get your groove back" exercise class. In other parts of the country are programs, lasting anywhere from a weekend to a season or longer, that feature fly-fishing, hunting, canoeing, running, basketball, even "boot camps" for survivors.[56] And while fund-raising bike rides, walks, and runs for various causes are not technically support groups, they, too, are often a source of inspiration, new skills, *and* consequential strangers.

Mary Benes, diagnosed with MS in 2003, manned a water station at the 2006 MS ride in Tulsa, Oklahoma. The grueling two-day event covers 150 miles—too much for many MS patients. Benes struck up a conversation with an employee of American Airlines where her husband also worked and told him that next year she wanted to *ride* in the event, not just watch. "He invited me to join their team, which I did. I couldn't have asked to have been in a more supportive group. One couple, who were more experienced in biking, always rode with me on the longer rides, to make sure I was okay. They pushed me to go up hills I didn't think I could make."

Customizing Our Convoys

Since the seventies, when epidemiologists first began to confirm the links between stress and disease, relationships and well-being, they have been trying to use that knowledge to improve health. The war on stress was a losing battle, so it made sense to shore up people's convoys instead. As one of the pioneers in the field put it, "We should start now to teach all our patients, both well and sick, how to give and receive support."[57] Since that call to action forty years ago, scientists have amassed scads of data on the importance of social ties, and the public is now savvier about prevention. But we have not learned nearly as much about *how* to help people enhance their connections.

What we do know for sure is that nothing works for everyone. Most people who have a disease don't turn to traditional support groups.[58] Two out of three cancer patients *never* attend them, nor do 85% of people with other chronic health conditions.[59] Richard Cohen is one of them: "Support groups are terrific, but it would take a sharp bayonet to get me to go there."[60] Even women, who are more likely than men to seek a support group, don't necessarily stay involved; some get what they need and move on. No one is (yet) tracking activity-oriented venues, such as dragon-boating, but both common sense and research suggest that these venues aren't universally effective either. When the dragon-boating experience was offered to overweight women, for example, stark differences emerged. Although all recruits felt better and got physically stronger when the twelve-week trial ended, the experiment was less successful from a social and emotional perspective. Unlike breast cancer survivors, the women didn't see themselves as "similar others."[61] Instead of bonding, they sniped and made comparisons based on body types: "Why is *she* here? She's not really overweight." The younger women, who ranged from twenty-seven to thirty-five, didn't want to sit next to the fifty-to-sixty-five-year-old participants. The lesson here, says Catherine Sabiston, is trial and error. "Over time, with learning and self-reflection, you figure out what kind of support you need as well as a general idea of who's going to provide it."

The answer is different for each of us. Cutting-edge research on resiliency—the ability to maintain a sense of mental equilibrium even as we go through a difficult time—indicates that people have different needs for support.[62] Also, the right *fit* is critical. Having someone come to your aid who is willing to loan you money may be useful if your medical bills are overwhelming, but of little help when you're struggling to understand what is wrong with you. When social support is inappropriate, it can actually do more harm than good, especially if the assistance somehow implies that you *can't* cope.[63] The more proactive strategy, then, might be to mobilize your own "natural network"—family members, neighbors, coworkers, medical advisors, and others who can give you what you need.[64] And if they can't give you the type of support that you ask for, they might be able to help you figure out who else can. This very practical and tailored approach makes even more sense in a culture of continuous connection: You can reach out to everyone in your network with a few keystrokes. To wit, after reading this paragraph, our editor remarked that she's often gotten emails from friends who have had cancer or their friends, "asking to help pay for someone to come in and clean the house while they're in treatment, to drop off meals, or to do whatever needs to be done." The ability to quickly tap helpers could never have happened a short ten years ago.

Natural networks were first conceived as a way to assist mental health patients living in the community. The idea was then extended to disabled people. One of the earliest documented cases involved Judith Snow, a Canadian woman with muscular dystrophy. The government had provided attendant care for Snow as part of her education. When she graduated from college, the funding stopped. Unable to handle even the basic everyday tasks of living, the once independent and employable woman had no choice but to move to a nursing home, where she languished for several years. Her condition worsened, and she might have died there had it not been for a brainstorming session with five of her friends who volunteered to take turns providing care and find others who'd pitch in as well. Half of the people who formed Snow's initial "circle of support" were friends, half consequential strangers. With their help, she was eventually able to move into her own apartment and take back the reins of her life. "Often," maintains Snow, "what we think of as health problems are really support problems."[65]

A natural network provides a safety net *and* puts the patient in charge—a good balance in any situation. Think of it as customizing your convoy. If people who are already on board don't have the information, experience, or empathy you need, you enlist others who do. You mix and match—intimates and CS, one-on-one support and group venues, people already in your convoy and new recruits, face-to-face and virtual encounters. Certainly, based on our interviews, it seems that the right person is often at the right place at the right time, saying the absolutely right thing—as long as you're ready to listen:

Paolo,* who had been taking the same weekly yoga class for years, informed his fellow yoginis as they trickled into the studio one day that he had been diagnosed with diabetes. One of them, who had a close friend with juvenile diabetes, told him about a comprehensive treatment center two hours away that Paolo's doctor had never mentioned and perhaps didn't know about.

Trudy* arrived at graduate school a good fifty pounds overweight and with dangerously high blood pressure and migraines. Growing up on the family farm where huge meals were a way of life, it had been impossible for her to lose weight. But in the new setting, surrounded by professors and fellow Ph.D. candidates who understood her plight, Trudy was able to change. Her colleagues removed sweets from the lab. A few even enrolled in pilates and yoga classes *with* her. She dropped thirty pounds in three months.

Customizing our convoys makes sense. For one thing, we need help sifting through the often conflicting information about health. One year we're told to drink eight glasses of water a day, and the next, drink only when we're thirsty. Take vitamins, but beware:

Too many can cause the blood to thin. Hormones prevent osteoporosis; but you might want to go off them to lower your risk of cancer. The confusion is worse if you actually *have* a condition: surgery or watchful waiting? a drug that might make you dizzy or one that puts you at risk for other problems? the doctor with a stellar reputation or the one with a good bedside manner? As if illness isn't enough, there's also the matter of insurance coverage. One woman, recalling the information she had to digest, expressed what the newly diagnosed often feel: "How much can one brain take?" However, if you can call on an array of people, it alleviates the stress on you and your caregivers.

When we consciously assess our personal networks, we can recruit *specific* people who have run the gauntlet themselves and whose experiences resonate with our own. They give us information, a fresh perspective, and suggest ideas we might not have considered. Virtually all of our interviewees remarked that their crisis or a chronic disease put them in touch with people who under ordinary circumstances they never would have known. Like all consequential stranger relationships, some have the potential to deepen into friendships, but most don't—in part because they are of a time. Laura Halliday, a children's clothing designer, single and now in her early fifties, had what felt like a friendship with a woman she met in her oncologist's office. "We ended up having radiation and a little chemo together. But when the treatment was done, that was it," recalls Halliday. "What you once had in common, you don't want to discuss anymore." Now involved in a group that is lobbying for the passage of legislation that would force insurance companies to cover lymphedema treatment, Halliday sees herself "at a different stage. I'd rather take on the advocate role."[66]

The Big Give: A Personality Booster and a Prescription

Elizabeth Edwards, the wife of 2008 Democratic presidential hopeful John Edwards, is a member of two clubs to which no one ever wants to belong: parents whose children have died and cancer survivors. In 2006, when she toured the country reading from her memoir *Saving Graces*, she explained her motivation: "People tell me, 'You're so strong,' but there's a secret to this strength. It comes from the spiderwebs we build and what we knit together, and I just wanted to tell that story." Everywhere she went, Edwards kept hammering home the same message: Keep family and friends close but also look beyond them. Call that waitress by her first name, take a moment to talk to someone who isn't like you, embrace people for who they are, and give back to them when you can. In short, connect and you will weave your own safety net. Edwards repeatedly acknowledges John and her children, as well as other family members and close friends who cared for her when her sixteen-year-old son Wade died and when she was undergoing cancer treatment. At the same time, she also stresses the importance of people on the periphery. "I am stronger because Edward the mailman smiles and Sam at the grocery store smiles."[67]

We become even stronger when we smile back.

Thus far, we have stressed the importance of *getting* support from consequential strangers. It's also beneficial to *give* to people outside our intimate circles. Henry Perlman was told early on by the old-timers in AA, "You only keep what you give away." If he wanted to stay sober, he had to "do service"—make the coffee, bring the donuts, clean up after a meeting, and perhaps most important, reach out to newcomers.[68]

Steve McCeney was twenty-four in 1984 when he learned he was HIV-positive. A psychologist, he went from isolation (telling only his brother and a close female friend) to socialization (getting involved with various support groups) and now has shifted his focus to outreach (leading yoga groups for people with AIDS). The progression parallels McCeney's self-acceptance and increasingly better health.[69]

Cindy Gibbs and twelve other cancer survivors she met when she relocated to a new neighborhood in Charlotte, North Carolina, dubbed themselves the "High Hopes." They first participated in Relay for Life—a twenty-four-hour fund-raising walk symbolizing that cancer never sleeps. They then raised money for the Ronald McDonald House, a place that had nothing to do with cancer. "Maybe it was a symbol of us trying to move on."[70]

Peggy Thoits, who has analyzed how people cope with negative events over the long term, grants that factors such as environment, socioeconomic status, gender, race, and the composition of our convoys can limit or enhance our options. However, people who are higher in "personal agency"—the ability to make choices, take action, and set a new course in the face of problems—often manage their circumstances in ways that improve their situation. Such individuals usually have better "personal coping resources," among them, high self-esteem, optimism, and a sense of "mastery" which allow them to believe they can handle the situation. They also experience fewer symptoms of depression or anxiety.[71] Coincidentally, many of the same strengths are found in people who are "sociable"—agreeable and able to seek out others—which is also associated with better physical health.[72]

When we rise above "seemingly unresolvable and inescapable difficulties," says Thoits, we often do so by transforming the meaning of the event. Think Mothers Against Drunk Drivers, or Autism Speaks.[73] Social involvement can change how we see our misfortunes, because it puts us into a new role. No longer feeling like victims, patients, sufferers, caretakers, or even survivors, we instead become activists, supporters, lobbyists, teachers, and leaders of self-help groups.

Judith Snow travels around the world lecturing on inclusion so that other disabled individuals can join society despite their differences. Sylvia Mackey's persistent phone calls and letters to the powers-that-be at the NFL resulted in "Plan 88" (named for the number her husband wore), which provides up to $88,000 worth of home health care for former players with dementia. Both women are using difficult chapters in their own lives to help others cope with theirs. But the "Big Give," to use Oprah's phrase, also benefits *the donor.* And like social integration (or perhaps because of it), dosage matters: The more people do, the greater the benefits. Their physical and mental health improves, and they experience lower levels of chronic pain and depression.[74]

But what enables those who are suffering mentally and physically, who are carrying large burdens to begin with, to reach beyond themselves and focus on a bigger picture, a more distant goal? Is it their personalities—are they more resilient, more caring? Or does the act of getting involved with a wide variety of others cause them to *become* the kind of person who then "pays it forward"? The question might never be answered, but increasing evidence suggests that the two factors—social context and personality—can work independently *and* influence each other.[75]

Consider Seventh-Day Adventists in Loma Linda, California, and people residing in Okinawa, Japan, and Sardinia, Italy—locales that seem to have little in common except that their residents live longer than the rest of us. In all three places, residents eat healthy diets and get lots of exercise. They are surrounded by family and friends.[76] But it's their strong *community involvement* that caused psychologist Brent Roberts to speculate that they also live more harmoniously and have more positive personalities to boot.

Roberts's conjecture is based on his "social investment" theory: "Those who invest more in social institutions," he explains, "tend to be warmer, more responsible and organized, and less anxious and depressed than others."[77] Roberts grants that certain people are more likely to engage in social investment—and more likely to be the types sought out by organizations—*because* of their personalities. Scientists call this the "selection effect." However, the fake-it-till-you-make-it principle—technically, the "socialization effect"—applies, too: Commitment to a particular role *requires* you to get along with others, take responsibility, and be even-tempered. If you don't naturally possess such traits, over time, being committed to the role will help you develop them. Although one can theoretically "invest" in solo pursuits, Roberts stresses, "most of these activities involve crossing paths. It's the ties and binds that impart the effect."[78]

Astrid Matthysse fits the profile. A pretty, petite, somewhat shy woman, her rich brown eyes exude warmth and compassion. She learned about diabetes as a child in Venezuela when she would watch her maternal grandmother suffer through a low-blood-sugar episode. "It completely changed her personality," Matthysse recalls. "My grandfather would have to force juice down her throat. Afterward, she wouldn't remember a thing. She was a very private and introverted person, and it caused her great embarrassment. Sometimes she cried to think of what she had put us through."

Ironically, two months after her grandmother died, Matthysse learned she, too, had Type I diabetes. Fortunately, it was 1993. Doctors knew much more about controlling the disease than in her grandmother's day.[79]

When Matthysse arrived in Miami two years later, she left her extended family and a career in computer science behind. She was determined to "start over"—a tall order for a recently separated thirty-three-year-old with two young children in tow. A perfectionist and child of divorce herself, Matthysse suffered "a bit" from depression during college and also flirted with an eating disorder. She has her "down moments," but they don't stop her. Indeed, she seems to be the kind of person John Cacioppo had in mind when he observed, "The secret to gaining access to social connection and social contentment is being less distracted by one's own psychological business."[80]

Matthysse humbly attributes her success to "luck." True, she stumbled on an advertisement for a postgraduate class on diabetes and nutrition that she might just as easily have missed. But it was she who took the initiative to call on the professor. "We ended up talking about what I was going to do in Miami. When I was in college, I didn't even know that there was such a thing as a degree in dietetics." The professor allowed Matthysse to sit in on the graduate-level seminar and encouraged the young émigrée to seek a second bachelor's degree. Three years later, Matthysse was offered the first job she applied for. Being bilingual didn't hurt in a city where 61% of the population is Hispanic and 8.6% of those in the Latino community have been diagnosed with diabetes.[81]

Today, Matthysse lives her disease, but no one could call her self-involved. She works as an educator for an insulin pump manufacturer and splits her spare time among various diabetes associations. In 2007, she won Johnson & Johnson's Volunteer Spirit Award and promptly donated her $1,500 grant to the summer camp program run by the Juvenile Diabetes Institute. "Having contact with people who live with this disease and seeing the consequences has really opened my eyes. It has pushed me into striving to take better care of myself. And I try to be an example, to show people that you can live healthful lives." True to Brent Roberts's theory, her "investment" in the diabetic community, which puts her in touch with a wide array of consequential strangers, has changed her personality. "I never imagined myself speaking in front of large groups of people, but because this is something I'm passionate about, all my shyness goes away."

It might be just a coincidence, but now in her early fifties and surrounded by an array of consequential strangers, Matthysse is also symptom-free. "Having diabetes doesn't stop me from doing anything at all."

5

Being Spaces

Some of the joys and blessings of being alive ought to be as easily achieved as a stroll down to the place on the corner—but there does have to be a place on the corner!

—*Ray Oldenburg,* The Great Good Place

The Power of Place

"I assumed everything would be easy," said Karen Robinovitz, speaking of her move to New York City after college graduation.[1] It was the mid-nineties. An aspiring fashionista, she had landed the requisite *Devil Wears Prada* job at *Women's Wear Daily*, a plum her peers would die for. Robinovitz was no Ugly Betty. She had the looks—a memorable face framed by long, well-coiffed dirty blond hair—and she knew what shoes to wear, which restaurants were hot, and how to jostle to the front of the line. At night, she went home to a comfortable apartment on the well-tended Upper East Side. But for all these superficial trappings, she was miserable. College chums had moved to the back of her convoy, and one by one began disappearing from the rearview mirror as each chose a different highway toward adulthood.

"I knew people in Manhattan, but they didn't have any resonance in my life. And I was coming from Emory [University] where I was a bigger fish in a small pond." Now she was surrounded by piranhas. "Women in the fashion industry tend to be competitive; they put other women down. So I didn't have a loose network of people around me. I just didn't feel good about myself. I was a writer but didn't feel motivated to write. And I had a string of bad boyfriends." Depressed and disappointed that she hadn't advanced beyond the reception desk, she truly hit bottom when she was diagnosed with Graves' disease, an autoimmune condition. "One day I walked into work and, without any plans to do so, I just quit my job. I had no clue about how I was going to make money."

Robinovitz moved downtown to the West Village, a neighborhood memorialized by urban activist Jane Jacobs in *The Death and Life of Great American Cities.* The book had inspired a generation of architects and city planners to look at the human element when designing a neighborhood or city, not just its buildings. Jacobs described how the mom-and-pop stores, coffeehouses, three-story brownstones, and tree-lined blocks allowed for the "intricate sidewalk ballet" performed daily on her beloved Hudson Street.[2] Some thirty years later when Rabinovitz arrived, the area had changed in some respects, attracting a more upscale, urbane crowd. But it was still an environment where neighbors bore witness to each other's everyday rituals in a reassuring yet unintrusive way.

When Robinovitz walked the zigzagging blocks of the West Village, she felt what Jacobs famously called "eyes on the street." People paid attention to one another. One of her favorite haunts was Shopshin's, a diner/deli. Within a month she knew the owner, Kenny, and chatted with assorted other neighborhood characters throughout the day—people at the dry cleaner, nail salon, and "the little candy store on the corner." She felt like she belonged. "I'd make eye contact and smile at people on the street, go out for lunch and be surrounded by others with laptops. Then, I'd meet one person, who'd introduce me to someone else. I started getting more motivated with my writing, started going out more."

Robinovitz's story exemplifies the power of "place." Where we live, work, shop, and mingle has everything to do with the weak ties we cultivate, and therefore our quality of life. We simply can't separate our relationships from the places we inhabit.[3] Here was a young woman who had grown up with social, material—and possibly genetic—advantages. Some of her earliest memories are of being on hotel vacations with her gregarious mother. "We'd meet other people, they'd have children, and my mother would say, 'Go and introduce yourself to those kids over there.' It was something instilled in me all my life." But even someone well schooled in social graces, who describes herself as "a major connector," can be thwarted by an inhospitable place.

Where we *are* matters. In 2006, after polling over 30,000 people in some 8,000 communities nationwide, urban guru Richard Florida found a strong correlation between happiness and place. As important as personal relationships and work are, he says, place is "the third leg of the triangle."[4] Context affects how we act and think, our roles, and the rules of engagement.[5] (Compare the "you" who walks through a run-down neighborhood with the self who enters a public park in anticipation of a free concert.)

It's almost impossible to develop casual relationships in an unwelcoming neighborhood, or in a competitive and unfriendly work environment. And if we can't connect, we don't feel like we belong. Was it mere coincidence that when she moved to the West Village Karen Robinovitz's mental and physical condition improved or that she began writing again and selling her work? An article in *Marie Claire* ultimately led to her first book, *How to Be Famous in Two Weeks or Less*, which she coauthored with Melissa del Cruz, an email pal. Fittingly, one of their chapters was entitled "The Schmooze Factor." Place had to have played a role in her metamorphosis. Although Robinovitz possessed the "goods" that had helped her succeed in the past, she needed to be in an environment that supported her—where she wasn't judged, where she felt free to express herself, where there were opportunities to meet people like her *and* different from her. A *being space*.

Futurist Reinier Evans coined the term "being space" in 2003 on his website, trendwatching.com, as a way of describing "living-room-like settings in the public space" where we can not only eat and buy products, but also socialize.[6] He credits Starbucks as one of the first retailers to allow—indeed, encourage—customers to linger, long a practice in the cafés of the West Village and Europe and the teahouses of Japan. We define the term more broadly as any physical environment—commercial, residential, or public—where a stranger can become a consequential stranger. A person you meet there might first become a casual acquaintance, and over time morph into a friend or lover. Most often, though, being spaces foster "anchored" relationships—ties associated with that particular place. Certain types of virtual communities qualify as well: cyberplaces where people can form "hybrid ties"—they meet online *and* in the real world.[7]

The concept also owes a debt to Ray Oldenburg, whose 1989 book *The Great Good Place* convinced a lot of retailers, real estate developers, and city planners to consider the importance of sociability. Oldenburg himself experienced the restorative power of place during the Korean War, when he was stationed in the south of France.[8] On the long walk from the bus stop to his apartment, he dropped into a tavern, where he chatted with the owner, "a femme fatale," before returning home. Years later, he would coin the term "third place," neither home (the first place) nor office (the second), to describe that tavern and other informal public gathering spots where people can engage in small talk, be playful, and escape the cares of the day. A third place is any arena in which "uncomplicated relationships" might develop.[9] The people you find there—a waitress, a neighbor, a salesperson, another patron—provide what Oldenburg calls an "easier version of friendship and congeniality."[10] They don't ask much of you, but their presence is more than reassuring. Oldenberg's description of these relationships puts them clearly in consequential stranger territory: "You find these people you really want to spend time with, but they wouldn't be comfortable in your home. And maybe your spouse wouldn't want them there either."

Because there are so many different types of being spaces, commercial and public, says trend-watcher Reinier Evans, it's impossible to gauge how many exist, but he adds with a wink, "Even if you just count Starbucks, the numbers are already pretty overwhelming."[11]

Build It and We Will Come: Variations on a Theme

If you happened to be in the Capitol Hill neighborhood of Seattle around dinnertime on the cold winter night in 2007 when the Braeburn condominiums lost electric power, you'd have found a group of residents in their communal kitchen/library area. Some were huddled around the one gas stove in the building, others cozied up to the fireplace, commiserating as a few stalwarts tried to salvage their partially cooked evening meal. What might have been a disquieting experience turned into an impromptu party as one resident ladled out her vegetable soup and another divvied up portions of stir-fry.[12]

It's hard to "neighbor" in a high-rise, but this was exactly what the developer, Dana Behar, had in mind when he designed this 153-unit complex that sits on a former supermarket parking lot. "When I was single, I always tried to live where other young people were, but I'm kind of shy. And in the typical apartment building, there was no place where I could inconspicuously hang out and start up a conversation. After work I'd be home alone watching cable TV and eating frozen pizzas."[13] Reasoning that "people have an easier time socializing when they're involved in an activity they like," Behar made sure the Braeburn had something for everyone—a Wi-Fi work space, a gym, a screening room, a community garden (or "P-patch," as it's known in Seattle),[14] and studios for yoga, crafts, woodworking. The building sold out in record time. Young hipsters and gay men, the demographic that typically propels gentrification, purchased some of the units, but to Behar's surprise, "it was mostly professional women in their thirties, forties, and fifties who wanted community, a chunk of seniors, some families with kids, some married couples." Not everyone bought in with the same vision, he grants, but the handful who like to garden now maintain the P-patch, movie buffs schedule films and keep the old-fashioned popcorn machine filled with raw kernels, and party-lovers plan the potlucks. "I think what we were trying to do here also speaks to one of the deepest desires we all have," maintains Behar, "which is for connection and belonging."

Connection was also the force behind an eclectic store on Manhattan's Lower East Side, the brainchild of two sisters from Southern California.[15] In her early thirties, Julia Werman had saved up enough money to quit working and backpack through South America for a few months. She was the girl who always relished the first day at school because she loved to meet new people. She had been drawn to social work for the same reason, but now knew she wanted to change careers when she returned from her trip. Meanwhile, her equally outgoing younger sister Nina, an actress and comedy writer, was working a desk job to pay the rent. Their emails during Julia's travels eventually centered on the idea of opening a business together.

Growing up in Studio City—"the valley"—was like coming from the wrong side of the tracks, at least in the eyes of some of the Werman sisters' well-heeled Beverly Hills classmates. It might not have been "hip," Julia grants, but it was "a hometowny place where people were accepted for who they were." And that's what the sisters ultimately re-created in Valley—a mad mix of merchandise and services—the kind of shopping experience they themselves "craved."

Julia explains, "Selling clothing was a no-brainer, but we didn't want just a clothing store. We wanted a place where you could walk in and not feel like the salespeople were looking you up and down, a place where you didn't feel pressured to buy. You could just enjoy the people who ran the store. And we didn't want to sell only high-end items." Accordingly, you can buy an eighteen-dollar T-shirt at Valley or the two-hundred-dollar blouse next to it. You also can sample a bowl of *acai*, an energy fruit that Julia discovered in South America or slip downstairs for a beauty treatment—nail art, pedicures, facials, and "painless" Brazilian waxing (another import from Julia's travels). Many customers say that being at Valley, which has a duplex layout, feels like you're in someone's home, which is exactly the point. The sofas and rustic wooden rocking chair, the family pictures, the cork floor are warm and woodsy, like their childhood home, "where people always felt comfortable," says Werman. "The idea was to create a place where women could come and relax and do it all. It's a place where you can just chill out and be in a space for more than fifteen minutes. You can linger for a couple of hours if you want."

The types of houses and communities we build, the stores and playgrounds we design, ebb and flow with the currents of history. Some eras are socially expansive, and others restrictive.[16] Today, being space is both in demand and on the rise. In some of the nation's hippest eateries, for example, you're likely to find a communal table. In part, a smart marketing response to the growing number of single diners and business travelers, it is open to anyone and is often the most popular spot in the house, says Marya Charles Alexander, a restaurant consultant and founder of SoloDining.com. "When you agree to sit at one of those tables, you enter in a social contract." Often the host or waiter offers to introduce people, which starts the conversation flowing. Communal tables speak to the zeitgeist, says Alexander: "The trend first became obvious in the late nineties, when the media began lamenting a lack of community."

If we were teetering in this direction before September 11, 2001, the attacks on the World Trade Center and the Pentagon may have pushed us over the edge. In the wake of the tragedy, the National Trust for Historic Preservation's National Main Street Center—a nonprofit group that has helped two thousand communities breathe life into abandoned downtowns—polled more than 1,400 businesses in 26 of its revitalized "Main Street" districts. Kennedy Smith, former director of the center, notes that whereas many shopping mall businesses experienced dramatic declines in retail sales that dark September, more than one quarter of Main Street businesses reported that their sales actually *increased*, and over half reported no change. Upward spikes were most dramatic in being spaces: Restaurants saw a more than 43% increase, bookstores 25%. "The interesting stuff," she adds, "was in the written comments, in which business owners reported that customers told them that they just wanted to be around other people after 9/11."[17]

Entrepreneurs recognize our desire to commune, rather than "cocoon," as we did in the early nineties. The strategy is simple: Make a place attractive, homey, intriguing, or exciting, let customers know it's okay to just hang out, and they will come. A decade ago, who would have dreamed of having a manicure in a clothing store? But mixed use is an important element of being spaces. Bookstores have become places to eat and check your email. Shopping malls sponsor concerts. Banks offer movies and yoga classes. Umpqua Bank in Portland, Oregon, even produced its own CD of a local band and sent the group on a five-city concert tour of its branches. Some supermarkets are going for what one consultant called the "linger longer effect" by providing seating, cafés, sushi bars, entertainment, and play areas to keep the kids amused.[18] There's no guarantee that you will actually *talk* to other patrons or the staff, of course, but the likelihood of doing so increases when you're in a place that brings you together with other people in a comfortable, relaxed environment—a human watering hole.

Back in the fifties, a time when female shoppers were described without apology or irony as "housewives," Chicago sociologist

Gregory Stone surveyed whether they preferred large chains to independent merchants and then asked what specifically drew them to one type of shopping experience over another. Based on their answers, Stone conceived four "types" of shoppers. One category, "personalizing," looked for stores that were warm and friendly, where they knew the sales staff and felt at home. They were quite different from the three other types: "economic" shoppers, who sought value and expedience over everything else, "ethical" shoppers, who were champions of mom-and-pop stores, and "apathetic" types, who shopped wherever they happened to be. Stone maintained that the personalizing shopper refuted the then popular notion that city dwellers didn't forge meaningful social ties. On the contrary, this was a woman who developed, and even sought out, "quasi-primary relationships"—consequential strangers—with "strong personal attachments . . . often approaching intimacy." It was her way of making the city less alien. Such a shopper would drive clear across town to frequent a store where she felt "known."[19] Fifty-five years later, although the marketplace has changed—among other reasons, because so many little guys have been driven out by giant retailers—Stone's four categories still ring true. And it is the *personalizing* experience that makes us come back for more.

That's the goal of Annie's Garden & Gift Store in Amherst, Massachusetts. When Annie Cheatham was first casting about for the raw ingredients from which she might fashion a country store, she looked to her past. She wanted the comfort and familiarity of Fred's, a favorite hot dog joint, Bernice's Beauty Parlor, Talton's Grocery, the Fashion Shop, and "other public places in my hometown of four thousand that meant home." These were places that provided "arm's-length caring" to all comers. In that tradition, Annie's is a "nursery" in the broadest sense, a place where humans, not just plants and flowers, are nurtured. Cheatham gives classes, sells local crafts and homemade preserves, sponsors radish-growing contests, and in countless other ways reaches into the community.

She loves it when people stop by just to sit a while, experience the beauty of nature, and have a bit of good conversation to boot. To get strangers' attention as they zoom along the state road that borders her six acres of land, Cheatham posts an ever-changing medley of eyecatching signs such as "Trees marked to move—help pay for our vacation." A particularly effective draw was "Come in—tell me what to have for supper." And people did.[20]

Being space in all its many manifestations is a win-win. Proprietors are rewarded because we spend, recommend, and become repeat customers. We benefit by shoring up our convoys with people who share our interests, enrich our knowledge of the world, and allow us to feel part of a larger whole. And society wins because people are more likely to care about each other and their neighborhoods when they get up close and a little personal. "It's just basic human common sense," Fred Kent explains. He is president of the Project for Public Spaces in Manhattan, the "placemaking" consortium that transformed Bryant Park from a seedy drug haven into an urban oasis where people now come to eat, sit, and attend concerts and movies. "We need places that people feel comfortable in and connect to, that they can be affectionate in, smile, laugh, engage, tell stories. It's about bliss, really."[21]

Ray Oldenburg adds that we actually laugh *more* in welcoming places. He analyzed descriptions of various taverns in a small Midwestern city to identify ones in which conversation was the main activity and where a dependable stream of regulars ensured a consistently friendly and often playful mood. Oldenberg wasn't surprised to discover that the more a given tavern met those criteria, the more laughter it inspired—the *Cheers* model of endless stories and good-natured banter.[22]

The fact is, when we're in a space that encourages us to slow down, we relax and have a greater chance of connecting. Which is why many hotels have cast aside formal check-in areas, replacing them with smaller, individual pods that allow for more personalized interactions. The Westin's "5–10 rule"—spend at least five minutes and walk ten steps with each guest—nudges the guest-staff relationship into consequential stranger territory.[23] "I always go back to hotels where they call me by name and go out of their way to connect," offers a food sales representative in her early fifties who travels frequently. "I remember the staff, and I feel like they know me."[24] Even the army has begun to design more diverse communities that make it easier for residents to meet. Herryford Village at Fort Belvoir, Virginia, is built around a central green and has a postal area in lieu of individual mailboxes. Starbucks and assorted shops are within walking distance. In contrast to the army's timeworn "no fraternizing" policy typical of base housing in the past, Herryford is a font of diversity, open to enlisted men *and* officers. It's a lot like the mythical base portrayed on the TV show *Army Wives.*

The philosophy of creating space that gently nudges people to linger and to make contact with each other has trickled into workplaces as well. This, too, is good business: If the physical plant of a company makes it easier to socialize, says Gallup researcher Tom Rath, you are three times more likely to have a close-knit work group. Just as important, when employees are encouraged to mingle in a casual way, productivity and profits go up, absenteeism and job disapproval go down.[25] Best Buy, for one, created a town square for the 5,000 employees at its headquarters in Minneapolis. You won't find coffeepots on each floor; to get your morning pick-me-up you *have* to come to the bustling center of the building, where you also can work out at the fitness center, play volleyball, or shoot pool. There's also a food court, gift shop, bank, pharmacy, health clinic, dry cleaner, and day care center.

A workplace being space doesn't have to be a multimillion-dollar installation—it's the intention and participation that matter. Boeing, the jet builder, provides meeting rooms at its seven offices nationwide for more than a hundred "clubs," devoted to everything from wine and beer making to square dancing. These clubs create being space *at work* by bringing diverse groups of people together in a stress-free social setting—a policy that, not so incidentally, helps reduce employee turnover.[26] Redesigning offices and factories and rethinking social policies are part of bettering the workplace in ways that foster "employee engagement."[27] The buzz phrase implies greater involvement with the job, but engagement results in more casual, nonwork interactions with *each other* as well.

Homes Away from Home

For our forebears, the arrival of a stranger was so rare it was cause, at the extremes, for celebration or assassination.[28] Ten thousand years later, cities and, on a smaller scale, suburbs and towns have become "worlds of strangers," as sociologist Lyn Lofland puts it. Being surrounded by unknown others is a fact of modern life. When Lofland, an admitted "cityphile," revisited the small town of her youth, population 8,000, she spent time with a childhood friend. Where it once took "forever" to walk a block of their downtown, the friend lamented, "I can walk down the street now without hardly ever seeing anyone I know. It's really changing."[29]

Like Gregory Stone's personalizing shoppers, we hunger for people in our daily comings and goings who know us. If you're lucky enough to live in an area that makes everyone's "most livable" list, you're probably surrounded by being spaces. But for all the flurry of placemaking over the last several decades, many of us still spend our time on blocks where we don't know our neighbors, in communities that lack welcoming parks and safe playgrounds, and in companies where socializing is not on the menu. To eliminate the "strangeness," we transform public or semipublic venues into a "home territory"—a being space we think of as our own.

For Tony Orum, it was the White Hen.[30] Every morning at seven, Orum, an urban scholar who has spent several decades pondering the nature of place, would announce to his wife that he was going out to get his coffee. "Wouldn't it be easier if you just brewed a cup here?" she often wondered aloud. But the White Hen offered her husband something the neighborhood lacked and that he couldn't get at home: a way of being "known" in the community. They were then living in a posh burg on the North Shore of Chicago, a place typical of many suburban tracts developed in the wake of World War II. Zoning regulations ensured that commercial enterprises and workplaces were separate from residential areas. Typical of so many Americans, Orum spent great chunks of time in his car. As the area grew more populous and spread out, malls put many small merchants out of business. The downtown area was left with few shops and little foot traffic. When Orum jogged on a path near his home or walked his two dogs, he hardly ever saw another person; when he did, the passerby rarely nodded in his direction. People who speed from here to there in cars are not inclined to be "custodians of their neighborhoods."[31] No surprise, then, that when a trash bin was knocked over, no one picked it up.

In contrast, the White Hen, a standing-room-only deli near the railroad tracks, was a cherished island of civility and connection. On the way in, Orum might hold the door for another patron, or one might return the favor. Pauly, the owner's brother who walked with a noticeable limp, knew Orum would fill up a 16-ounce cup with Colombian Supreme, step up to the counter, and when it was his turn, ask for an all-seasons bagel and his favorite string cheese. Orum knew Pauly would always make sure the string cheese was in stock. A few years back, the two dieted together. Every day they'd check in. "How much today, Pauly?" Orum would ask. "Oh, about a pound, but it sure is coming off slowly." Orum admired Pauly for his matter-of-fact sense of decency and generosity, like the time he gave a local homeless man a job because "the guy needed work and money."

Orum would also mix it up with Marco, who had worked at the White Hen for years. The young Mexican immigrant had a habit of offering a customer a dollar bill and then playfully yanking it back. The prank invariably made Orum smile—another predictable moment at the White Hen. The summer Orum took a crash course in Spanish, he practiced on Marco. "Me, a white Jew, and he, a dark-skinned Mexican immigrant—we became something else—almost like friends, more like acquaintances—when we began to talk in Spanish."

The guys at the White Hen probably weren't people Orum would entertain at home, "but they reassured me that the sun came up every day." When he traveled to China to study its public spaces, he brought back key chains for Pauly and Marco. They were a part of his convoy—so different from him but so important to his quality of life.

Orum has since moved to Evanston, a suburb of Chicago that has grown into the kind of small, dense, walkable city of which Jane Jacobs would have approved. He doesn't "need" the White Hen nowadays (although he sometimes drops by for old times' sake), because there is life on the streets of Evanston and many being spaces. For those of us in less inviting locales, Orum suggests that we "look around ourselves, in the morning, or in the evening. There are corners and shops, grocery stores and newsstands, bars and playgrounds where the sense of our identity as well as that of our community are constantly replenished."

Healing at Kappy's

Finding such a place was literally a lifesaver for fifty-seven-year-old Toby Rosenbaum when her husband Jerry, a high school teacher, died of lung cancer.[32] The dimpled, effervescent redhead was alone for the first time in thirty-five years. She began to have panic attacks and developed geriatric anorexia, a frequently overlooked by-product of depression sometimes seen in surviving spouses, particularly women.[33] It wasn't as if she'd been strictly a mother and homebody. She'd spent twenty years as a shoe salesperson and another ten behind the jewelry counter in a department store. Still, she had been *Mrs.* Rosenbaum since she was twenty-two. Now, without Jerry at her side, who was she? With her lost identity went her desire to eat. She also was the first of her close friends to lose a husband. Not wanting to be a "fifth wheel," she repeatedly turned down invitations. Going to a restaurant, which she and Jerry did almost every night once their children had left the nest, was even worse, because "everyone was coupled."

No place was emotionally safe. She hated being at home for all the reminders of Jerry but was also afraid to leave. "I was very lonely. I wasn't eating at home, and I kept having panic attacks. I was afraid I was becoming mentally ill. I thought to myself, *If I stay in my house any longer, I'll get worse.* I had to start doing something to prove to myself that I could take care of myself. The hardest step was getting out the door."

The door she chose to enter was Kappy's, a Greek diner in her neighborhood. "The owners and staff weren't really strangers. They had always made us feel welcome. When my husband got sick, they knew about it and were very supportive. They'd always tell him, 'Jerry, you're looking better today.'" Once when Jerry was hospitalized, she had stopped in to pick up a piece of pie for him. "When I said, 'How much do I owe you?' Big George, one of the owners, wouldn't take my money. 'Please,' he said, 'whatever we can do for you.' I remembered their kindnesses."

Big George was at the door the night Rosenbaum returned as a widow. When she asked for a seat at the counter, he was puzzled. "I told him, 'I'm just a one,' and he said, 'Oh no. You're going to sit at a booth. A lot of people here are ones.'" She had never noticed. On the way to the table, she recalls, "He told people, 'This is Toby,' and it kind of made me feel like, *Hey, it's okay.*" Okay, that is, until the waiter brought her dinner. "I was eating the food, but I felt panic coming over me. I thought I was going to choke. Then I looked up and saw Big George and the others, and I thought, *I'm not alone.*"

Eventually she met the morning crowd as well. A sociologist

would say she became one of the "colonizers" at Kappy's. Her frequent visits and connection to other regulars set her apart from "patrons," who spend time and know the place and its characters better than mere "customers" but don't quite see the place as "home."[34] Rosenbaum's fellow colonizers, Andrea, Alice, Dory, and Marilyn, each had their troubles too. Comparing herself with the others, Rosenberg began to feel better about her life knowing that hers wasn't necessarily the worst situation. Just as important, where the outside world once felt alien to her, she now felt comfortable in it. Although she wasn't close to the other regulars in the best-friend sense, they inhabited what was now *her* territory—a social world unto itself—and she was part of the "in" crowd. To her surprise, she even felt at ease with the couples, and when others lost their spouses to cancer or Alzheimer's, it made her feel good to support them. "During that period of time when you're grieving you feel like there's nothing, and then all these new people are around you—I guess you'd call them consequential strangers. They make you feel like you're somebody again."

Bagels and Barbells: What Makes Kappy's Run?

Rosenbaum's transformation was so dramatic that her son Mark, a professor of marketing who had been studying how social considerations impact consumer behavior, undertook a study of Kappy's. He found that although "commercial friendships" are weak ties, they provide a surprising degree of companionship and emotional sustenance. Eighty-three customers ranging in age from thirty-six to eighty-seven volunteered to be part of the study. Admittedly, this was a "self-selected" group of people who might have been more inclined to stress the positive role of their diner relationships. Still, a place that fosters a sense of community allows such connections to deepen. Bereaved and divorced customers found that the majority of their emotional and practical support came from people at the diner.[35] One might then jump to the conclusion that a place like Kappy's is best for lonely or older people. Certainly socialization is a boon for seniors and a balm for loneliness. But customers who weren't in the throes of a life crisis received 25% of their support from their connections at Kappy's, too. And later, when Rosenbaum surveyed 207 members of a Gold's Gym franchise, he found that young men and women in "prime health" also forged relationships with staff and other gym rats that provided them with companionship (workout partners) and emotional support (people with whom they shared feelings and concerns).[36]

Another fascinating finding emerged from Rosenbaum's research: The regulars at Gold's reciprocate by giving of themselves to *the place.* They pick up towels, wipe equipment after using it, cooperate with employees, and follow the rules. They are the good citizens, the ones who more readily help out other gymgoers, for instance by showing them a new stretch or how to use a machine. Similar "customer voluntary caring" occurs at Kappy's. At 4:30 a.m. on most mornings, a group of older men sit in their parked cars outside the diner until Harriet, the morning waitress, shows up and unlocks the door. They follow her inside, mumbling hellos to one another, and set to work refilling the saltshakers, sugar containers, and ketchup bottles and restocking the cups of crayons given out with the children's menu. By 5:30, when the restaurant officially opens, they are at their usual seats at the counter where they eat and joke with one another until around nine, when they begin to depart.[37]

Countless studies have shown that we develop relationships with places in much the same way as we do with human beings.[38] And just as our relationships to certain people change over time, ties to a place can also transform as circumstances intervene. After two years of almost daily visits, for instance, Toby Rosenbaum began to care for her first grandchild so that her daughter could go back to work. She could no longer spend as much time with her diner posse, but every evening she headed back to Kappy's for dinner.

Many of the regulars credit Big George for setting the tone at

Kappy's. "He makes you feel like you belong, like you're part of his family," remarked one, who then clarified, "his extended family, not his immediate family."[39]

To be sure, if you peek into the back office of any establishment that keeps consumers coming back (and employees happy), you'll find an affable owner or manager to whom connection is important. Zingerman's Deli in Ann Arbor, Michigan, is a case in point. Now a lucrative "community of businesses" that grosses $38 million in sales and employs just under 600 employees, it was built by two consequential strangers who met in 1982 while working at a local restaurant. Paul Saginaw, the general manager, and Ari Weinzweig, the kitchen supervisor, quit their jobs and leased an old grocery store. "In our minds, we were performing a community service by creating a space where people could come," Saginaw recalls. "A place where you had world-class academics, delivery truck drivers, and high school kids. We wanted it to be like a Japanese tea ceremony where there is no status. We imagined everyone the same, looking silly with Russian dressing streaming down their faces."[40]

Even as the business has grown, the partners have not lost sight of that vision. "Providing really wonderful service to our staff, our customers, and the community is not a means to an end, it's an end in itself," says Saginaw. Whenever a new customer comes in, staffers have been taught to look that person in the eye and find out where she's from, what brought her here, and, most important, what they can do for her. "After all," Saginaw admits, "we don't sell anything that anyone needs, or that people can't get at a dozen other places within five miles. No one says, 'If I don't get a twelve-dollar corned beef sandwich, I'll die.' So we service the hell out of you. We make you feel like you're the reason we got out of bed."

Of course, every place has personal meaning to those who frequent it. Its value is in the eye of the beholder. Your home territory could be a mere pit stop or even a place others avoid. For instance, when New Yorkers learned in 2008 that the mayor was planning to close the Off-Track Betting parlors that had operated in the city for the last forty years, observers weighed in with their opinions. To some, the dingy spaces were a blight on the neighborhood, a hangout for hustlers. To others they were homes away from home—"unofficial social clubs with core groups of regulars."[41] It was as if they were describing two different locales.

Reneé's Place of Beauty

Seventeen years ago, Reneé Harris was twenty-eight, a single mother of two little girls, working at one of the downtown hotels in New Orleans as a housekeeper. The work was mind-numbing and physically demanding. She pitied Miss Louise, an elderly coworker who'd been on the job for years. "I used to finish my work and then go help her finish hers. One day I said to her, 'Miss Louise, I don't want to be old like this.' But I had no skills, no interests, not even a high school diploma. I wanted to learn to do *somethin'* so I could make a decent livin' for me and my children."

A few weeks later, a flyer from a vocational school sat atop the pile of mail at her front door. She began reading it as she walked inside. One of the offerings was a nine-month hairstyling course. Harris, who is five-five, cute, coffee-colored, and always "well put-together," as a former client described her, immediately thought of Danneel's Beauty Shop and Miss Rose, the owner. "She'd do me and my sister and my mom's hair. My sister wore an Afro and it looked *go-ood*," she says, drawing out the *o*'s as most people in Louisiana do. In high school she went to Danneel's with her girlfriends and was styled by Claudine, who "did all the teenagers."

Like her older sister's hairdo, Danneel's was a product of the seventies, a time when black beauty shops had emerged from invisibility to become not just profitable ventures but a profession to be proud of.[42] No longer self-taught "kitchen beauticians" who ironed and curled their neighbors' hair, Miss Rose and her peers were trained and licensed as hair*stylists.* They were developing a professional *and* political consciousness, for instance, using "curly" or "wavy" to refer to clients' hair. They didn't "wash," they "shampooed." As one well-schooled master stylist put it, "We are like doctors; we diagnose and treat sick hair."[43] Beauticians had a loyal following. Their clients talked to them and trusted them. Just as important, a beauty salon was one of the few professions in which a black woman could call the shots and be financially independent.

The tipping point for Harris that day was the realization that beauty school might help her re-create what she had loved most about Danneel's: "They all looked like they was havin' fun. Back in the day, everyone had a TV in the shop while you were waitin'." She could catch up on her soap operas and the latest happenings in the community. "You'd find out who had parties, what happened there, where the next hangout was goin' to be."

The appeal of such a place is apparently universal, at least when compared to a machine shop, says Richard Florida. In the late nineties, when Pennsylvania was, in the words of one state official, "turning out too many hairdressers and cosmetologists and not enough skilled factory workers," Florida set out to determine why. He posed an intriguing question to his first-year public policy students at Carnegie Mellon University: "If you had just two career choices open to you, where would you work—in a machine shop, with high pay and a job for life, or in a hair salon, with less pay and where you were subject to the whims of the economy?" The students—and, later, audiences across the country—invariably chose the hair salon. Why? The work is creative and independent—there's just the stylist and his or her client. Lower pay, perhaps, but the novelty and stimulation would more than compensate. There are always new techniques to learn, new styles, and "every customer is a new challenge."[44]

Harris loved it. She did hair out of her house initially, first come, first served, then turned her garage into a salon. She'd put out lemonade and cookies and, for "entertainment," tuned into talk shows or played videos of inspirational speakers. Finally she was able to open her own shop, Reneé's Place of Beauty. She had no shortage of clients. "In those days, I could do hair all night." One Easter it was so busy, she worked straight through until six-thirty the next morning. "People was draped all over the chairs, waitin' for their turn. The sun was shinin' when we left." When she could no longer handle the overflow herself, she hired three female and one male stylist and opened a larger shop, called Designing Women because her "cast" was just like the TV series.

When Hurricane Katrina hit in 2003, Harris relocated to Atlanta, Georgia, and now works out of a department store salon. It's harder to build up a steady clientele in a transient city and to create a being space in a shop run by a corporation, but like Stone's personalizing shoppers, the regulars are willing to drive miles to see her. Harris is most proud of the fact that so many of them seek her advice and open up to her. It seems to go with the territory. Studies have shown that we spend over one-third of our "talking time" revealing personal problems to our hairdressers. We discuss children, health issues, marriage, romantic partners, depression and anxiety. We're pampered and at ease, far away from the responsibilities of home or work. Certainly the setting itself, especially an owner-operated shop, encourages us to open up, as does the stylist. "I'm a hairdresser but I'm more of a counselor," says Harris. She does what many hairdressers do: She's sympathetic and listens intensely. She might show the lighter side of a situation or offer advice. "I feel like I've been called to minister. I'm a high school dropout, and I don't have anything 'cept hair trainin', but I have a lot of wisdom. I know things just from bein' out in the public. I ask a lot of questions, I watch *Oprah*, and I know how to make people feel good." Interestingly, science bears her out on this point. Hairdressers who have these skills are often as helpful to their clients as trained mental health counselors.[45]

And just like the good citizens of Gold's Gym and the elderly gentlemen at Kappy's who pitch in, Harris's clients have given to her as well. One evening as she was closing Reneé's Place of Beauty, she was robbed at gunpoint. Shaken, she decided not to renew her lease. "I never stopped doin' hair. I just went back into my garage. I lost some business, but people who'd been comin' for years understood and stuck with me. They knew I was afraid, and they did everything they could to make me feel comfortable."

Acquaintanceship: Tales from the Softball Field

On any given spring or summer day virtually anywhere in the United States, men and women are playing or watching amateur softball—a sport that began when a bunch of Harvard and Yale alumni discovered that it was great fun to hit a boxing glove with a broom handle. Today, an estimated 25 million players compete against their neighbors, coworkers, and loosely connected groups of acquaintances.[46] Over the course of a season, the playing field is like a giant petri dish where a scientist might observe the way strangers congregating in a public being space move into consequential stranger territory—and beyond.

Allison Munch, then a Ph.D. candidate in sociology, did just that.[47] She spent a four-month season studying the "Astros," an amateur men's fast-pitch team in a medium-sized city in the Southwest.[48] Their games were played in a public park located in a neighborhood that can best be described as marginal. The spectators, like the team and the city itself, were equally divided between whites ("Anglos") and those of Hispanic heritage. Some of the Astros spectators knew each other from previous seasons, of course, but each year brought a crop of new players and their fans. How, Munch wondered, would these fans, a diverse group who had close ties on the field, also build connections with one another?

When we step into a crowd of strangers, knowledge of the place helps us brave a potentially stressful situation. It can also shortcut the process of acquaintance.[49] We know who is "supposed" to be there and are therefore less wary. At the Astros games Munch attended, police sirens constantly blared in the distance and women were urged not to return to their cars without a male escort. But the ball field was a sanctuary in the midst of the chaos, where families congregated and good-natured rivalries were played out. Although first-timers didn't know other spectators personally at the outset, they could at least "place" them in a known *category*—fans of Astros.[50]

Still, newcomers sat alone at first and "protected" themselves by practicing what sociologist Erving Goffman called "civil inattention"—a kind of ritual ignoring of others.[51] We stare blankly, acting as if we're not really looking or listening so as not to appear impolite, yet not inviting conversation. First-timers also created a "physical and social boundary," Munch noted, by having their children sit with them. Similar to putting belongings on an adjacent chair, burying one's nose in a newspaper, or chatting on a cell phone, it's like wearing a sign that says "I've made this my personal space."

We mean that literally. Even birds keep a certain distance from one another. Forty years ago, anthropologist Edward T. Hall went so far as to quantify four human "distance zones" that, in his opinion, correspond to increasing levels of closeness. In "public" zones, Hall maintained, we keep twelve feet or more apart, in "social," four to twelve, "personal," eighteen inches to four feet, and "intimate," eighteen inches or less. The closer you are to another person, the more you see, hear, feel, and—yes—smell. When someone moves in, it usually means he or she wants to *be* closer.[52] Today, some modern social scientists still cite Hall, whereas others now dispute his theory, among other reasons because of individual difference—how close we stand in conversation varies from person to person. In any case, we probably keep most of our consequential strangers in the social zone at first, but as we get to know them, might allow them into our personal space as well. And it's a pretty safe bet that when the distance between two people doesn't jibe with the level of their relationship, it can be uncomfortable, even stressful. That's why we tend to squirm in crowded elevators or in subway cars filled with strangers.

At the Astros games, Munch began to see distances shrink and differences between newcomers and old-timers "dissolve" after only three weeks. A typical first exchange between two Astros fans was usually to ask which player the other had come to see. Although these initial forays were "halting and hesitant," Munch noted, "a first conversation could become intimate in minutes." One encounter is often all it takes.

Then, too, communication is not just a matter of how far apart two people stand and what they say to one another, it's also *how* they talk—tone of voice, delivery, attitude—and what they *do.* A step forward or back speaks volumes, as do certain gestures. Munch now observed more eye contact, nodding, smiling, extended arms, and open hands. Greetings and one-liners ("My, how your baby has grown") gave way to small talk—the currency of everyday relationships—which helped launch a conversation the following week. Such "tie signs" are evidence of a relationship.

Erving Goffman, who identified tie signs in the course of observing several decades of public behavior, gives the example of a couple in a movie line. If one turns to address the other face-to-face instead of "merely orienting with half-turns, we can assume that the relationship is new enough to warrant attentiveness—a courtesy that will later be foregone" as the two become closer.[53] A mere glance can define a relationship, or redefine it, as seen in this passage from the 2007 novel by Afghani writer Khaled Hosseini, *A Thousand Splendid Suns*:

> And when Aziza woke up crying and Rasheed yelled for Laila to come up and shut her up, a look passed between Laila and Miriam. An unguarded, knowing look. And in this fleeting, wordless exchange with Miriam, Laila knew that they were not enemies any longer.[54]

By mid-season, almost everyone who routinely came to the Astros games was part of what Munch describes as a "floating community." Fans, who had met only weeks earlier, now shared snacks, beverages, blankets, and clothing. They gossiped, traded tips about parenting, and talked about the best service people in town. More willing to allow people into their personal zone, the newcomers sat with others and allowed their kids to play alongside the bleachers where everyone kept a collective watch on the children. Now that the mothers had become consequential strangers—and some were progressing toward closer ties—they urged their young ones to address the adults as "aunt" and "uncle" or "*tía*" and "*tío*."

Although group events often don't lend themselves to intimacy-building, two of the women Munch observed seemed to deepen their connection. Each week, they deliberately sought out one another. Despite the fact that they were in a public setting, they created an island of privacy for themselves. Munch could catch only snatches of their conversation. But the little she heard, in concert with their body language, made it clear that the two women were sharing intimate details about their marriages, speaking "in hushed tones, turning their bodies toward each other and slightly bowing their heads so that their voices would not carry."

Munch's observations underscore the fact that shared time and the right setting can enable a diverse group of people, who might not otherwise connect, to develop at least casual ties. Not every fan partook. Some politely said hello each week and moved on. But where seeds of relationships were planted, the regularity of the games provided fertile ground for them to grow. The stands became a place to learn about one another, have a good laugh, get a tidbit of information, and for some, bring their troubles. Bridges were built between individuals and across family units as well. And yet, fans and players had little contact with each other beyond the ball field—the hallmark of an anchored relationship. As one fan put it, "Our back porch [is] the stands. We come from all over [the city] to play and meet each other, but we don't hang out much in each other's homes. Maybe that's why people keep coming back year after year."

Close . . . But Only in the Gym

The question of what makes us open up to another human being fascinates laypeople and scientists alike. A recent *Wall Street Journal* headline declared "So Close . . . and So Separate: Gym Friends Are Among Our Most Personal Confidants . . . But Only in the Gym." Some 41.5 million Americans schedule visits to a fitness club as part of their regular routine.[55] Those numbers have climbed steadily over the last twenty years, in part because exercise keeps us healthy and in good shape. That would be reason enough to work out. But a fitness facility is also a social venue, and some of the anchored relationships we forge there become surprisingly intimate. "Gym friends talk about their coworkers and their spouses, their dating dilemmas and their diets," wrote the *Journal* reporter. "They blurt directives they might never say to a lifelong friend (dump him! you're overreacting! quit! don't quit!). Gym friends don't judge, regardless of whether you take their advice. And gym friends make time for each other." One thirty-five-year-old woman, who tries to arrive fifteen minutes early for a warm-up chat with her gym buddy, admitted, "She probably knows more about things going on in my life than some of my lifelong friends that are supposedly best friends."[56]

What's going on here? While it is *generally* true that we reserve our confidences for our loved ones, many social scientists suggest that the complexities of relationships require a more nuanced view. People don't easily divulge personal information in any case. Even with close friends and at later stages of relationships, most of us are reluctant to talk about intimate matters.[57] So why at the gym?

First, let's consider the question of self-disclosure—the engine that drives relationships. In the "initiating" stage, we size up the stranger, put our best foot forward, and at the same time, try to find out who she is—her background, values, details of her daily life—the "safe" stuff. We then segue—sometimes quickly, sometimes at a snail's pace—into the "experimenting" stage where the "breadth" of disclosure expands. We begin to talk about a greater variety of subjects—and possibly also increase the "depth" of disclosure by revealing more about ourselves.[58] With each encounter, we must decide whether we actually want to let the other person "in," past our public persona, to see the layers underneath. It's like an intricate dance: If we trust, we take one step forward, then pause to get our bearings; and if we feel too vulnerable, take one step back. We ask ourselves, What's in it for me? Favors? Fun? The "shoulder" of someone who understands where I'm coming from? An impartial listener who doesn't know much about me? A future mate? Will I get what I need and want—and at what price? What will this person ask of *me*? Assess, interact, assess, interact again.

Ultimately, our willingness to "engage"—talk about ourselves, rely on others, allow them to become part of our convoy—is affected by more than our personal baggage or even what goes on in a given relationship. It also matters *where* we are—ideally, a being space, a place that is familiar, lends itself to privacy, and features an atmosphere and activities that inspire us to connect. Given our increasingly fragmented lifestyles, the gym can be a place where you often run into the same people. You also feel better mentally when you exercise. The people you encounter are likely to be in a good frame of mind, too. And you already know you have something in common.

Moreover, disclosure is not an either-or proposition. Within each of us are opposing and yet complementary desires: to share ourselves *and* to guard our borders. When we first meet, we might be willing to disclose parts of ourselves, but we also hold back. Even within an established relationship, we need both togetherness *and* breathing room. Both are necessary to control our own boundaries and sustain relationships. At any given time—and here we mean everything from time of day to time of life—we are open *and* closed, and we cycle between the two with one pole typically taking prominence over the other.[59] For many people, being at a health club inspires openness. A thirtysomething quoted in the *Wall Street Journal* article, for example, described her workout time as "always kind of the most positive part of my day."

Hence the irony of certain consequential stranger relationships, particularly those that develop in being spaces: Although we are more likely to expose our deepest secrets to people close to us, we are also inclined to offer bits of our private selves when we're set apart from others, when we feel safe, and when we feel like we can get away from the other person if we need to.[60] Confidants at the gym or fellow dog walkers who are far removed from each other's intimate circles can be secure in the knowledge that once they leave the building or the park, their lives won't intersect. In a similar vein, the aptly named "stranger-on-a-train" phenomenon occurs when we divulge secrets to people we don't know but happen to sit next to for an extended period of time.

Studies conducted in bus terminals and airport lounges also indicate that we're more likely to tell our troubles to a stranger if the other person opens up first.[61] It stands to reason that a similar dynamic operates with consequential strangers. For example, you're at a lunch with a colleague in the same industry. It's typical to talk about business or the NBA playoffs; whereas complaints about your respective partners are usually off-limits. But imagine sitting in a cozy booth, out of earshot of other diners. If your colleague shares something deeply personal about his life, you're more likely to respond at an equal level of disclosure. It's like that old game we played as kids: You show me yours and I'll show you mine. Of course, intimate relations demand this kind of reciprocal disclosure; with consequential strangers, the choice is yours.

The promise of no-strings social connections motivates Los Angeles–based Jourdan Biziou to return to an art studio in Laguna every Saturday, even though it means spending a grueling hour, or longer, on California freeways. Biziou, a handsome man in his mid-thirties, with straight hair down to his shoulders, could just as easily draw and paint for five hours at home—and save gas at that. But he's come to appreciate the benefits of practicing with peers. His first experience was a weekly three-hour figure-drawing class. "They all had different reasons for being there," he says, recalling his classmates. "But like me, they just wanted to get back to drawing. It was a really diverse group, from their late twenties to their eighties. Accountants, businesspeople, professional artists, one worked in a hospital. Men, women, black, white, everything. That was the only place I saw them. But by drawing together, we experienced this deep mutual passion, and we were very present with each other. We shared this one thing that brought us together, and then we'd go our separate ways."

Biziou suddenly understood something his mother had always told him. "She said if you want to meet people that resonate with you, just do what you love. That's the way to find people who are much closer to your own sensibilities. That's how people form communities. They do what they enjoy." His art mates were all consequential strangers, some to whom he might have become closer had he not moved back to Los Angeles to work on another film. All the same, he says, "I opened up a lot to them on different issues, because I could see that they were very real."

To Talk or Not to Talk to Strangers?

Scott Heiferman admits to a "peculiar" hobby. For many years, he has been taking photographs of strangers. "I just ask people if I can take their picture on the subway platform. I like the idea of getting past that don't-talk-to-strangers mantra. It [has led to] some of the best stories I've heard."[62] Heiferman's hobby is not so strange when you realize that he is one of the cofounders of Meetup.com, a web community launched in 2002, now with close to six million members worldwide and still counting.[63] Visitors to the site plug in their zip codes and then look for others who are similarly devoted to their chihuahuas, Cajun cuisine, the Texas two-step, or any of 3,500 other interests listed there. The goal is to eventually meet in person.

"I was shocked that after 9/11, New York was like one big community, and I remember how good that felt," Heiferman says. He was inspired, too, by the dire assessment in *Bowling Alone*: "[Robert Putnam] put a challenge out there to bring back the good parts of an era where there was more community." Meetup.com probably wasn't what Putnam had in mind. But offline sociability is a natural extension of what had been happening since the earliest online communities, support groups, and dating sites appeared: people reaching out to each other around a shared activity, a need, or an interest.

As we said at the outset of this chapter, a website can qualify as a being space—a place where people seek out strangers with the hope of turning them into consequential strangers. Although the scientific jury has only begun to construe the complexities of communicating online, it seems that relationships in virtual places have a lot in common with brick-and-mortar venues. They are influenced by a range of factors which can matter more than, or certainly as much as, the medium.[64] For one thing, personality. Some of us naturally reach out more than others. Also, to progress from one point on the relationship continuum to the next is, in part, a matter of chemistry. We might have different "styles" of interaction, too. You could be the kind of person who immediately dives into a personal topic, who talks a lot or loudly, and is emphatic about your opinions—a presentation that might repel someone who is more reserved. It might also depend on the other person's mood and what kind of day he or she is having. Many of these factors, which help us decide whom we want to socialize with, come through in computer-mediated conversations as well.

Connection in any kind of being space is also a matter of *motive*. What do we hope to get out of the encounter—companionship, information, support? Are we more interested in our own private world, or are we in search of wider connections? Given the widespread use of cell phones, PDAs, and laptops in public, the line between physical and virtual space can blur, and motive may not be immediately apparent. Drop into any Internet café, for example. The clickety-clack of keyboards is as redolent as the smell of fresh brewed espresso. At first glance, all the laptop users might look the same, typing, surfing, answering email.

But if you take the time to observe and question them, as urban sociologists Keith Hampton and Neeti Gupta did in Boston and Seattle, you'll see that some of the laptop users are not necessarily "there." A café is the stereotypical being space, but "true mobiles," as the researchers called them, have no intention of making acquaintances. Place is irrelevant; they could be at home or at the office in front of their computers. To them, the café is a place of productivity, an extension of their workplace, and they ignore whatever activity or conversation swirls around them. If someone glances at their screen—either out of curiosity or a desire to connect—true mobiles don't even notice.

In contrast, "placemakers" often use such moments to start conversations. They are not only open to meeting others; it is *why* they're there. The laptop is a mere prop—an admission ticket to a social arena. Placemakers return almost daily—many are colonizers. They tend to live or work nearby, whereas local true mobiles (as opposed to business travelers) will pop in only once or twice a week, merely for a change of scene. Half of the placemakers will, in fact, meet someone new at the café; true mobiles almost never do.[65]

There are analogous situations in cyberspace. Some people are just looking for information. Others would like to chat but not on a particularly deep level. Still others seek more intimate connections. It's like the old saying, "You don't buy oranges in the hardware store." You go where you are likely to get what you need. You might join a "new in town" Meetup.com group if you were interested in making local acquaintances but not if you were just diagnosed with Hodgkin's disease. Not surprisingly, the latter type of Internet community—a place designed for fellow sufferers—is the kind of being space where people are more likely to seek solace, which is usually not the case in discussion groups, such as a site where people talk politics. "Conversations" on these different types of sites evolve accordingly. Also predictably, the posts (messages) in online support groups are much more revealing, intimate—and lengthier—than those in discussion groups. The depth and breadth of online conversations are usually reciprocal, too—again, mirroring what happens in real-life encounters.[66]

Naturally, there are also important *differences* between virtual and "meat" space—a term used by Netizens to describe physical places where you can literally see the meat on your bones. Online chats tend to be more casual, offhand, spontaneous. They're colored by the fact that we can't "read" the other person's face, hear her tone of voice, or see her body language. We also might say and do things in cyberspace that we might not do in person—a phenomenon social scientists call the "online disinhibition effect."[67]

The absence of physical cues can cut either way. We sometimes disclose too much and later regret it. Or we let someone in, and discover that he is needy and demanding—or worse, not who he says he is. On the other hand, we are less afraid to talk to strangers online, and can quickly move into consequential stranger territory. Meeting online also makes it easier to transcend conventional social boundaries.[68] Scott Heiferman recalls a young Meetup.com member who joined an *anime* (Japanese animation) group: "Before the group met, he expected that everyone would look like him. But now some guy in his sixties is his buddy. Except for their shared interest, he would have no other excuse to talk to someone older unless it was his boss, a professor, or a family member, no less relate to that person as a peer."

Some evidence also suggests that first meetings online bode better for relationship-launching than face-to-face encounters. Pairs of students who didn't know each other at the outset were given twenty minutes to become acquainted—a reasonable amount of time to give a complete stranger. Some met in a chat room, others in person. As it turned out, chat room conversation partners felt they knew more about each other, could predict their attitudes better, could move easily from one topic to the next, and were able to share both breadth *and* depth in their conversations. They also *liked* each other more than the pairs who had spent the same amount of time getting acquainted in person. The effect held even when the participants met one another twice, both in the flesh and via the Internet, unaware that it was the same person in each situation. This is not hard to believe when you consider that in face-to-face encounters, superficial factors such as physical appearance tend to overshadow other social assets. In contrast, "quality of conversation" was often cited as the reason for liking the other person in a chat room.

Of course, young adults, who are typically used in these experiments, are generally comfortable with the medium; results might be different with less-acclimated users. Also, these findings apply only to male and opposite-sex meetings. When women meet for the first time, the opposite is true: They like each other more when they meet face-to-face, and tend to distrust new female acquaintances online.[69]

Unfortunately, no one knows what happens *after* an Internet meeting—whether the closeness engendered by not having to face one another then allows a couple to be more intimate in person. Chances are it depends on the two people involved. For some, laying the groundwork online will be enough to ease into real-life relationships. This, after all, is what a site like Meetup.com banks on.

But what about people who are uneasy in social situations? Some research suggests that virtual being spaces can be a boon for the introverted. For example, young people at both extremes—those who found it either very easy or very hard to dive into new situations—were assigned to meet a group of three strangers, which is certainly a more complex social challenge than a one-on-one encounter. Some foursomes met face-to-face, some in Internet chat rooms. Predictably, the outgoing students felt equally comfortable in either venue. But the socially anxious, whose usual feelings of insecurity surfaced in face-to-face encounters, reported feeling "like nonanxious extroverts" in the chat rooms.[70]

Questions still remain: Might those successful cyberencounters eventually build up an anxiety-ridden person's confidence—at least online? If so, might such people find electronic communication so appealing that they become even more inclined to withdraw from real-life social situations?[71] Science doesn't yet have those answers, but the experiences of Roger Hobbs, a self-confessed "Internet geek," might offer some clues.

Instant Karma's Gonna Get You

Describing his high school self as "a plump, silent, painfully awkward dweeb who clung to his Latin textbook as if it held the secrets to existence," Roger Hobbs was in his sophomore year when he accidentally discovered that his cybercharm could more than compensate for a lack of charisma in person.[72] It started with five painfully awkward, sweat-inducing minutes with a female classmate he'd wanted to meet. Daunted by his own clumsiness, he nevertheless managed to blurt out a request for her screen name. After two nights of chatting with the girl via instant messages, she typed out the words, "Would you like to go out with me?"

Hobbs was shocked—and hooked. "Online I could shuffle off the nervous coil that had previously bound me to failure. As soon as my fingers touched the keys, I was not just another face in an endless crowd. With words on a screen, I would never stutter. I could take as long as I wanted to think of the perfect answer to every question, and the perfect response to every flirtation." He soon began to woo other female classmates, sometimes chatting with five at once. Each thought she was the Only One. "I didn't want another girlfriend per se, but rather I wanted the affirmation that would come with being able to get another girlfriend."

Hobbs was able to explore a part of himself that was difficult to express in person—a common occurrence online, but also with consequential strangers in any context. The Internet is like a vast playground for those multiple selves we discussed in Chapter 3. Some experts theorize that in cyberconversations the "true self" emerges—characteristics we possess but are generally unable to express to others in social settings.[73] Certainly, because of the disinhibition effect, we sometimes say and do things we wouldn't do in person. But we don't always think through the consequences of unleashing the words of one of our lesser-known selves. As with most things technological, it's a double-edged sword. On the one hand, we feel freer to share fears and buried emotions. On the other, we might also let loose criticism, anger, even threats, without seeing, or caring about, their impact on the other person. Hobbs was less a perpetrator with malicious intent than an anxious teenager in search of self. After his first successful online conquest, he kept going because he "needed to know that the cool person I became when my finger caressed the keys was actually me."

So he racked up a virtual harem of girlfriends, going out on real dates with some of them, developing "deep and steady" online relationships with others. His biggest challenge was not getting caught. Three years into his odyssey, he received a text message from one of his first "girlfriends" that made him realize he wasn't playing a video game. It read: "I love you."

Love was never part of *his* equation, Hobbs admits. Until that point he had thought about the Internet as a retreat from the real world. "The Internet is the real world," he suddenly realized. "Only faster."

When Hobbs flew off to college the following September, he decided to "find a way to be both charming and true to the person I really am." Arguably, his online experiences helped, or at least taught him a lesson about social responsibility.[74] A few months into his first semester, he struck up a conversation with a young woman at a midnight screening of *The Rocky Horror Picture Show.* Their face-to-face chat went well enough for the young woman to offer her screen name. Hobbs promised that she would be the only one on his contact list.

6

The Downside

The art of being wise is the art of knowing what to overlook.

—*William James*

When They're Bad . . .

In February 2006, the fifth season of *According to Jim* chugged into its final weeks. Viewers who watched the "The Grumpy Guy" episode that aired at the end of the month, had no idea that the plotline, which centered on a long-standing feud between neighbors, was lifted from a real-life drama.[1] Why would they? Such disputes are the stuff of situation comedy. In this one, Jim Belushi, playing the title role, discovers that the irritating seventysomething woman next door has profited from his anger all those years by writing a series of children's books in which the main character is a grumpy old man—based on him.

The actors' true-life story was far juicier.

Belushi and his guest star, veteran actor Julie Newmar (of "Catwoman" fame), lived a mere ten feet apart for nearly nineteen years and had been battling over property rights for most of them. She complained that his loud carryings-on forced her to wear soundproofing earmuffs. She also wanted the fence between their houses lowered—it was depriving her prize rosebushes of light. At one point Newmar attempted to tear it down herself. Another time, she threw an egg at his house. Belushi then sued her for harassment, defamation, and vandalism, asking for four million dollars in damages. He claimed that she was attempting to force him out of the neighborhood. They finally settled out of court, and as a gesture of forgiveness, Belushi invited Newmar to appear on his show to play his next-door nemesis—this time for laughs.

Thankfully, real-life neighbor set-tos aren't everyday occurrences, but they certainly happen. When they do, they rarely have a Hollywood ending. While writing this chapter, Blau happened on a Facebook minifeed (one-liners about other members' activities and whereabouts) posted by a "friend" (read *acquaintance*): "Paul is hoping that the U-Haul parked across the street is really gonna take his neighbors away." Paul Kellogg,* a public relations professional who lives in a working-class neighborhood outside Boston, later elaborated in an email:

> I fear my neighbors are too "over the top" for your book. My issues are many: selling drugs in the street, engaging in massive fights with their rivals, house being raided by police, snarling pit bulls in the driveway . . . bad news. When they get bored, they will just come over and sit on my porch for the day, throwing their debris in my little garden or trampling my flowers. If we wanted to sell our home, we couldn't. Nobody would buy it with this group of troublemakers malingering on their porch all day.[2]

Actually, Paul, you're not alone. A 2002 "rudeness" survey of adults eighteen and older found that while 64% found their neighbors friendly and helpful, 37% have been so offended that they thought about moving just so "they can live in a community where people are nicer to each other."[3] Moreover, feuds with neighbors and landlords are often the precipitating cause of eviction—and homelessness.[4]

As we've stressed throughout this book, the majority of consequential stranger relationships are positive, among other reasons because we can walk away when the relationship no longer serves us. If the maître d' at Joe's Bar and Grill slights you, you go to another restaurant. If someone you meet on the golf course turns out to be a blowhard, you make sure he's never in your foursome again. But what happens when circumstances don't allow us to escape people on the periphery who drive us crazy? If not a next-door neighbor, it might be the dependably disruptive resident in a co-op, condo, or neighborhood association who complains constantly but never volunteers to help. In the office, it could be the coworker in the next cubicle who doesn't know how to use his inside voice, or the boss who belittles. It might be an overbearing coach, an insensitive teacher, or the mother of your daughter's best friend who is rude and perpetually late. Then there are the random people who glom on to you as if they're long-lost soul mates—at a social gathering, the nettlesome friend-of-a-friend; at church, the resident busybody.

This chapter is a cautionary tale. We all have to put up with people we'd rather live without—and some of them are consequential strangers. In a recent large national survey, people were asked about the arguments and strains in their lives: Who were those difficult interactions with and how did they react to them? Relatives were mentioned most often, but "nonfamily relationships" accounted for approximately 40% of the reported daily hassles with other people (as opposed, say, to your car breaking down or a health issue).[5] And whereas we are frequently ambivalent about the people closest to us, Fingerman's research suggests that consequential strangers usually evoke either positive *or* negative emotions. Which brings us back to the reason why most of these relationships are positive: We end the unpleasant ones—unless we can't.

Bit players though they may be, "bad" consequential strangers are by turns embarrassing, annoying, intrusive, inappropriate, or unreasonable. They can color your perceptions of a job or a place, make you avoid an activity you love. And if you're the kind of person who can't "let it go," as friends often advise when you complain about the latest episode, there's a reason these people feel like such a drain: We tend to weigh negative social exchanges more heavily than pleasant ones. Bad relationships also have a greater impact on our well-being than positive ones.[6]

Troublesome people not only test our mettle, our reactions to them also tell us something about ourselves. What part do *we* play in these unpleasant encounters? Have we been too trusting or naive, or perhaps moved too quickly to deepen the relationship without the other person's consent? Have we ourselves been guilty of bending the truth, gossiping, or jumping on the bandwagon when others expressed a negative opinion—all the more likely when we're dealing with consequential strangers? And when we interact with someone who is very different from us, are we really as open-minded as we thought?

No Way Out

When Blau asked people (after exacting a promise of anonymity), "Have you ever had to deal with a 'bad' consequential stranger?" their answers frequently involved stories about coworkers, bosses, and colleagues. Of course, many of us make good friends on the job. However, depending on the size and nature of our place of business, a large number of workplace connections usually fall in consequential stranger territory. You might interact frequently; you might eat and even travel together. But once you're out the door, you usually don't give coworkers much thought—unless they upset you.

Our interviewees found themselves at the other end of rudeness, sarcasm, hostile glares, disrespect, shouting, backstabbing, insults, and sabotage. Their tormentors often undermined them in passive and subtle ways, such as "forgetting" to send a report or omitting a necessary piece of information. They were made to feel incompetent while their aggressors advanced their own agenda.[7] And because the perpetrators were coworkers or even supervisors and their infractions were hard to prove, there was often no way out.

How prevalent are situations such as these? In a poll of nearly eight hundred, one in ten U.S. employees witnessed incivility on the job, and 20% said they themselves were targets *at least once a week.*[8] The statistics on bullying—a term that typically indicates the more aggressive range of negative behaviors—are less clear because experts in various fields tend to define it differently. Most agree, however, that bullying is uninvited and happens repeatedly over time; an occasional lapse of behavior isn't bullying. In the United States, the range for bullying that occurs weekly is between 14 and 36%. Even greater numbers report *witnessing* such behavior, leading the authors of one scholarly review to conclude, "Clearly and sadly, bully is an enduring part of many employees' work lives."[9] Incivility and bullying are a by-product, among other factors, of more time spent at work with less time to get the job done. As one expert put it, we don't believe we have time to be nice.[10]

Robert Sutton, a professor of management science who explored this issue in his controversially titled book *The No Asshole Rule*, recalls an experience he had early in his career at Stanford University. Having received a rash of poor teaching evaluations his first year, Sutton worked hard to improve his skills and was delighted when students later voted him "best teacher" in his department. Minutes after he accepted the award, a jealous female colleague whispered in his ear, "in a condescending tone (while sporting a broad smile for public consumption), 'Well, Bob, now that you have satisfied the babies here on campus, perhaps you can settle down and do some real work.'"[11]

It doesn't take brawn to inflict psychological damage. The stereotypical bully is a man, but according to Gary Namie, director of the Workplace Bullying Institute, women often target other women, whereas men are more likely to be equal-opportunity bullies.[12] Namie maintains that men "use the hierarchy" to inflict psychological damage—for example, they badmouth fellow employees to their superiors and to colleagues. Women, he says, "play divide and conquer. They use the power of the social group to ostracize."

The director of a psychotherapy institute recalls walking into his office manager's office one morning to find the man slumped over, with his head resting on the desk. "I asked what's wrong, and he looked up and said, 'You have no idea what I go through with these women.' He was talking about the support staff, which is all women—all consequential strangers, to use your term. They were treating each other badly, inviting one out for lunch and not the other. Their behaviors were very subtle and sophisticated. And it is incredibly common."[13]

In most reported cases of bullying, the perpetrators are either supervisors or coworkers.[14] But "upward" nastiness, where a worker takes on the boss, can occur as well.[15] When Kelly Naybor,* at twenty-eight, was brought into a charitable foundation to handle multiple responsibilities—trial by fire for someone relatively new to management—she was stymied at every turn by Jim Sampson,* a project director she supervised. Bristling at the idea of working for someone younger *and* a woman (this happened nearly twenty years ago), Sampson made her life miserable. Using the foundation's letterhead, he signed Naybor's name to press releases that criticized the organization. He also ingratiated himself with certain members of the board and tried to wage a smear campaign against Naybor, hoping to get her fired. It took nearly a year, but Naybor finally honed her managing chops—and fired Sampson instead.[16]

In Ellen Roth's* case, the "worker" was one she had invited into her home, and the "workplace" was her kitchen.[17] She met Ralph Durane* when he was doing the final inspection on a home she was about to buy. He seemed knowledgeable, precise, and thorough, so when he mentioned in passing that he was also a carpenter, she seized the moment. Would he be willing to take down the wall between the living room and kitchen and replace it with a counter? He agreed; she thought they had a shared vision. Theoretically at least, it was an even exchange: her money, his expertise. But half-way into the project, Durane suddenly "got busy" elsewhere and it was impossible for her to track him down. "There was no way to fire him. I'd never find a replacement for such a small job." He finally showed up again, always at night. When she tried to talk to him, begging him to "simplify" the project, he took her suggestion as an insult. What Roth originally saw in him as "precision and thoroughness" now bordered on obsessive compulsion. Often he'd tear down his previous session's work. "The guy never yelled at me or made me fear for my life, although he also gave new meaning to the term 'moonlighting,'" quips Roth. "Sometimes he continued to work after I'd gone to bed. He made my life miserable, and I had no choice but to suffer through it."

Inside the Control Tower: The Day-to-Day Fallout

The long-term reverberations of negative interactions is well-documented. However, most surveys look at social conflicts retrospectively, not when they're actually happening. Psychologist Rena L. Repetti took a different approach. She monitored the *daily* stress of fifty-two air traffic controllers at a major international airport. Each day, Repetti asked the men to complete a questionnaire about interactions with coworkers and supervisors, how they felt about these exchanges, and whether they had any physical symptoms of stress, such as headaches and stomach pains. Because job-related factors such as weather, traffic, and landing patterns are rigorously recorded at airports, Repetti could rely on those objective measures rather than depend solely on the ATCs' descriptions of their "perceived workload."

Air traffic controllers like to describe their work by saying,

"It's just like any other job, except when we screw up people die."[18] Even on a good day, the task of monitoring a precisely choreographed ballet of aircraft is extremely stressful. It requires unremitting concentration. With his eyes trained on a screen, a controller must communicate with pilots through a headset and, with his free ear, listen to the ambient sounds of radar blips, all the while conversing with fellow ATCs. In larger airports, there's often a supervisor on duty as well. Decisions have to be made in split seconds, often on very little sleep, thanks to harrowing schedules that typically include a string of nights and weekends.

You would expect that in such a high-stakes occupation, adverse job conditions would exact a great toll, and to some extent that's true. But it's far from the whole story, especially when you throw an unpleasant, deceitful, or psychologically aggressive colleague into the mix: On days when the ATCs felt tense about, or argued with, their supervisors or each other, not only did their moods plummet, they were more likely to withdraw at home and, a subsequent study showed, were also more inclined to discipline their children. Certainly a heavier workload made for a more stressful day, but Repetti notes that "the effect of interpersonal relations on daily mood may be even stronger."[19]

Repetti's study was published in 1993, and looked at only male controllers. Still, ATCs on the job today, 18% of whom are female, not only agree with her counterintuitive conclusion, they believe an annoying or incompetent coworker can also compromise their ability to do their job well—a risk that affects all of us.[20] "Heavy traffic and thunderstorms can be dealt with," explains Chuck Adams, who works out of an airport in Grand Forks, North Dakota. "You can talk about those kinds of problems and figure out what you can do better next time. You also can control the number of airplanes you're gathering in a section. On a runway, you can limit the number of departures. And you can ask everyone to stop while you assess what's going on. But with a coworker situation, you don't have much control. It's a loose-cannon variable."[21]

Other ATCs point out that conditions continually change—bad weather gives way to sunny skies, a busy Monday is followed by a lighter Tuesday—but coworkers don't. And as in many high-risk professions, the kind of person drawn to this job is demanding and prone to perfectionism. As one controller put it, "Controllers are Type A personalities. We do it best, and if you don't do it that way, you don't know what you're doing. There's a lot of behind-the-back talk about people."

Adams, a muscular gray-haired guy in his late forties, is a former military man who, like many veteran controllers, joined their ranks in 1981 when President Reagan fired 11,000 ATCs for staging an illegal strike. He likens the job to being in a foxhole. "You depend on the other person to watch your back. If another controller does something to you or talks badly about you behind your back, it breaks that confidence, and there's a feeling of animosity that can really affect your job." As he speaks, a particular coworker comes to mind: "He's someone who'd stop at nothing to stab you in the back. Whenever he is in the cab, I don't feel safe. I don't feel I can be myself." Adams finds it physically and mentally exhausting.

Depending on the size of an airport, a controller might work in the tower, where takeoffs and landings are monitored, or in a ground-level radar command center which begins to track planes once they reach an altitude of ten thousand feet. Typically, ATCs work in teams of two to four, sometimes with a supervisor looking over their shoulder. There's no way to avoid a disagreeable coworker; each day, you go where you're sent.

"You come into work and you see the arrows pointing up for the tower or down for the radar room with everyone's initials next to it," explains Mike Patterson, a twenty-year veteran stationed in Evansville, Indiana, "and you're either happy or you groan, because certain people are a pain in the neck. You dread working with them, usually for one of three reasons: They have a negative personality or no personality, or they're not very good controllers." A less competent coworker can add to the workload, says Patterson.

"I'm sitting there watching my airspace and watching his too." He also recalls a particularly nasty supervisor who second-guessed everyone else's decisions: "He had no respect for his fellows. With a guy like that, you would come home, and you'd kick the dog and scream at the wife, and then you'd grab a lot of shots to calm yourself down." (Ironically, Repetti referred to her findings as the "kick the dog" phenomenon.)[22]

If you're studying stress, as Repetti was, male air traffic controllers were certainly a good place to start. But when the psychologist then explored a different population—a group of predominantly low-income working mothers whose children were in preschool—she also found a "robust" correlation between the mothers' daily social interactions earlier at work and their subsequent behavior toward their children. For five days she had the mothers rate statements about their workload ("I felt like I barely had a chance to breathe," "It was a fairly slow day"). As with the ATCs, she questioned them about their daily interactions with coworkers and supervisors. Each evening, the women also completed a questionnaire about interactions with their children. Luckily, Repetti was also able to videotape mother-child reunions at one of the centers, which allowed her to *see* how a stressed-out mother greeted her child.

Repetti found that mothers who were prone to depression or anxiety, as well as those who exhibited Type A behavior, were affected by heavy workload. But those who had better coping skills actually thrived when their jobs were more demanding. However, *none* of the four subgroups was immune to the impact of social stress. Like the ATC dads who tended to discipline their kids after a day of social stress, some working moms who had altercations with coworkers became more irritable and impatient with their children. However, most simply withdrew. This "negative spillover" meant that the little ones were "less happy" on those days, too.[23]

Throughout Chapter 4, we stressed that supportive relationships can be a boon to health. But the reverse is true as well: Irritating relationships can jeopardize well-being on a day-to-day basis, especially in situations where we have an unfair superior and little control. In England, for example, scientists focused on female health care assistants in hospitals, nursing homes, and residential homes because they were responsible to different supervisors, depending on the day of the week. The aides were asked to indicate the extent to which they agreed or disagreed with forty-seven statements such as, "My supervisor encourages discussion before making a decision," and "I am treated fairly by my supervisor." For three days, they wore portable blood pressure monitors that automatically took readings every thirty minutes. As it turned out, on a day when an aide worked with a superior with whom she didn't get along, her blood pressure climbed significantly higher than when she worked a shift under someone she considered a good supervisor or, not surprisingly, on her day off. Certainly other factors such as family history and lifestyle also raise workers' risk of coronary heart disease and stroke, but tense relations with bosses and overseers might also contribute to the mix.[24]

Groups, Gossip, and the Donald Effect

The late George Carlin told Larry King in an interview, "People are great one at a time, because in them you see all the beauty, all the potential for this species, but as soon as they get in groups, I get scared—of two people even. They say, 'I like Bob but not when he's with Linda.'"[25] Remembered best for his astute comic riffs on humanity, Carlin was spot-on in this case, too. When people in casual relationships are part of a closed network such as an office or a community group, the effect of gossip is magnified. They're more likely to believe stories about you if the facts seem consistent with stories they know about people *like* you—others of your gender, your ethnic group, your occupation, for example. (How many of us laugh at lawyer jokes and make judgments when we first meet someone in that profession?) And they are more likely to trade in, and to believe, gossip and lies.[26]

Consider this: In a small lab at Princeton University, student volunteers were given a few minutes to digest a written description of "Donald," who, they were told, was a fellow undergrad. The write-up revealed distinctly positive behaviors about Donald (for instance, a statement that indicated he was a "good athlete") and clearly negative traits (short-tempered behavior) as well as ambiguous information about him (an action that could be interpreted as either "confident" or "conceited"). Each student thought he was taking part in a communications experiment in which he would digest the information and then use his own words to describe Donald without naming him. The point, or so the volunteers believed, was to portray Donald in a way that another student—allegedly someone who knew him from one of the university's eating clubs—would be able to identify him. In actuality, the other student was a shill who was part of the team. And right before he was shown into the room, the researcher let it "slip" that the other student either liked or disliked Donald.

The results might remind you of social life in the seventh grade: When students were told ahead of time that the other guy—the shill—liked Donald, they described him as if they liked him, too. They barely mentioned Donald's negative traits and put a positive spin on ambiguous qualities—for instance, portraying him as "confident." But when they thought the other guy didn't like Donald, the volunteers' descriptions again mirrored their audience. They flipped the ambiguous traits—now Donald was conceited—and relayed mostly the negative information they had read.

The fact is, most of us play to our audiences and, therefore, *selectively disclose* what we know. We also begin to believe our own spin. A week later, when asked their own impressions of Donald, volunteers tended to remember what they had *said* about him—the tailored version, not what they had read. They actually *felt* that way about Donald, too. In effect, saying was believing.[27]

People can selectively disclose in any type of relationship—for example, failing to mention a spouse's conservative political leanings while talking to a staunch liberal. But among a group of consequential strangers, biased stories are often readily believed, and the fallout can make or break a person's reputation. Also, in casual conversation, it's polite to go along with everyone else. Before you know it, people who don't know Donald very well jump on the bandwagon, making it less likely that any one person will express a different view. So if you're Donald and someone is out to tarnish your name, you'd better hope someone at the watercooler—a colleague who knows you and already likes you—has your back.

In effect, Stephen Carter turned Luke Bridges into "Donald." Bridges,[*] thirty-five, married, and the father of two, landed a promising job with a two-year contract, a generous salary, and the chance to create a new Internet division.[28] He answered directly to the CEO. On his first visit to the home office in San Diego, Bridges met Stephen Carter,[*] the vice president of sales who'd been with the company for ten years. Carter greeted Bridges warmly and insisted they go out for drinks. Bridges saw forty-five-year-old Carter as an equal and an ally, and the VP did nothing to disabuse him of that notion—at first.

"He was very honest about his situation," Bridges recalls. "He'd never been in media before joining the company—he once sold drapes for his father-in-law. Then his wife left him. So he tells me all about this stuff and gets pretty personal with me. At the time, I thought, *I guess he's trying to be friends*. But sometimes it made me feel awkward, like when he'd casually mention that he had a taste for hookers or would want me to go to a bar with him to pick up women. *I* didn't want to do that, but I didn't want to offend him either. When he started asking questions about my life, I didn't think I had anything to hide, but I realize now that opening up to me was part of the manipulation."

Inexplicably, the friendly VP then started to ignore Bridges, dodging phone calls, not answering emails for a week. At one point he told the young man he should run everything through him first, instead of emailing the CEO directly. He insisted that

Bridges prepare an "action plan" they could discuss over the weekend. Bridges stayed up all night to complete it, only to have a week pass before Carter finally called. On the phone, he was more than complimentary, telling Bridges it was the "best" action plan he'd ever seen. Later, Bridges would find out that he told the CEO and other executives just the opposite. "Stephen was on this mission to destroy me," Bridges now realizes. "I felt like I had to keep looking in the rearview mirror."

Clearly, Carter was gunning for his younger rival. But Bridges, who was rarely in the office, unwittingly made himself an easy target. He was frequently on the road, meeting with potential customers. Otherwise he worked mostly from home. He didn't get a chance to "manage" his own reputation; in his absence, Carter did it for him. Planting a doubt here, a lie there, he let everyone know he didn't like Bridges. As a VP who had been with the company far longer than Bridges, he knew his audience. So it didn't take much for him to get their coworkers and even their superiors to believe *his* portrait of Bridges.

Another reason that men and women like Carter get away with such Machiavellian tactics is that people bond over negative attitudes. Gossip promotes closeness. When you reveal a shocking tidbit about Rita to Harry, it energizes your tie to Harry (especially if your story fits Harry's opinion of Rita). It lets Harry know you're on the same team, which makes him feel good and strengthens your relationship. Also, negative information (like negative emotions) usually trumps positive. We give greater weight to unflattering portrayals of people and more attention to "bad" events than "good" ones. We even stoke our relationships at the early stages by sharing what we *don't* like about others.

In one study, people were asked to recall and list the positive and negative attitudes they shared with their current closest friends when they first got to know each other—in effect, at a point when they were still consequential strangers. Whereas the participants *believed* that their shared positive attitudes about people had deepened their relationships, they actually shared a larger number of *negative* attitudes. They both viewed Amy as a tactless boor or thought that Ralph Nader should stop running for president. Of course they shared many positive attitudes, too—but most were about *things*, such as movies, activities, and beliefs, not opinions about people. Shared dislike can foster "in group" solidarity.[29] As sociologist Ronald Burt puts it, "Gossip is not about information. It is about creating and maintaining relationships."[30]

Some scientists liken gossip to primates' grooming. After all, apes and chimps are social creatures. They form coalitions. They sometimes gang up on a third party. And they apparently keep track of favors given and favors received. In one of his studies, the famed Dutch psychologist and primatologist Frans de Waal, who has written extensively on the parallels between apes and humans, kept detailed records of grooming behavior. He began to see an interesting difference between apes who groomed each other often and those who associated for the occasional grooming session—in ape society, a gathering of consequential strangers. Grooming mattered little between apes who spent a lot of time with each other. But with more infrequent encounters, the apes seem to recall the favor, later "rewarding" a groomer with food. De Waal says humans do it, too: "We are more inclined to keep track of give-and-take with strangers and colleagues than with our friends and family. In fact, score-keeping in close relationships, such as between spouses, is a sure sign of distrust."[31]

Much is made in scholarly circles of "exchanges" in a relationship. We may not like to think of it in these terms, but social ties function like an economy—there's some level of trust between the two parties, and each gives to and gets benefits from the other. When we lived in tribes and simple communities and you could observe the people around you, "trust" wasn't as much of an issue as it is today. Other people's actions are now hidden and separated by time and space.[32] When we trust someone, it means we're willing to put forth effort or money, or reveal information before we actually know how the person will behave. With each interaction, trust either builds or is broken. The stronger the relationship, generally, the stronger the trust.[33] But like primates, we're not so sure when it comes to consequential strangers, which brings us back to the power of gossip.

Gossip whets the social appetite. And most of us are more than willing to partake. Sometimes gossip is merely idle chitchat, and the results are fairly benign, even beneficial. It can be a way to spread word in a workplace or a community, or to let people know what's expected of them. Gossip, therefore, can keep people in line. Continental Airlines banked on this when it began offering employees a $65 monthly bonus for on-time arrivals. Although the scholarly term is "mutual monitoring," in effect coworkers began to gossip about people who weren't pulling their weight—so-called "free riders"—which pressured other employees to stay on task.[34]

Gossip also can act like an early warning system, alerting others about an unreliable babysitter, an unfeeling doctor, or an abusive coworker. But what if the circulating story is *not* true? As we've seen, gossip can, at the very worst, be a powerful weapon in a bully's arsenal. Once rumors gain a life of their own, they can be difficult, if not impossible, to combat.[35] Thus, gossip produces an "echo," reinforcing a negative reputation rather than shedding new light on the person. The parties become "erroneously certain"—and so, biased information is taken as truth.[36]

The Vampire Liar

Allyson Beatrice was twenty-seven in 2001, camping out on a friend's floor in Los Angeles, when she began her seven-year obsession with fandom—partcipating in a community that revolves around a particular interest—in this case, the TV show *Buffy the Vampire Slayer.* She had just moved from the East Coast and had no job, no prospects, and kept getting lost whenever she ventured out on the freeways. "My self-worth was in the toilet."[37] But at least she had her fellow fans at www.buffy.com. "I could write, 'I'm scared. I think I made a terrible mistake,' and twenty strangers would tell me it was going to be okay, and tell me stories about their own lonely lives, or how they survived cross-country moves. It was the only constant I had, the only thing that looked the same, worked the same."

For the uninitiated, a brief explanation might be needed: *Buffy* featured a posse of teenagers in mythical Sunnydale, California, whose school library just happened to sit atop "Hellmouth"—a gateway to the demon realm. Every week, the title character and her buddies fought an assortment of otherworldly bad guys. Some reviewers saw it as a cross between *My So-Called Life* and *The X-Files.* If none of this is clear, you had to be there. And while many of us who are over thirty-five weren't there when the show ended its seven-year run in 2003, some three to five million loyal fans were. *Buffy* has since been spun off, satirized, and showcased at an annual academic symposium entitled—no kidding—"The Slayage Conference on Buffy the Vampire Slayer."

Allyson Beatrice's social life wasn't totally limited to the Buffistas she met on "the Bronze," an Internet community named after the teen hangout in Sunnydale, but it was soon dominated by them. Many of her virtual relationships migrated offline. She met fellow fans who lived in L.A.; she even met friends of her online pals. Every year on Presidents' Day weekend, Beatrice and her cohorts, some now close, some still casual, would gather in Los Angeles for the "Posting Board Party." Her growing role at these parties morphed into an event-planning business with another Buffy enthusiast. The community was "a lot like high school" except that Beatrice, a former teenage loner who slid by on her reputation as the "art chick," was now one of the cool kids.

Online or in real life, being tied to people *only* by one common thread, or as Beatrice puts it, "the tiniest scrap of shared experience," means that there might be other surprises in store. Such was the case with "Penlind," whom she considered one of the more intelligent, well read, and insightful community members. Penlind peppered her posts with literary references and "intriguing theories" about the show and its metaphors. Gradually she also let pieces of her identity slip, and then her scholarly comments made sense: She was an adjunct professor at Harvard, related to a band member in the Barenaked Ladies, and married to an archaeologist. They had two adopted children with exotic names. When Penlind wrote that a neighborhood kid taunted her daughter "Cairo," saying, "Black girls can never play the heroes because there are no black heroes," it roused the community's collective ire. More to the point, Penlind had everyone's attention.

A few weeks later, poor Penlind, alone because her archaeologist husband was off on a dig, wrote that her dear little boy "Djoser" had a fatal disease. Details followed, each one garnering more sympathy for Penlind and her son. The Bronzers held a prayer vigil. Hearing this, an offline friend sarcastically suggested to Beatrice that Penlind was suffering from "Munchausen's by Internet." (People who have the real-life syndrome, named after a Baron who made up fantastical tales, exaggerate or lie about their own or a loved one's illness. The Internet has spawned a virtual version.)[38] Beatrice found it hard to believe that Penlind would lie. But then she began to reread old posts. As her doubts increased, she worried that people might start sending checks to Penlind, which had happened in the past when a community member lost a job or had a baby. Once, members of the community raised three thousand dollars to finance a whirlwind tour of the United States for Willy,* a fellow Buffista whom everyone loved. But in each of those cases *someone* had met the person in the flesh. No one had ever met Penlind. A "secret team of cynics"—members Beatrice trusted with her doubts—decided to delve into each of Penlind's claims.

Not only was Penlind lying about her child's illness, she didn't even have a child, or a husband for that matter. She *was* well read, but she was a librarian, not a professor—a librarian who had been fired for stealing computer equipment. Word spread, as it only can on the Internet, and the fierce debate that ensued threatened to disrupt the entire community. Some defended Penlind and bad-mouthed the investigators who exposed her. Others accepted the information more readily. Beatrice understood the range of emotions: "No one wanted to believe that they lent their heart to a fraud. No one wants to be played for a fool."

Oh, the Tangled Web We Weave (No Pun Intended)

Most distortions of the truth fall far short of the kinds of serious trust-breaching lies Penlind told. We might be inclined to dismiss her deceitfulness as extreme, therefore, or perhaps as an Internet phenomenon. To some extent, the medium does affect the message-giver. One aspect of the "disinhibition effect" (see page 160) is that an online self can take on a life of its own.[39] But lying is also part of the social dance. Call it what you will—bending the truth, exaggerating, embellishing, misrepresenting, making false promises, deliberately deceiving. When asked to review their daily social exchanges, people "intentionally mislead," on average, once or twice a day.[40] And the bulk of these everyday lies, especially the ones that make us look better, are directed at—and come from—consequential strangers, according to psychologist Bella DePaulo. Her research suggests that we tell more lies per social interaction to acquaintances and strangers than to our friends or best friends and feel more comfortable *about* lying to them. There are, of course, big lies and little everyday lies. Serious lies seem to be reserved for those we love. We lie rather than disappoint, or lie when the truth poses a bigger threat to the relationship than the lie, as in, "I'm not having an affair."[41]

Lying can be a form of "impression management." Recall the last time you were in a room full of consequential strangers—at a cocktail party, on a vacation, or among coworkers. If you exaggerated or put a more positive spin on anything about yourself, that would be considered *self-oriented* lying. Twice as often these are the kind of lies we tell. They're designed to protect or enhance ourselves or give us an edge—for example, implying to a client that you have a project under control so that you don't appear incompetent or invite further scrutiny. However, the extent to which we go to impress others also depends on who is in earshot. If just one person who knows you well is part of the conversation, you are likely to be more modest about yourself than you would with an audience comprised solely of strangers or acquaintances.[42]

Lying is also a social lubricant, explains psychologist Robert Feldman. He found that among adolescents aged eleven to sixteen, those who have better social skills lie more convincingly and are also more popular. Girls are better liars than boys, and both get better at it with age.[43] As adults, we lie in interviews and on blind dates. It's how we get jobs and keep friends.[44] We may think of ourselves as "being tactful" when we respond untruthfully to questions such as, "Do you mind if I sit next to you?" "Do I look my age?" or "Do you think Brian likes me?" But they are lies nonetheless. While they are half as frequent as self-serving fibs, one in four lies are *other-oriented*. Women tell more of these lies than men.

Although both kinds of lies can erode a relationship in the long run, they also can be effective, which is probably why they're so common.[45] As Feldman points out, "If you're totally blunt all the time, in many ways you're difficult to be around. No one wants to hear, 'Oh, you look terrible today,' or 'Wow, did you put on weight!'"[46]

To assess rates of lying, Feldman invited undergraduates at a large state university to take part in a study allegedly designed to examine how people interact when they meet someone new. Following ten-minute meetings, the students were asked if their statements to the other person were "accurate"—Feldman wanted to avoid using the more loaded term "lying." After hearing these directions, he recalls, "many participants spontaneously said that they were sure they had been totally accurate." But when they were then shown videotapes of these encounters, they saw the truth: Overall, 60% lied at least once and those who lied told an average of two to three lies *in just ten minutes.* Mirroring the "Donald" experiment, students often said they liked a certain person simply because the other person did. Others spun bigger deceptions, such as falsely claiming to be the star of a rock band—a form of extreme impression management.[47]

These participants didn't know each other at the outset and might have been affected, Feldman grants, by "the awkwardness of having to speak with a stranger for a period of time in a laboratory setting." Still, in a bar, café, online, or wherever people first meet, he says, such ten-minute conversations mark the beginning of a casual relationship. It's a good bet that a lie, however "white," will work its way into the conversation—and the person on the receiving end might never be the wiser. And lest you dismiss these findings because the volunteers were young, both Feldman and DePaulo have found almost comparable rates of lying in older people.[48]

DePaulo used a different approach: She asked groups of students and community members to keep a weeklong diary of conversations lasting ten minutes or more—with family members, best friends, friends, acquaintances, and strangers—and to record "any intentional attempts to mislead, including nonverbal ones." The college students told one lie for every three social interactions, the community members, who ranged in age from eighteen to seventy-one, told one for every five ten-minute (or longer) encounters. Their lies fell on a continuum from "very trivial, unimportant" to "very serious," with far more at the mild end. Had they planned to lie or did they do so spontaneously? And given the same circumstances, would they tell the same lie again? Regardless of whether they were lying to a close friend or a consequential stranger, people told mostly unplanned lies, felt somewhat bad while they were lying but had little to no regret afterward. Seven out of ten *would* lie again.

One reason we get away with these deceptions—with intimates and consequential strangers—is that our radar for lies is not particularly well-developed. In fifty or more laboratory tests where a "receiver"—the person being lied to—is asked to judge whether a "sender" is lying, most people do no better than the flip of a coin. As it turns out, even experts trained to spot liars only get it right around 56% of the time. As one researcher concluded, we are "at best inaccurate at deception detection."[49]

DePaulo and other experts maintain that our culture has "truth bias"—we are socially inclined to take at face value what others say.[50] Skepticism is discouraged. This helps explain why some Buffy fans were more upset with the detectives who uncovered the truth about Penlind than with Penlind herself. We are even more inclined to believe those in our inner circles. "People can be especially clueless in reading the lies of partners because they have an investment in them," says DePaulo. But it is also a matter of degree. Although Penlind was a consequential stranger to members of the Bronze, they had put in time with her. Even some of the cynics were invested. Therefore, DePaulo points out, "the relationship was going in that direction [toward greater intimacy]."[51]

Allyson Beatrice, who has since watched other Internet communities go through growing pains, would agree. At first members are thrilled to discover others who feel the same way as they do. They see no risk in opening up to each other, and their guard is down. "Our only experience till that point was that people were telling us the truth. In the life of an Internet community, when a Penlind comes along, it's paradise lost. We had people who were jerks. But even a jerk will tell you that he's been a jerk. This was the first time we had someone come in who was not at all who they said they were. People felt a huge connection to her. I felt a sense of empathy. We know that people can lie, but I thought in my own arrogant way, *How is it possible to take me in a scam?* Feeling duped is a horrible feeling, and some people's reaction was not wanting to see the truth. It made them feel worse. It shakes your faith in people, and that's a hard thing to swallow if that never happened to you. There was a lot of hurt."[52]

Miscues and Disconnections

Many consequential relationships go "bad" in far less dramatic ways. The flip side of living in the age of networked individualism, where connections are not necessarily dictated by family or organizations, is that potential social partners also have the right *not* to interact with us—or we with them. Extricating ourselves can be uncomfortable. As we pointed out earlier, social ties tend to ebb and flow. While two people can become increasingly open and intimate over time, they can also withdraw—either because of circumstances or personal differences.[53] Someone you were drawn to initially turns out to be harder to take in large doses than you anticipated. We don't usually bother to "break up" with consequential strangers, which is why Dana Cummings* was so surprised to receive a call from an acquaintance announcing that their "friendship" was over. Although Cummings enjoyed seeing the woman, which wasn't often, she never really thought of her as a friend. Good thing, because the woman made it clear that she no longer wanted to socialize with her![54]

Missed signals are perhaps more likely in consequential stranger relationships. Because these wash-and-wear relationships generally don't require too much maintenance, we may not bother to set boundaries—until someone steps over the line. An office mate you have lunch with on occasion expresses a desire to take in a movie on the weekend. A neighbor with whom you've had impromptu conversations invites you to Sunday dinner with the family. A fellow game-watcher at the local tavern asks you to help him prepare his taxes. Each wants more than you're willing to give.

Intimate ties can deteriorate when one person operates according to one set of unspoken rules and the partner another.[55] But the same can be said of casual relationships, says psychologist Irving

Altman.[56] "I think it's very frequent. People often call each other 'friends' or 'associates,' but they're in segmented relationships—what you call consequential strangers. There are all kinds of segmented relationships, and there may or may not be agreement on the rules. It fits with social penetration theory. It's saying that there are relationships that only go to a certain level of intimacy and only involve certain parts of a person. Confusion can occur, theoretically, when the two parties don't have a mutual definition of the relationship."[57]

Relationships that involve paid services have a built-in imbalance from the outset. Say you're very fond of your masseuse—she has such a soothing voice and great hands. Although she might genuinely like you and enjoy the conversation when you're there, she rubs fifty bodies a month and thinks of you only when she is readying the table for your visits. Likewise, your therapist is the keeper of your deepest secrets, someone who has helped you through difficult times. His voice is in your head as you make your way through the day. You might even dream about him. But he is bound by codes of professional conduct *not* to let personal feelings enter the relationship, so as much as you might 'adore' him, you are his "Monday at two o'clock."

Mentoring relationships can be tricky, too. Although some types of mentoring programs in Europe feature "learning partnerships" where both parties theoretically further each other's career development, in the United States, such relationships are typically more traditional: a senior person helps a newbie learn the ropes. A relatively new trend in mentoring is to be part of a "developmental network," rather than relying on a sole person. But the idea, which has been embraced by some organizations, is still in its infancy.[58] In any case, savvy up-and-comers often take the initiative, hoping to get the person or team that best meets their needs. Laura Wander* was one of them.[59]

In her early twenties at the time, Wander was working at a data-search company when she met Alice Houghton,* a vice president at a law firm in the Midwest. "My job was to make sure she had everything she needed from our company. Alice was in her mid-forties, one of those women you look at and you think, *This is the type of executive I'd like to be.* She was outgoing and attractive in a Texas businesswoman kind of way—big hair, lots of makeup. She juggled motherhood and wasn't bitter about it. I'd see her twice a year. We usually went to lunch whenever she was in town, and we talked around once a month."

The two women chatted mostly about business, and when Wander brought up the subject of mentoring, Houghton volunteered. Although they lived in different cities, the beginning of their relationship was textbook-perfect. In their first phone conversation, Houghton posed all the right questions, gave Wander assignments, and helped her set goals. "I was really pumped, made my lists, and did everything she asked me to do." For around eight months, Houghton made herself available. Wander, meanwhile, gained enough confidence to strike out on her own. "Alice seemed excited and supportive when I left the company, but that was when the calls started to trail off," Wander recalls. "I tried to be understanding and patient. Her business was not doing well, so I figured she was busy."

Wander came to feel as if she had "jumped off a cliff" and Houghton, who had promised to supply a parachute, was nowhere in sight. "I'd call her two or three times, and then I'd worry that she would think I was stalking her. She stopped returning my calls and then, out of the blue, I'd get a very positive email. It's like when you're dating a guy and he falls off the end of the earth. When you run into him again, you have that glimmer of hope. So I'd reply with a long email, and then I wouldn't hear from her again."

Wander eventually stopped trying. We'll never know Alice Houghton's side of the story, but Wander suspects that there might have been some professional jealousy. Despite initial good intentions, some mentors bristle when mentees begin to rise. Wander also admits that there were things *she* did wrong. "I shouldn't have replied with long emails." And although a mentor outside the company is theoretically more objective, Wander adds, "Had she and I worked in the same company, it might have been different because there would have been built-in incentives." Perhaps her mentor also had second thoughts: "I think she felt that as a successful female manager, she *should* be mentoring someone like me—it fit her profile. But as our relationship developed, she probably felt like she wasn't getting anything out of it."

Reciprocity matters, perhaps even more so with consequential strangers since it's so easy to drop them. Just like de Waal's apes, who groomed their occasional partners but expected something in return, humans make similar assessments of each other—apparently, quite early on in their relationships. A study that followed college freshmen who met for the first time in a communications class found that within the *first ten minutes* of a conversation, each party formed an opinion about the "future value" of the other. The students based their judgments on looks, brains, popularity, personality—or any other quality about the person that might be of some benefit in the weeks to come. Those who thought well of their partners acted in ways that strengthened the tie. Those who wrote their partner off in the first moments did just the opposite. Nine weeks later, their opinions, negative or positive, hadn't changed. It's also telling that the student with the *negative* opinion held sway over the relationship: Once he or she decided this wasn't a relationship worth pursuing, the other person could do little to change the situation.[60]

Crossing Social Divides: Mind Bugs and Hidden Realities

Even if there is an apparent imbalance between two consequential strangers—say, one is richer, more powerful, older, more knowledgeable—the relationship can still work as long as both parties are somehow rewarded in favors, promotion, accolades, money, emotional fulfillment, or spiritual benefits. But even for those of us with the best intentions, some social divides are not easily crossed.

Katherine Morgensen* befriended the maintenance man in her building, a low-rise on Main Street in a small Midwest city, where she worked for a publishing company.[61] Sam Smith* was a sweet guy who seemed to be down on his luck—the kind of person many of us regularly pass by without seeing. Morgensen always took a few minutes to make small talk. Sam would share a tidbit of his life; and she'd listen appreciatively. But before long he started visiting her office on his breaks. He'd park himself at her desk, eager to snag a few more minutes of her attention.

There were days when Morgensen was swamped with work, and Smith's brief visits felt like a burden. "I'd think, *Why did I have to be so nice to this guy?* Sometimes I could say, 'Sam, I'm really busy,' and he would leave with a dejected look on his face." On his next visit, she'd try to be more patient. "His life is minimal, and I'm an element in his daily existence. He gets so much pleasure and sociability out of it. I say to myself, *You can stop what you're doing for a few minutes. This person is in need—it's no big deal.* But it's not always easy to find that balance between giving of yourself and giving to another person. That's hard enough in an intimate relationship! It's exhausting."

Science helps explain Morgensen's quandary: According to the theory of "ego-depletion," we don't have unlimited reserves of attention or self-control. One can sap the other. Certain social situations make us anxious and require more self-control. That is, we monitor our thoughts, feelings, or impulses, and perhaps modify our typical behavior in some way. It's part of impression management—we don't want others to think badly of us. But at such times, we have less energy left over to then attend to a task that requires mental acuity. It works this way: Give yourself a taxing social assignment, such as meeting someone for the first time or acting uncharacteristically boastful with a friend—situations social scientists have used to test this theory on college students. If you are then asked to do a series of complex math problems, there's a good chance that you'll be less accurate or need more time to finish. In effect, the social task robs attention from the mental task.[62]

Arguably, for Morgensen to maintain her connection with Smith, especially at times when he enters her space uninvited, she has to expend extra energy to fight those inner voices that say, *I don't have time for him*. She also has to act in a way that encourages him to see her as compassionate and open-minded. She may be all of those things, but she has to work harder to showcase those parts of herself with Smith than she would with good friends. She doesn't know him very well, and they come from different worlds, so she even has to talk in a different way than she would with members of her inner circles. Thus, the irony: Difference itself—one of the most rewarding and growth-inducing aspects of connecting with a consequential stranger—has a downside. Despite her avowed desire to reach out to others and connect with a broad swath of humanity, Morgensen also might have attitudes of which she's not even aware that can prevent her from carrying out her good intentions.

Whether you consider it an accident of birth or a spiritual assignment with lessons to be learned, we're all born into and later choose certain social groups. And these larger groups, as we noted earlier, affect the way we think about ourselves and about others. Although we may *believe* we are open to people who are different, the "implicit association test" (IAT) suggests that most of us harbor unconscious biases. Different versions of the IAT, which takes less than ten minutes to complete, are designed to reveal hidden attitudes toward gender, ethnicity, religion, sexuality, body type, disability, age, and political leanings—the "isms" that often get in the way of forging relationships in the first place. The IAT on race, for example, displays white and black faces and directs you to pair them—as fast as you can—with either positive or negative adjectives. If you more strongly associate "white" with "good," the assumption is that it should take you less time to pair them that way as opposed to "black" with "good," or "white" with "bad."

Six million IATs later, "Project Implicit"—a virtual laboratory launched in the late nineties to test our unconscious attitudes—has found that whites, Asians, Hispanics, even blacks show a pro-white racial bias, although this preference is weakest among blacks. Most people also prefer thin over fat, straight over gay, the able-bodied over those with disabilities. We link males with science and career, females with liberal arts pursuits and family. And the strongest preference of all is youth over old age. With few exceptions, implicit attitudes *don't* correspond to our conscious, or *explicit*, preferences.[63] Thus, while we might *say* we believe that all are equal, our brains tell us that the dominant group is better. (You can go to www.implicit.harvard.edu to take the IAT and a short survey that assesses your explicit attitudes about various isms.)

Harvard scholar Mahzarin Banaji, one of the founders of Project Implicit, shies away from the word "prejudice," and instead calls these knee-jerk preferences "mind bugs"—glitches in the software of our brains, honed in part by environment and in part by evolution. Our ancestors' lives depended on their ability to distinguish between us and them. It's part of our hardwiring. "We see recognition of self and other in babies. They seem to come prepared to be able to acquire very rapidly the kind of information that says, *This is me, and this is not me.*" Banaji stresses, "So we have a lot to work against: many millions of years as our species, as well as societal stereotypes and our own experience as individuals."[64]

Putting these two ideas together—that we are affected by unconscious attitudes about "otherness," and that our ability to focus may be compromised when we are around people who are different—has powerful implications about consequential strangers, who by definition are often dissimilar or at least have had experiences that are unfamiliar to us. The process of getting to know them can be stressful and depleting. Social psychologist Jennifer Richeson demonstrated this when she gave groups of white and black students the IAT and then, in a seemingly unrelated activity, had each person interact with an interviewer, either of the same or a different race. Finally she had the students take the "Stroop test," which involves quickly naming colors printed in noncorresponding inks—for example, the word "green" is printed in red—which requires a great deal of concentration. Whites typically performed more poorly on the Stroop after meeting with an interviewer who was black than with one who was white. And the greater their implicit bias—attitudes they might not even be aware of—the more poorly they performed after such interracial interactions. For blacks, it was much the same story. The more negative their attitudes toward whites, the poorer their performance after interracial, as opposed to same-race, interactions. Both performed well after same-race meetings.

On each side of the divide, Richeson stresses, are different reasons for individuals' discomfort: Whites or members of any dominant group are typically concerned about appearing prejudiced, whereas blacks or individuals who belong to another minority group worry about being the target of bias or somehow confirming a negative stereotype. Either way, Richeson and her colleagues concluded, interactions that cross barriers—in this case racial divides—"can be cognitively costly."[65]

Although these studies involve first-meetings and none have looked at the prickly issue of interclass interactions, the findings might help explain why sometimes Katherine Morgensen finds encounters with Sam Smith "exhausting." They also shed light on low-paid workers' relationships with more affluent supervisors, coworkers, or customers, which can be similarly tiring and difficult. The question is, Can riding out the discomfort of getting to know a consequential stranger ultimately help bridge these difficult divides?

Morgensen keeps trying. She sees it as a spiritual imperative: "I guess the lesson is not to be too nice to someone you barely know if you can't carry it through day after day. In the long run, I've been able to maintain my end, and on most days I feel good about it."

She has the right idea: We make "otherness" more accessible and therefore less strange through friendships and acquaintanceships. Most social scientists agree that having firsthand contact with members of out-groups or with people who defy the stereotype has been shown to reduce bias over time (although findings vary as to what type, intensity, and duration is most effective).[66] But as we've seen, these efforts can backfire, especially when we're thrust into situations and don't want to appear biased. (Morgensen admits, for example, that she finds it most taxing when Smith drops by unexpectedly.)

An alternative is to be proactive—that is, to *seek out* people who are different. Richeson found that individuals who were told to "avoid prejudice" during an interracial interaction performed more poorly on the Stroop than those who were told to "have a positive intercultural exchange." The first group went into the exercise with their backs up. They had to be more vigilant than the other group. Sadly, that's the default strategy many of us use in these "politically correct" times. Richeson suggests that we shift direction. Instead of trying to control ourselves so as to *avoid* appearing prejudiced—a strategy that can exact an emotional and cognitive price—we might adopt what she calls "approach behavior," which involves "intercultural learning, friendship development, and honest dialogue in the service of mutual understanding." That sounds a lot like forging relationships with consequential strangers.

7

The Future of Consequential Strangers

> There will be possibilities for the rapid development of closeness between and among persons, a closeness which is not artificial, but is real and deep, and which will be well suited to our increasing mobility of living. Temporary relationships will be able to achieve the richness and meaning which heretofore have been associated with lifelong attachments.
>
> —*Carl Rogers (1968)*

Silent Rave Strikes Back

On Friday, April 18, 2008, some 2,000 people, mostly teens and college students, converged in Union Square, a historic park in downtown Manhattan. The gatherers came by foot, bus, and subway from the five boroughs of New York City, from the suburbs, and from points beyond. Some wore street clothes; others looked like they were headed for a night out at the clubs. A few, like the guy in the banana costume, dressed for Halloween. A buzz of expectation filled the space. Suddenly conversation ebbed and all eyes turned to the center of the park, where an eighteen-year-old Englishman, straddling a bronze statue of George Washington on horseback, began the countdown. On cue, at precisely 5:28 p.m., the revelers flicked on their MP3 players and began to dance, giving new meaning to the notion of marching to the beat of your own drummer—in this case, your own playlist. And yet, the swirling, booty-bumping, fist-pumping dervishes felt a strong connection.

The young man with the watch was Jonnie Wesson, a prep-school exchange student who had attended similar silent raves in London. He proposed a New York version of the BYO music event via Facebook and hoped friends would tell friends and they would tell their friends: "Imagine the pure liberation at dancing however you want to," he wrote, "to whatever music your heart desires from Ozzy Osbourne to Justice, and not caring what anyone else thinks!" He assured Facebook members that everyone was welcome:

> Punks; Goths; Ravers; Space-Cases; Indie-kids; Electro-heads; House fiends; Commuters; Teenagers; Retirees; Businessmen; Musicians; Emos; Jocks; Geeks; Teachers; Students; Christians; Jews; Muslims; Atheists; Agnostics; Upper East Siders and Coney Islanders; this event is for anyone who wants to dance and experience something truly wonderful![1]

Mass gatherings such as this silent rave, organized via social networking sites, email, cell phones, and instant messages fall under the rubric of "smart mobs." The term was coined years ago by longtime Internet observer Howard Rheingold, who presciently declared it "a new form of social organization."[2] One or more people get the ball rolling, but they don't consider themselves leaders. Some smart mobs are spurred by free agents like Wesson, a kid with a fun idea, others by rogue "prankster" groups. The participants start out as strangers but quickly become a powerful collective. The net effect might be a political statement, the conversion of public space into mass playground, or the execution of a harmless prank—like the time 111 shirtless and not particularly fit men invaded an Abercrombie & Fitch store, a subtle spoof on the company's ads showing bare-chested hunks.[3] "We may not be interested [in participating]," Rheingold told a reporter in 2002, "but today's 17-year-olds are."[4] How right he was.

Yuna Shaughnnessy, a junior in high school at the time, was "pissed" that she couldn't make the first silent rave in Union Square. Her church youth group had chartered a bus to see Pope Benedict XVII, who was then visiting New York. Shaughnnessy (a random teen plucked from Facebook) attends Staten Island Tech, one of the more rigorous and competitive high schools in the city, but she can't be easily classified. She loves to meet new people and "do spontaneous things" with her friends. She is also a serious student. That year, she had a heavy courseload, was in the thick of college applications (reaching mostly for the Ivies)—and feeling very "high-strung." She had already missed the pillow fight in Union Square and the bubble battle in Times Square. So that summer, shortly after her seventeenth birthday, when she saw an announcement for "Silent Rave Strikes Back," scheduled for August 17, she knew she *had* to be there.

At first blush, a silent rave seems to embody our worse fears about technology's effect on young people. But the event was neither silent nor isolating. One girl walked around with an icebreaking sign that read "What's on your iPod?"—the 2008 incarnation of "What's your sign?" Several people carried posters offering "free hugs." When Shaughnnessy's friend's batteries died, other dancers shared their earbuds with her. An unsteady conga line jerked its way through the crowd. Even as they bobbed and shuffled, dancers whipped out their cell phone/cameras, documenting the moment. At one point Shaughnnessy, dressed in a black spangled flapper dress, burst into a "pit"—a circle of dancers—and started "skanking" to a Reel Big Fish song. "They're a ska band," she said, elaborating for her considerably older interviewer. "Skanking is basically flailing around." Later she would see images of herself on YouTube, looking a lot like a commercial for iPod.

True, no music could be heard in Union Square that night, but friendly conversation and laughter punctuated the night air.

And while the term "rave" generally connotes a wild affair with everyone drunk or high on Ecstasy, this wasn't the case. "One guy I know smoked up before, but for most of us, the event itself was a natural high," says Shaughnnessy. "And it was very social. I danced, but I also talked to a lot of people when we listened to each other's playlists or just when we were sitting on the sidelines, resting. The people who organized it set the tone. They asked you to respect the park and clean up afterwards, and people did." The crowd was as diverse as Jonnie Wesson had hoped—a cross section of every conceivable identity. It may have been this generation's Woodstock, but no one had a bad acid trip. No one got arrested. And the only punches thrown were aimed at keeping several huge multicolored beach balls aloft.

The New Heroes

If there's any one group whose lives and habits might give us a hint about the future of consequential strangers, it's the Millennial generation—kids like Yuna Shaughnnessy. Compared to the young adults who preceded them, rebellious Baby Boomers and disaffected Gen Xers, Millennials will disprove the assumption that each new generation is "more alienated and risk prone than the one before," according to historians Neil Howe and the late William Strauss, who have written extensively on cyclical patterns of generational change.[5] They maintain that Millennials, whom they place as being born between approximately 1982 and 2005 (other sources define them slightly differently), will be less motivated by self and more oriented toward teamwork, less inclined toward high-risk behaviors, and more disposed to do good.[6] Ultimately they will become our next "heroes," a role vacated by their GI-generation grandparents.

A lofty forecast perhaps, but research on Millennial voting habits and political consciousness supports their prediction. Among other factors, the historians point out, a generation is shaped by the public events they witnessed in adolescence.[7] The oldest Millennials were barely out of high school when the Twin Towers went down in flames. Sociologist Robert Putnam attributes a possible "rebirth of American civic life" to these young people for the same reason: "Just as Pearl Harbor had spawned the civic-minded 'Greatest Generation,' so too September 11 might turn out to produce a more civically engaged generation of young people."[8]

In terms of their social lives, Millennials, now between the ages of four and twenty-six (using Howe and Strauss's designation), are already displaying an unparalleled sense of *inter*dependence. Many have been in day care and participated in play groups from the time they were born. Those who have since reached their teens and early twenties have strong bonds with their buddies, and at the same time have remained close to their parents—emotionally if no longer geographically.

Millennials are über-connected—some fear, *over*connected.[9] They don't remember life without computers: To them, the cyberworld is merely an extension of their real-life social space. Once they're old enough to read, they email and IM; then it's on to texting, Twittering, and checking out each other's home pages to see what's up. As Howe and Strauss describe them, "Millennials expect nonstop interaction with their peers."

Their offline lives are just as social. They travel in packs and date in groups. They're aware of the power of their own convoys. "These young men and women want to have their dating lives simulate the way they meet people in real life," a *Wall Street Journal* reporter recently observed, "through concentric circles of friends."[10]

Many network scholars suspect that "cybernetworks" represent an important aspect of our relational future, giving us access to information and the ability to coalesce around common interests and causes.[11] The Internet Generation, as Millennials are sometimes called, is already there.[12] In fact, some of the oldest members are propelling that future. Mark Zuckerberg was a college sophomore in 2003 when he launched his first social networking site, a precursor to Facebook.[13] Daniel Osit, twenty-six, and Adam Sachs, twenty-five, founded Igniter.com, which enables gaggles of twentysomethings to meet and plan group dates.[14] Twenty-three-year-old Jordan Goldman recently snared funding for Unigo.com, a student-generated guide to colleges. In the planning stages, his focus groups consisted of high school students; now that the site is up and running, most of his twenty-five employees are younger than he is.[15]

Millennials see the world and their relationships through a broader lens than their elders. A silent rave naturally appeals to them because it extends their social reach. They sense that when they join forces they can rev the motor of social change. Just as important, they were born *after* the various liberation movements and in an era that has seen a dramatic increase in ethnic and racial diversity—a trend that is projected to increase even more in the decades to come.[16] They've grown up (or are now growing up) watching TV shows that routinely feature multihued and differently abled casts of characters.[17] Many of their own families are untraditional.[18] Some live with a single parent or parents of the same sex or have mothers and fathers of different nationalities or races. Others are children of immigrants and must navigate two cultures—an experience aptly described by a Cuban-American as "life in the hyphen."[19] Arguably, many Millennials backed Barack Obama in the 2008 presidential election because, unlike former candidates (in either party), his background and rhetoric epitomized a blurring of racial lines. Obama also provided them with social networking tools and trusted that their online loyalty (and dollars) would translate into offline activism. He gave them, in the words of a veteran campaign organizer, "seats at the table and allowed them to become players."[20]

The Millennials, admittedly new to that table, are less socially conservative than generations before them—a 2007 poll conducted by the Pew Research Center for the People and the Press found that young people born after 1976 agreed with an average of only 2.4%

of conservative values.[21] That said, you'll still find some staunch political conservatives among them, like the young Republican in Yuma Shaughnnessy's high school who is "convinced he's going to be president one day." There are bigots, too, as well as cliques of kids who hang together and exclude others as a way of insulating themselves from prejudice. Moreover, children in rural areas or impoverished neighborhoods often don't have the same real-life access as their more privileged peers. But as a whole and certainly through the Internet, Millennials have unprecedented opportunities to connect around cultural interests and life choices, in addition to, or instead of, the usual social divisions, such as race or religion or ethnicity.

Yuma Shaughnnessy, who describes herself as "100% Korean," is the adopted daughter of an Irish father, a computer programmer, and a Korean mother who has worked as a pharmacist throughout Yuma's childhood. Her school, like Staten Island itself, is mostly white, but from the looks of her Facebook page, Shaughnnessy's convoy is quite diverse. "I base my relationships on personality," she explains, "not race." Attending a summer program at Brown University in Rhode Island, where she took a class in "writing the academic essay"and spent a week in fencing camp, she added new acquaintances from all over the world. And if the experts are right, her "multicultural competence" is just what she'll need to thrive in the future.[22]

Social skills have always been important—in school, at work, or in any situation that requires communication and cooperation. Beyond that, the need for "social versatility" is greater today than at any time in history, according to a team of social scientists who looked at family and work trends in order to determine what adolescents would need to be prepared for the social challenges of the twenty-first century. Forging and maintaining adult relationships, the scholars concluded, will require a "secure and flexible internal self that allows one to shift between worlds."[23] To some extent, of course, these abilities are acquired at home through a sociable and empathic parent or grandparent who models connection. But children, like adults, derive different benefits from their interactions with consequential strangers—babysitters, teachers, advisors, coaches, clergy, as well as other kids. When teenagers are exposed to, and open to, diverse groups—especially in situations that put them all on equal footing—they learn how to talk to peers who skirt the periphery of their cliques or who happen to travel in similar cybercircles but are otherwise worlds apart. They gain the social currency that comes from being a bridge between groups. And they develop the confidence to handle the sticky situations that might arise when dissimilar worlds collide.

The truth is, all of us need these skills. Even as we have sorted ourselves into geographic enclaves that allow marketing masters to pitch directly to us and political pollsters to predict how we'll vote, even as we do what humans have always done—gravitate toward people who are like us—we still live in a world of social complexity.

The More Things Change, the More They Change

Michael Ventura, an Italian-American in his early sixties, a former "kid from Brooklyn" who sports a long gray ponytail, is an unlikely resident of Lubbock, Texas. His look would seem more at home in a city like Austin or Seattle, locales favored by the so-called "creative class."[24] His journey to Lubbock started quite serendipitously, back in the early seventies. He was twenty-seven. "I was doing a poor kid's version of Route 66, out to explore America." Sitting at Christmas dinner at the home of a boyhood buddy who had since moved to Santa Cruz, California, Ventura mentioned in passing that he was planning to hitchhike to a wedding in Nashville after the holidays. "Come with Irene and me," said Crash, one of the consequential strangers at the table, a new friend of Ventura's old friend. "Lubbock is halfway there."[25]

The three reached Lubbock in time for one of the worst snowstorms in history. By the time the streets were cleared, Ventura had decided to take his time passing through.[26] That he could play poker quickly put him on common ground with the locals, but everyone knew he was "not from around here." He didn't have long hair in those days—a conscious decision given his love of hitchhiking. Still, because of his olive-toned skin, even his new acquaintances didn't think of him as "white."

"I had occasional problems in town," he says, recalling the barber who "accidentally" sliced his neck. "People didn't know what a Sicilian looked like. Some called me a 'spic' to my face." The Lubbock of 1973 was full of white folks, most of them the descendants of Celtic, Irish, and Scotch pioneers who traveled to Texas by covered wagon. They didn't mix with Hispanics or African-Americans. Irene was the only Jew Ventura knew in Lubbock, and she left before he did. Indeed, the locals bragged of having "more Christian churches per capita than any city in the world."

So what kept Ventura in Lubbock for the better part of that year? Certainly not the cuisine, which was Texas diner food. Rather, it was the tight-knit group of fascinating homegrown musicians and artists Crash and Irene lived with and whose sensibilities were surprisingly close to Ventura's. "These were some of the most interesting, intelligent, and creative people I'd ever met. The conversation was brilliant. And they were also culturally quite different." His new acquaintances took him to the Cotton Club, where Elvis used to appear. "The band was playing a mix of rhythm and blues, rock and roll. There were people my age on the dance floor, but also little kids and people who could have been my parents. There was a continuity of generations I hadn't seen back home."

Ventura would later move to Austin, where he launched his career as a writer. Since then, whenever he's had extra money in his pocket, he's hopped in his car to "explore America," and by now has "looked around in every state but Michigan." He was living in Los Angeles when he decided to move back to Lubbock five years ago. By then it was a far different city. Its population had doubled to 200,000. It was still a Christian town—the following year it would be ranked the second most conservative U.S. city after Provo, Utah.[27] But it had become cosmopolitan as well, featuring a medley of ethnic markets and grocery stores, a mosque, a synagogue with a visiting female rabbi, and a university and medical center that drew people from all over the world.

Ventura maintains that Lubbock, Texas, 1973, would never have agreed to become Lubbock, Texas, 2008. Sitting in a Mexican café, he watched "a classic, well-dressed, West Texas Anglo-Saxon old lady, her blue-white hair in a firm bubble 'do," playing with her biracial granddaughter. No one else in the restaurant took notice. "When that woman was born," Ventura observed, "every school, restaurant, bathroom, and bus in this state was segregated, and most Anglo-Saxon Texans meant to keep it that way.

"Thirty-five years ago, Lubbock *was* Texas," says Ventura. "Now a strong accent is as unusual as a cowboy hat." When Ventura first began his American odyssey, accents, attire, and behavior spoke volumes about a locale. Ethnic diversity was reserved for big cities. "All that's changed," he says, "and the traditional images of a Southerner, a New Yorker, a Texan are fading further and further from the daily reality. This is especially true of the middle class and affluent."

It has happened in Lubbock, and it's happening everywhere, the result, in Ventura's view, of an "uncontrollable tidal shift in economics, culture, technology, and perception." It is no longer a white world, a man's world, a monocultural world, or a straight world for that matter. And there's no going back. In worst-case scenarios, these changes will drive us into walled communities, literally and metaphorically. Some observers think that's already happened.[28] But it's also possible, and perhaps long overdue, that we will come to embrace diversity and create new kinds of alliances that capitalize on the strength of our weak ties. (Arguably, those who supported Barack Obama would like to see us go in that direction.)

Billy's Buddies: Hidden Solidarities

When his son Billy was born, Jim Hourihan remembers the nurse whisking the baby out of the delivery room. "He was gray and not breathing right. Christine knew something was wrong, but no one said anything. By accident, I saw 'Down Syndrome' on a paper I had to sign, and I ran out after the doctor."[29] Although in the years to come, the family would come to view Billy as a gift, a child who would inspire an unexpected sense of grace and acceptance of others, Hourihan admits, "It was like a funeral for the first few days." The "turning point," he recalls, occurred a few months later when he, Christine, and several members of their extended clan attended a "buddy walk" in Plainfield, New Jersey. They had learned about the event through the National Down Syndrome Society, which cosponsors hundreds of annual buddy walks to raise money and awareness. "It was a comfort for us to talk to parents who've been there, and to see older kids having fun, playing baseball," Hourihan recalls. "But there was no group in Bergen County, where we live. So my mother said, 'Let's start one.'"

In an era of networked individualism, our personal convoys exist in our minds, unconstrained by time, place, or institutional allegiances. However, we are also part of larger groups and collectives that represent particular niches—this slice of our life, that interest, an aspect of our identity. Most of us, therefore, are members of *multiple* communities. The more we "join"—a word we must use loosely—the more we bring new consequential strangers into our lives. And when a challenge arises, we can also *create* a community, as Jim and Christine Hourihan did.

At their first planning meeting, Christine, her mother-in-law, and three sisters-in-law sat in Starbucks and set what they thought was a realistic goal for their first year: twenty walkers and $20,000. Instead, four hundred people showed up, and the take was $60,000. "It was like a domino effect," Jim says. "I had sent out emails to office mates, clients, players on my softball team. Of my fifteen teammates, eight showed up." Christine, a chiropractor on extended maternity leave, tapped into her network of mothers. Jim's sister, a journalist, knew the director of the local YMCA. Through that connection, the Y, which already had a program for children with special needs, agreed to cosponsor the event. Other Hourihan friends and acquaintances continued to spread the word until it traveled to the far reaches of their respective convoys and beyond. As a result, the walk has grown considerably every year, raising over $200,000 to date, enough to seed Billy's Buddies, a new outreach program at the Y. Hourihan, a partner in a consulting firm, has always had many consequential strangers in his life; thanks to Billy's Walk, he has even more. "There are people I barely know who are now tied to the event," he admits, "people I meet maybe twice a year."

Their buddy-walk community has given the Hourihans support, hope, and a glimpse into Billy's future. And they get to return the favor, lighting the way for others just starting out on the journey. "People you've known for a long time say, 'I understand,' but they don't really," says Jeanne Kelly, sixty-three, Jim Hourihan's mother, who works for a local school board. At a recent walk, a mother of twins showed up with her large extended family. One of the twins, a boy who has Down's, was in the hospital recovering from open-heart surgery. But she showed up anyway. "The mother was in tears after the walk," Kelly recalls. "She told me, 'We needed to be here, to see this. You have no idea what this did for our whole family.' She promised me she'd be back next year as a volunteer. If we had done the buddy walk with just that one person, it would have been worth it."

The Hourihans' efforts represent what British sociologist Ray Pahl calls "hidden solidarities"—new forms of compassion and commonality that "stretch across the world."[30] These are the connections we collect when we look beyond our intimates. Reflecting on the outpouring of support in response to recent international disasters such as the tsunami that erupted in the Indian Ocean in

2004, Pahl notes that both the number of charities and volunteerism are on the rise. Swims, runs—events like the Bergen County buddy walk—are "everywhere" in Great Britain. "That we are able to treat people anywhere in the world as our neighbors-in-need," Pahl suggests, "is surely grounds for hope."

A similar trend is unfolding in the United States. The Millennials are responsible for the greatest increase in civic engagement.[31] And their elders seem to be trending upward, too. As this book is being written in 2008, the first of the boomers are turning sixty-five. Coddled children of the fifties and hell-raisers of the sixties who famously didn't trust anyone under thirty, they are inching up the generational ladder. But they are not likely to go gently into that good night, Howe and Strauss note. Rather, they're "determined to transform elderhood in some meaningful way."[32] Some have joined the Peace Corps.[33] Others are still at their old jobs, not even thinking about retirement, or they're launching "encore careers." Nearly 60% of those who leave full-time careers will move into "bridge jobs," which ease the transition from work to retirement.[34] Baby boomers are also likely to engage in volunteer work.[35] Both trends are likely to link this rising senior generation to new reservoirs of consequential strangers.

The societal drift today favors interdependence. We are able to connect in forms—and at speeds—that our forebears could never have imagined. Researchers in many scientific disciplines affirm that we are "social animals," not merely directed by our individual minds, but also by our relationships.[36] That is not to say that we have vanquished selfishness, greed, prejudice, or loneliness. And no one is suggesting that we bring back love beads or blindly assure ourselves that we are in the "age of Aquarius," a time, as the old song from *Hair* promised, when "harmony and understanding, sympathy and trust abound."[37] Then again, is it a random coincidence that the recently revived forty-year-old musical has been drawing sellout crowds of nostalgic Baby Boomers with their adult children and grandchildren in tow?

Ray Pahl, an Englishman, wonders aloud whether government

might have a stake in maintaining a society in which people feel insecure and wary of various "bogeymen," a mind-set that makes us less willing to be sociable and helps maintain the status quo. It's not so farfetched an idea. The alternative—people banding together in service of a mutual need or goal—isn't as predictable and "can take unexpected direction." Smart mobs, for example. Pahl blames media, too, for both encouraging us to "view the world in a fearful and pessimistic way" and for obscuring these hidden solidarities by focusing almost exclusively on "human-interest stories that show us always acting as individuals."

Well, not all media. A central goal of this book is to bring those solidarities *out* of hiding.

Shelter from the Storm

The future begs the question, Can we survive without each other? The short answer is no. It *does* take a village—even if the villagers are miles apart and quite diverse. The longer answer is more complicated, as Blau discovered when she became part of an ad hoc hurricane relief group in November 2005. She and the two women she'd traveled with from Massachusetts stood in the parking lot of the New Zion Baptist Church in Eunice, Louisiana. Clipboard in hand and surrounded by a group of Katrina survivors, Blau, ever the in-charge New Yorker, asked each of them, "What else do you need? Clothes? Cleaning supplies? Diapers?"

Mary Washington,* an outgoing heavyset woman in flip-flops and capri pants, had already gone through the cartons of donations. "Curtains," she offered as Blau's eyes met hers. "I need curtains. You got any?"[38]

Blau looked at her. "Curtains? You're kidding, right? Not sneakers or a mattress or something for your kids?"

"Nah, just curtains."

Blau and her companions were puzzled. Having talked with Washington as church volunteers were unloading the truck, they knew her story. She had been working in a New Orleans nursing home when the owners of the facility herded her and several other aides onto a bus filled with residents. They were given no food, no medical supplies, no destination. The bus finally ran out of gas in Eunice. By then, one of the residents had died in Washington's arms. So how could someone so traumatized, and so angry at the system, a woman—a mother—who had lost *everything*, now joke about needing curtains? But every time Washington saw the volunteers, she'd ask, "Did you get my curtains?"

They never did. So many needed so much, and curtains just didn't feel like a priority *to them*. But days later, the relief team had occasion to visit the run-down housing development where Washington and other evacuees were temporarily living. The one-story houses were crowded together; many windows were broken. Finally the three could grasp why Washington considered curtains a basic need. If people couldn't see in, maybe they wouldn't break in.

The three volunteers were changed by their experiences in Louisiana. When they left, their organization continued to send money, supplies, and Christmas gifts. Blau stayed in touch by phone with Washington's very shy younger sister, Violet Simmons,* a mother of eight. But most of Simmons's problems in the year after Katrina couldn't be solved by donations. The kids were doing poorly in school; her blood pressure was high; and everyone wanted out of Eunice—it just wasn't "home." Blau listened, asked questions, made calls on Simmons's behalf, and occasionally offered what seemed to Blau like trivial advice ("Take a walk. It might clear your head"). Between Simmons's reticence and their different dialects—fast-talking New York meets Deep South drawl—it was impossible to know whether those phone calls meant anything to Simmons, no less made a difference in her life. Three years later, Blau finally mustered the nerve to ask.

"It was the best thing that happened to us," thirty-nine-year-old Simmons answered without hesitation. "You are the first person I know from out of state. It is nice to have a friend from out of town all these years, to know someone else other than family. I get a lot out of it, because I have someone to talk to."[39]

If the very differences that make consequential strangers so valuable to us can also be a barrier to relationships, the solution, it would seem, is to invite a variety of people into our lives. If we can't get past our differences, we might at least come to feel more comfortable with them and understand what our own limited experiences can't possibly teach us. Our survival might depend on trying.

"People in relationships can reach goals that would have been far beyond the grasp of individuals," Robert Putnam wrote in *Better Together*, his sequel to *Bowling Alone*. With the exception of the Millennials' growing civic-mindedness, though, Putnam stands by what he wrote in 2003: "We do not yet see evidence of a general resurgence of social connection or involvement in the public life of a community." But he also acknowledges that "hidden within that broad statistical truth of the erosion of social ties is a tremendous variety of particular experiences."[40]

Peering through the lens of consequential strangers, we found a range of those very experiences—individuals and groups connecting online, meeting in person, dancing, comparing notes on their dogs, trading strategies for saving the planet. Neighbors in Netville rising up against a developer who broke his promises. Nepalese women stemming the tide of smallpox in their village. Red Hatters skydiving into a new phase of life. Such alliances reflect an expansive notion of "community"—people dedicated to problems or to making life a little easier, more interesting, or fun. They exemplify the hidden solidarities that, Ray Pahl claims, social commentators "rarely consider," yet they are "the actual set of enduring relationships within which people live out their lives."[41]

We found newspaper articles that told similar stories: a musician on Long Island offering free Latin drumming lessons on Saturday mornings to all comers. In April, six people showed up; by August the crowd reached well over a thousand.[42] A blind ninety-four-year-old woman, healthy but homebound, hosting a steady stream of young people who stop in daily to read to her. "Reading to the blind and elderly is hardly novel," the reporter who happened on this story acknowledged. "But the casual, organic way in which this particular group came together around Ms. Goodyear is a window into the way New York can be a small town, the way strangers become a community."[43]

Indeed, the line between stranger and consequential stranger has blurred. Consider the article "Dear Stranger: It's 4 a.m. Help!," the last of Michelle Slatalla's ten-year-old "Online Shopper" columns in the Circuits section of the *New York Times.* She muses that when she first started writing about the Internet in 1998, buying online was rare. Now, she doesn't know anyone who *doesn't* make online purchases or turn to the Internet for advice: "In other words, we've reached an age in which it doesn't seem at all weird to get help from strangers."[44]

Online helpers are consequential strangers, too. But regardless of how you *label* these assorted others, what matters is that you pay attention to the broad swath of humanity outside your inner circles. *Each of the people you connect with gives you something different.*

When we view our lives through this wider lens, we see how far our connections extend. We watch the cast of players who walk on and off our center stage, which gives us both a sense of belonging and a sense of promise. We can get things done because we're not alone. We can help and heal others and be taken care of as well. We can discover ideas and experiences that are "beyond our familiar." Because of their consequential strangers, Karla Lightfoot has been able to cobble together an unconventional career, and Doug Davis, a quadruple amputee, doesn't see himself as disabled. Drawing from the edges of their corporate convoy allowed Procter & Gamble to find Swiffer hiding in the cracks between divisions. Understanding their interdependencies and connections helped a ragtag group of government types and tribal leaders to better understand the challenges they faced in regulating water use in Ghana.

Ideally, these pages will inspire you to take notice, too—to appreciate *all* the people in your convoy and to broaden your definition of what an "important" relationship is. Our hope is that by giving this diverse group of social relations a name—"consequential strangers"—it will make you more cognizant of their power. If Theo Stites is any indication, it works. The tech-savvy twenty-something you met in Chapter 1—our "Beatrice" who guided us through the ethers of the Internet which, to her at least, was Paradise. That was back in 2006—ancient history in web time. Stites sent this message to Blau via Facebook two years later:

> I've been having some crazy consequential stranger experiences recently (this book will make people suddenly realize how many they have!). What I've found is that the more personal the relationship, the more the consequential strangers give, which makes sense from a human understanding perspective, but not economically. In the last two days, I've received two free cab rides, free coffee three times, a bagel, gum and a magazine, and soup from a deli—all from people I check in with on an almost daily basis. On all occasions I tried to refuse. On all occasions they brought it up independently and offered to give. And this was not just men; half the people were women. It's amazing what human connection can mean on the other side for people who end up being many people's consequential strangers, I guess. In all cases, the giving happened after the consequential stranger told me something personal about their life, and it was like they wanted to give in exchange for that experience/opportunity.
>
> Sorry to go off on a tangent. Sometimes humanity . . . is really nice.

EPILOGUE

The Postscript Is Personal

> The really important kind of freedom involves attention, and awareness, and discipline, and effort, and being able truly to care about other people and to sacrifice for them, over and over, in myriad petty little unsexy ways, every day.
>
> —*David Foster Wallace, commencement speech, Kenyon College, 2005*

I

On Tuesday, September 30, 2008, the first day of the year 5769 on the Jewish calendar, I walk down the embankment behind my house to the river. Bogey, my six-pound canine companion, is happily at my side. I get to the bottom of the hill and notice a bigger-than-usual crowd coming toward me on the dirt path, mostly families with kids. This is a place Bogey and I visit almost daily. I normally see maybe five other walkers, ten or twelve on the weekend. Now I count at least thirty. My only thought at first is this: *I hope Bogey doesn't get stepped on.*

Suddenly a hand is on my shoulder. I turn, and it's Dorothy, also a former New Yorker whom I adore. We haven't seen each other for longer than either of us can remember. "Come with us," she says, pulling me into the steadily growing stream of walkers. "I'll give you some of my bread," she adds, holding up a plastic bag. I finally get it. On Rosh Hashana, Jews symbolically purge themselves of their sins by throwing pieces of bread into a body of water—a ritual known as *tashlich*.

"How perfect," I say. "I just finished my book."

"Good for you!" I knew she really meant it.

As we walk, the two of us catch up on each other's lives. When we reach the small beach area, there are what feels like a hundred or more people milling about. I spot Robin, another New York expat, and Rob. I usually see them once a year at Leah's holiday party. They know Dorothy, too—also through Leah. *Everyone* knows Leah, but that's another story. Rob is really smart and loves to discuss ideas, and Robin is a writer and editor, so I know both will get it when I say (because I can't help myself), "I just finished the book."

Dorothy, Robin, and Rob are people I encounter only occasionally. But whenever I've seen them over the last several years, they've always asked, "How's the book going?" Their questions and comments work themselves into my thoughts, and my ideas become more concrete in the telling of them. Sometimes I'm self-conscious about holding forth, fearing that my chatter about the nuances of consequential strangers is monopolizing the conversation, so I ask, "Are you sure you want to hear this much detail?" A "yes," whether out of politeness or genuine interest, keeps me going.

Finishing a book is better than any drug; it's the best altered state I've ever experienced. But now I feel like I've also wandered into a movie—Fellini meets *Fiddler on the Roof.* The gathering itself symbolizes what I've been writing about for the past year: people drawn together by their commonalities. Most are strangers, but I know something *about* them: They are here to participate in a centuries-old custom. I'm more a cultural than a religious Jew, but I like the idea of ritual in general and this one in particular. It makes sense to start a new year by letting go of your sins. A bearded guy in sandals hands me a white sheet of paper with the Cliff Notes to *tashlich.* It tells me that the only "supplies" I will need are "a bag of bread (a few slices will do) and a humble, willing heart."

So here I am, with a ten-minute-old book about consequential strangers on my desk (actually, in my computer), surrounded by people who don't seem to matter, but today of all days really do. Yesterday I had to cancel Rosh Hashana plans with my dearest ones. I was inches from finishing the book and too exhausted to make the three-hour drive. Feeling a little sorry for myself, I set out to polish the final chapter. Staying in Massachusetts had been the right decision, but when I typed the last sentence, no one was around to congratulate me. Then I walked into this surreal scene.

Dorothy reaches into her baggie and hands me a slightly stale piece of beige bread.

"Whole wheat?" I ask, and then, exaggerating my "New Yawk" inflection in the presence of a *landsman,* add "What, no challah?" (Robin and Rob have pretzels, because Rob's been on the Atkins diet.)

As I throw pieces of bread into the river, I silently express my thanks. For a new year, for all my blessings, for the ritual itself, for my consequential strangers and the book they inspired. I'll think about my sins later. I don't know what or who controls the universe, just that it's not me. And I certainly couldn't have conceived of an ending better than this.

—Melinda Blau

II

Hillary Clinton made famous the idea, adopted from an old African proverb, that "it takes a village" to raise children. Actually, it takes a collective of consequential strangers. When my son was a baby, it was the connections between parents in the parking lot of his day care center that first sparked my interest in peripheral ties. And as this book nears publication, I realize that many of those same consequential strangers and countless more I've met through the years and who are part of my children's universe—mothers, fathers, teachers, coaches, janitors, clergy—have shepherded me through a rich and sometimes confusing world that my prior childless self never could have imagined. People I barely know have provided models for parenting, led my children into confidence, and connected me to a larger world.

My daughter—our second child—was born the year I published my first scholarly work on peripheral ties. We had just moved to Indiana and felt very isolated. But days after her birth, my neighbors arrived with tuna casseroles and pasta salads. My realtor, one of our first consequential strangers in West Lafayette, introduced us to her daughter, who became our nanny. On the playground, we garnered connections to children whose parents have lived on four different continents (and taught us to sing "Happy Birthday" in six different languages). In my department, I met a graduate student who loves to babysit and knows a rhyme that ends "cut the pickle, tickle, tickle." And as my daughter has grown older, we enrolled her in ballet classes with a teacher who somehow manages to convince dozens of fathers to dance in the recital every April.

In the cold harsh winters of the Midwest, I am thankful for women like Ethan's mother. She is an important medical researcher, ranked among the top fifty American scholars in her field—many of them Nobel laureates, few of them raising young children. I don't know her well, but I greatly admire her ability to juggle work and family. Her son is enrolled in half a dozen extracurricular activities, which she manages by combining forces with a cadre of car-pooling parents. In February, when the demands of our respective jobs are greatest and the weather bleakest, public schools let out early for several half-day vacations. To handle them, Ethan's mom organizes a "child swap"—the children at her house one afternoon, my house the next.

And it's not just my children's activities that have broadened my convoy—sometimes it's a need. In preschool, for example, my son was terrified of the water. My sister's pediatrician—one of *her* consequential strangers—advised her that teaching a child to swim is as important as vaccination: nearly three quarters of the Earth is covered in water. But getting my little boy, who hated being wet, into the water was more challenging than any shot. I turned to the parent grapevine for help. I can't even remember which one eventually told me about Jackie, the child whisperer of swim instructors. I marveled at her ability to coax my hesitant son into the water. Thanks to the freestyle kick Jackie helped him develop, my son eventually landed a spot in a prime lane on a competitive swim team. I, in turn, now sit in the bleachers, grateful for his success and even more for my own connections to the parents of other little swimmers. With one eye on the kids, we chat about where to buy team swimsuits, the math curriculum in first grade, and the schedule for roadwork downtown. Certainly, consequential strangers enrich my research and help me manage my daily comings and goings in academia. But in my mothering work, they provide a tether that at once keeps me grounded in what's important and allows me to explore the unknown.

—Karen Fingerman

APPENDIX I

Twenty Questions

We live niched lives, and in each arena are people who sustain us in varying degrees. The person who helps you weather emotional storms may not be the same one who does favors or gives you career guidance or a good laugh. If you analyze your social convoy, as described in Chapter 2, you might inadvertently omit individuals who serve important functions in your life but aren't part of your inner circles. One way to grasp the bigger social picture is to ask yourself the kinds of questions researchers pose about "rewarding interactions," suggests sociologist Claude Fischer, one of the pioneers in this approach.[1] What kinds of exchanges occur between you and the various people in your life? Some happen during everyday moments, often on a regular basis, others only when a particular need arises.

The following are general questions, adapted and updated versions of those conceived by Fischer and his colleagues. They are meant to jog your awareness, but they won't get at people who have a negative impact on your life. They also may not capture your weakest ties nor people who serve a particular function that's unique to your situation. Still, they will give you a fairly extensive portrait of the people who support you and make life more enjoyable, those closest to you as well as your consequential strangers.

There are no right or wrong answers here. Feel free to list more than one name after each question:

1. Who would take care of your house if you went out of town?

2. With whom do you engage in social activities—movies, dinner, group travel?

3. With whom do you discuss personal worries?

4. From whom do you get advice before making important life decisions?

5. If you needed a large sum of money, from whom could you borrow it?

6. Who would you call if you were out for the day and thought you left the stove on?

7. With whom do you participate in leisure activities, such as sports, hobbies, or games?

8. With whom do you connect via the Internet—email, web communities, blogs, video chats?

9. From whom did you last get a product recommendation?

10. Who provides you with services—cleaning, gardening, repair, maintenance?

11. Who are your teachers or has someone recently taught you a new skill?

12. Who takes care of your physical problems?

13. Who provides grooming services such as haircuts and manicures?

14. Whom would you call if you need information about a health issue?

15. If you're caring for an older relative, is there someone else who helps?

16. Who helps you remember, and nurture, your spiritual self?

17. Who has similar interests in a political activity or a cause?

18. Who mentors you—or whom do you mentor?

19. If your car was in the shop, whom would you ask for a ride?

20. If you're a parent (or a pet owner), who is also involved in your child's (or pet's) care?

APPENDIX II

The Occupation Test

Put a checkmark next to each profession in which you have a relative, friend, or consequential stranger—anyone you know well enough to talk to, even if you are not close to him or her. Then turn the page to see how your answers compare to national samples.

Profession	**Relative**	**Friend**	**Consequential Stranger**
administrative assistant			
babysitter			
bellboy			
bookkeeper			
CEO			
computer programmer			
congressperson			
factory operator			
farmer			
janitor			
hairdresser			
lawyer			
middle school teacher			
nurse			
personnel manager			
police officer			
production manager			
professor			
receptionist			
security guard			
taxi driver			
writer			

Social scientists have devised various ways to assess the extent and variety of people's social convoys. Asking you to list the names of people in your life—a "name generator"—is one approach (see pages 36–38). A "position generator," such as this occupation test, asks you to name your contacts in various *fields*. Theoretically, the more people you know up and down the socioeconomic ladder, the greater your ability to access information and resources.

The list of twenty-two occupations shown here was used in a survey of 3,000 employed or previously employed adults, aged twenty-one to sixty-four, conducted by sociologist Nan Lin, who devised the method.[2] The best-known occupation was nurse—nearly 70% of the respondents knew at least one. Forty-five percent or more respondents listed a hairdresser, lawyer, police officer, computer programmer, or middle school teacher. The least-known occupation was hotel bellboy (2.7%); fewer than 20% knew a taxi driver, CEO, production manager, or a congressperson.

Where do *you* stand? In this particular study, people knew, on average, someone in six or seven occupations. Sixty-three respondents, or slightly more than 2% of those surveyed, knew none. No one knew people in all twenty-two jobs—19 was the upper limit. But around a third knew people in eight or more occupations.

Bonnie Erickson (see pages 76–78) adapted Lin's method by adding another step: asking participants to sort their contacts into columns indicating *how* they knew each person. In this way, she found that weaker ties—consequential strangers—"give substantially greater access" to a variety of occupations, and therefore to people in different economic classes. For example, in her study of the security industry (using a list of nineteen different occupations), people had relatives in "only about two" occupations, friends in two to three times as many job categories as relatives, and weak ties in twice as many occupations as friends.[3] You'll probably find that your list is heavy on consequential strangers, too.

NOTES

1 The Ascendance of Consequential Strangers

1. Joel Stein, "Meet the Other 100," *Time*, May 8, 2006, 176. http://www.time.com/time/magazine/article/0,9171,1189176,00.html.
2. Joel Stein, "The Other 100," http://www.time.com/time/magazine/article/0,9171,1190759,00.html.
3. Letters to the Editor, *Time,* May 29, 2006. http://www.time.com/time/magazine/article/0,9171,1197931,00.html.
4. Joel Stein, interview with Blau, June 17, 2006.
5. Karen L. Fingerman, "Consequential Strangers and Peripheral Partners: The Importance of Unimportant Relationships," *Journal of Family Theory and Review* 1 (June 2009); Fingerman, "Weak Ties," in *Encyclopedia of Human Relationships,* edited by H. T. Reis and S. K. Sprecher (Thousand Oaks, Calif.: Sage, in press); and Fingerman, "The Consequential Stranger: Peripheral Relationships Across the Life Span," in *Growing Together: Personal Relationships Across the Life Span,* edited by F. R. Lang and K. L. Fingerman (New York: Cambridge University Press, 2003). The term "familiar stranger," coined by psychologist Stanley Milgram in 1972, refers to someone we regularly observe but with whom we do not interact—like a traffic cop. If you personally connect with a familiar stranger, he or she becomes a consequential stranger.
6. Karen L. Fingerman and P. C. Griffiths, "Season's Greeting: Adults' Social Contacts at the Holiday Season," *Psychology and Aging* 14 (1999): 192–205. In an article by Kate Murphy, "In Case of Disaster, Have a Backup Plan for Your PC," *New York Times*, May 14, 2006, Janet England, a marketing executive in New Orleans, who lost valuable and possibly irreplaceable digitized daguerreotype photographs, added to her lament, "I know it sounds silly, but I also lost my Christmas card list, which really upsets me."

7. Karen L. Fingerman and Elizabeth L. Hay, "Searching Under the Streetlight? Age Biases in the Personal and Family Relationships Literature," *Personal Relationships* 9 (2002): 415–33. Of studies on intimate ties, 44% focused on spouse relationships, 25% on unmarried romantic ties, 26% on families with young children, 17% on parents, and 13% friend or best friend relationships. The 10% figure represents all the other types of nonintimate relationships *combined.* (The percentages don't add up to 100 because some studies covered more than one topic.) This bias has been noted by a handful of other researchers: Calvin Morrill and David A. Snow, "The Study of Personal Relationships in Public Places," in *Together Alone: Personal Relationships in Public Places*, edited by Calvin Morrill, David A. Snow, and Cindy H. White (Berkeley: University of California Press, 2005); Lyn H. Lofland, "Social Interaction: Continuities and Complexities in the Study of Nonintimate Sociality," in *Sociological Perspectives on Social Psychology*, edited by. K. S. Cook, G. A. Fine, and J. S. House (Boston: Allyn & Bacon, 1995); Robert Milardo, "Theoretical and Methodological Issues in the Identification of the Social Networks of Spouses," *Journal of Marriage and the Family* 51 (1989): 165–74. In his 1989 paper, Milardo observed: "Social scientists have long held that close and intimate friendships are the *sine qua non* of personal relationships, and no doubt they are important, but ties with acquaintances are equally important."

   Most of us intuitively know that peripheral relationships matter, and yet Ph.D. researchers who study social ties resist this idea. In a subsequent study, Fingerman asked her peers what type of relationships were important and compared their responses with people who hold advanced degrees in other fields (law, medicine, the humanities) and people who had no more than a college degree (some had no more than a high school degree). Less educated individuals rated peripheral relationships (church members, neighbors) as more important than did the researchers who study social ties. Even highly educated participants in other fields thought that consequential strangers were important. Fingerman suspects that this disparity, at least in part, is because social scientists spend entire careers focusing on intimate relationships to the exclusion of other ties.

8. Morrill and Snow, "The Study of Personal Relationships in Public Places"; Calvin Morrill, interview with Blau, July 7, 2008, and follow-up emails.
9. Several scholars and researchers have attempted to categorize different types and levels of nonintimate relationships: Claude Fischer, *To Dwell*

Among Friends: Personal Networks in Town and City (Chicago, Il.: University of Chicago Press, 1982); Ray Pahl and Liz Spencer, *Rethinking Friendship* (Princeton, N.J.: Princeton University Press, 2006); Tom Rath, *Vital Friends* (New York: Gallup Press, 2006). Japanese sociologist Hidenori Tomita also coined the term "intimate stranger"—a person with whom one shares intimate and yet anonymous contact—to describe "new relationships born through the new media." See Hidenori Tomita, "Keitai and the Intimate Stranger," in *Personal, Portable, Pedestrian: Mobile Phones in Japanese Life*, edited by M. Ito, M. Matsuda, and D. Okabe (Cambridge, Mass.: MIT Press, 2005).

10. Claude Fischer, "What Do We Mean by 'Friend'? An Inductive Study," *Social Network* 3 (1982): 287–306.
11. Morrill and Snow, "Taking Stock: Functions, Places, and Personal Relationships."
12. David Morgan, Margaret Neal, and Paula Carder, "The Stability of Core and Peripheral Networks Over Time," *Social Networks* 19 (1996): 9–25.
13. Chicago Historical Society, Studs Terkel/Conversations with America, biography, http://www.studsterkel.org/bio.php.
14. From the introduction to *Division Street: America* by Studs Terkel (New York: Pantheon Books, 1966).
15. Mark Granovetter, "The Strength of Weak Ties," *American Journal of Sociology* 78 (May 1973): 1372, and interview with Blau, May 2006.
16. Mark Granovetter, interview and emails to Blau, May–July 2006.
17. Granovetter, "The Strength of Weak Ties," 1372.
18. Erin White, "Profession Changes Take Time but May Be Worth Wait," *Wall Street Journal*, November 27, 2007.
19. Robin L. Jarrett, "Successful Parenting in High-Risk Neighborhoods," *The Future of Children* 9 (Fall 1999); R. L. Jarrett, P. J. Sullivan, and N. D. Watkins, "Developing Social Capital Through Participation in Organized Youth Programs: Qualitative Insights from Three Programs," *Journal of Community Psychology* 33 (2005): 41–45.
20. Aleks Muñoz, interview with Blau, October 20, 2007.
21. Ilse van Liempt and Jeroen Doomernik, "Migrants Agency in the Smuggling Process," *International Migration* 44 (2006): 165–90.
22. Social scientists have also investigated the concept "social capital," encompassing the general benefits of connections between social partners or community organizations. For discussions of social capital, see Robert M. Milardo, Heather M. Helms, and Stephen R. Marks, "Social Capitalization in Personal Relationships," paper presented at the Theory

Construction and Research Methodology Workshop, annual meeting of the National Council on Family Relations, November 2005, Phoenix, Ariz.; Nan Lin, *Social Capital: A Theory of Social Structure and Action* (New York: Cambridge University Press, 2001).

23. The Bureau of Labor and Census Bureau statistics provide a mixed view of the number of hours that Americans work, but one table from the Census Bureau using Bureau of Labor data suggests that 82% of working Americans work "full time." http://www.census.gov/compendia/statab/tables/08s0590.pdf.
24. Theodora Stites, interview with Blau and subsequent emails, July 2006–January 2007. Unless otherwise noted, all subsequent remarks by Stites are from these exchanges.
25. Michael Schrage, "The Relationship Revolution," *Merrill Lynch Forum* (1997), and interview with Blau, October 30, 2007. http://www.cooperationcommons.com/node/406.
26. Keith Hampton and Barry Wellman, "Neighboring in Netville: How the Internet Supports Community and Social Capital in a Wired Suburb," *City and Community* 2 (Fall 2003); Keith N. Hampton, "Grieving for a Lost Network: Collective Action in a Wired Suburb," *The Information Society* 19 (2003): 1–13.
27. Keith Hampton, interview with Blau and emails, July–October 2007.
28. Jon Shannon, former director of technology at Northfield Mount Herman, interview with Blau, October 3, 2007.
29. According to Stites, Mount Herman alums now have an "I Miss SWIS" group on Facebook in which they compare the two sites. Several anonymous authors' descriptions of features they love on both sites underscore Michael Schrage's insistence that electronic communication captures our hearts more than our minds: "While giving up SWIS was hard, we gained an almost perfect replacement: facebook. . . . facebook doesn't have a 2 hour time limit. On facebook you can be an even more successful stalker because there are pictures and profiles and 'walls.' . . . facebook never lets you forget an important birthday (or let you live down a humiliating night). . . . so [although] facebook may have better graphics, and more to discover while procrastinating, some things will always be better on SWIS. . . . instead of 'poking' people, we 'SWIS-bombed' . . . when you sent someone a message, you could actually see if they read it . . . you could tell who was online, AND talk to them too. . . . you could find out about snow days, super fun school events, who got into college, who had a birthday (and not pay to share a happy thought),

and even what was on the menu for breakfast, lunch and dinner for the week! . . . So while you may not miss much else about your alma mater (or you do and wont admit it) dont be embarrassed to say that YOU MISS SWIS." http://www.facebook.com/group.php?gid=2204868992.

30. Robert Kraut et al., "Internet Paradox: A Social Technology That Reduces Social Involvement and Psychological Well-being?" *American Psychologist* 53 (1998): 1017–31.
31. J. P. Barlow, "What Are We Doing On-Line?" *Harper's*, August 1995, 35–46, quoted in Barry Wellman, "Personal Relationships: On and Off the Internet," in *The Cambridge Handbook of Personal Relations*, edited by Anita L. Vangelisti and David Perlman (Cambridge: Cambridge University Press, 2006), 711.
32. Barry Wellman, who has written extensively about this debate, sums up the early accounts of the Internet's role in personal relationships in "Personal Relationships: On and Off the Internet," 709–23.
33. Hampton and Wellman, "Neighboring in Netville."
34. Toronto Real Estate Board, Average Single Family Historical Home Prices and trends for Toronto and Mississauga. http://www.mississauga4sale.com/TREBprice.htm. This calculation is based on an annual increase of 4 to 5%.
35. Elaine Carey, "In Netville, Good Nexus Makes Good Neighbours," *Toronto Star*, November 14, 2000, section B2.
36. Barry Wellman, "The Glocal Village: Internet and Community," *Idea&s* (University of Toronto) 1 (Autumn 2004).
37. Barry Wellman, "The Community Question: The Intimate Networks of East Yorkers," *American Journal of Sociology* 84 (1979): 1201–31.
38. Hampton and Wellman, "Neighboring in Netville."
39. Hampton, "Grieving for a Lost Network: Collective Action in a Wired Suburb," interview with Blau, and follow-up emails.
40. Ibid.
41. Walter J. Carl, "<where r u?> <here u?>: Everyday Communication with Relational Technologies," in *Composing Relationships: Communication in Everyday Life*, edited by J. Wood and S. Duck (Belmont, Calif.: Thomson Publishing, 2006), 96–109.
42. Schrage, "The Relationship Revolution."
43. Theodora Stites, "Rock My Network," in *Twentysomething Essays About Twentysomething Writers* (New York: Random House Trade Paperbacks, 2006), 142–48. When one of Stites's IM buddies—a consequential stranger—emailed her about an essay contest sponsored by Random

House focusing on what it means to be part of her generation, it didn't take her long to figure out her topic.

44. Jeffrey Boase et al., "The Strength of Internet Ties: The Internet and Email Aid Users in Maintaining Their Social Networks and Provide Pathways to Help When People Face Big Decisions," Pew Internet & American Life Project, January 25, 2006, http://www.pewinternet.org. Only around 10 percent of users first meet online; and unless distance or infirmity prohibit, most enduring relationships migrate into real life.
45. Keith Hampton, Oren Livio, and Lauren Sessions, "The Social Life of Wireless Urban Species," draft, November 10, 2008.
46. Keith Hampton, "Glocalization: Internet Use and Collective Efficacy," draft, June 24, 2008; and Hampton, emails to Blau, August 2008.
47. Miller MacPherson, Lynn Smith-Lovin, and Mathew Brashears, "Social Isolation in America: Changes in Core Discussion Networks Over Two Decades," *American Sociological Review* 71 (June 2006): 353–75. The study was a comparison of responses to the 1985 and 2005 General Social Survey.
48. Although in other periods of history Americans have been distrustful, the Harris Poll's 2007 "Alienation Index" (http://www.harrisinteractive.com/harris_poll/index.asp?PID=829), which has been measured almost every year since 1966, shows a considerable uptrend since 2006 on three questions: "Most people running the country don't really care what happens to you," from 53 to 59%; "Most people with power try to take advantage of people like yourself," from 54 to 57%; and "The people in Washington are out of touch with the rest of the country," from 68 to 75%. At this writing, it is too early to report the effect of an Obama presidency on the Alienation Index.
49. Those who study the U.S. service economy point out that we have two types of jobs: (a) well-paid and secure jobs that include long hours and demands of email and computer tasks at home; and (b) poorly paid, insecure jobs that may include underemployment. The well-paid Americans are working longer hours and have the sense that their work is impinging on their home life. By contrast, poorly paid workers may have fewer hours, lower pay, and work that is neither engaging nor rewarding—with changing shifts and corporate policies that allow few opportunities for connections with coworkers. See J. A. Jacobs and K. Gerson, *The Time Divide: Work, Family, and Gender Inequality* (Cambridge, Mass.: Harvard University Press, 2004). The Family and Work Report: http://www.familiesandwork.org/site/research/reports/brief1.pdf.

50. Peter Bearman and Paolo Parigi, "Cloning Headless Frogs and Other Important Matters," *Social Forces* 83 (December 1, 2004): 535–57. As part of the North Carolina Poll, an annual survey representative of adults residing in North Carolina, the researchers asked people if they had discussed "an important matter" with anyone in the past six months, and if so, what they had discussed. Only 20% of participants reported that they hadn't discussed any important matter in the past six months. Half of the "silent" participants indicated that they had no one to talk to, but the other half indicated they simply didn't have anything important to talk about. The silent isolates with no one to talk to tended to be people who had lost partners (due to divorce) or had no jobs. The authors conclude that social isolation may be less pervasive and more pocketed in specific segments of the population than the GSS suggests. Also, people are likely to discuss what we might deem "important" issues (life and health, money and house, children) with their spouses, and more likely to discuss community issues, politics (e.g., cloning headless frogs), and work with their acquaintances.
51. Boase et al., "The Strength of Internet Ties."
52. Ann Hulbert, "Confidant Crisis," *New York Times*, July 17, 2006.
53. Claude Fischer, "*Bowling Alone:* What's the Score?" *Social Networks* 27 (2005): 155–67.
54. Robert Wuthnow, *Sharing the Journey: Support Groups and America's New Quest for Community* (New York: Free Press, 1994), and *Loose Connections* (Cambridge, Mass.: Harvard University Press, 1998).
55. Robert Wuthnow, *After the Baby Boomers* (Princeton, N.J.: Princeton University Press, 2007).
56. Karen S. Cook, "Charting Futures for Sociology: Structure and Action," *Contemporary Sociology* 29 (September 2000): 691: "Globalization and global culture are terms that have currency in ways not imagined even a decade ago, and the implications for new modes of social interaction and forms of social organization have yet to be fully comprehended."
57. Gwendolyn Bounds, "Entrepreneurial 'Therapy': Deals, Divorce, Downsizing," *Wall Street Journal*, November 6, 2007.
58. Meetup.com website and Dawn Mateo, interview with Blau, August 1, 2008.
59. Rob Walker, "Good Disguise," *New York Times*, February 4, 2007.
60. Susan Warren, "Inspired by a Joke, One-Arm Dove Hunt Is a Tradition in Texas," *Wall Street Journal*, September 19, 2006; Doug Davis, participant, interview with Blau, November 4, 2006.

61. Morrill and Snow, "Taking Stock: Functions, Places, and Personal Relationships."
62. Mark Granovetter, email, September 21, 2008. We have always had some degree of mobility, Granovetter points out, even in medieval times. The stereotype is that people lived in one small house their whole lives, but historical demographers have found that the proportion of people who lived in a particular village ten years or longer was actually quite low. Likewise, they have found that in China, multigenerational families that provide a sort of "cocoon" for its members are actually quite uncommon.
63. Barry Wellman, "The Persistence and Transformation of Community: From Neighbourhood Groups to Social Networks: Report to the Law Commission of Canada, October 30, 2001, 16. Wellman writes, "Most personal communities are essentially sparsely knit and loosely bounded." Although no recent statistics are available, between 1987 and 1997, mean network density—the number of people who know each other divided by the total number of people in the network—declined from 0.33 (which means that a third of the people are acquainted) to 0.13 (only 13% know each other).

2 The View from Above

1. Kurt Vonnegut, *Cat's Cradle* (New York: Dell Publishing, 1963).
2. Barry Wellman, "Challenges in Collecting Personal Network Data," *Social Networks*, January 14, 2007, introduction.
3. Charles Kadushin, "Some Basic Network Concepts and Propositions," in *Introduction to Social Network Theory*, online draft, February 12, 2004. http://home.earthlink.net/~ckadushin/Texts/Basic%20Network%20Concepts.pdf.
4. Used here, the phrase "social convoy" is synonymous with "egocentric network," "personal community," or "individual network," terms also used by social scientists to describe a web of relationships in which an individual or institution is at the center. However, the *convoy* image best captures a sense of movement and change over time.
5. Wellman, "Challenges in Collecting Personal Network Data." Wellman points out that "every whole network can be analyzed as a series of personal networks, just by viewing the network from the standpoint of specific persons in it." The difference is that an institution, organization, or country is a *bounded* entity, whereas individual networks are not.

6. Toni Antonucci, interview with Blau, October 23, 2006.
7. Karla Lightfoot, interviews with Blau and follow-up emails, August–December 2007.
8. Ronald S. Burt, "The Social Capital of Structural Holes," in *New Directions in Economic Sociology*, edited by Maruro F. Guillén et al. (New York: Russell Sage Foundation, 2001), 201–47.
9. Katherine Rosman, "Clinging to the Rolodex," *Wall Street Journal*, November 24, 2007.
10. Robin Moroney, "BlackBerry Contacts Go Stubbornly Undeleted," *Wall Street Journal*, December 13, 2007. http://blogs.wsj.com/informedreader/2007/12/13/blackberry-contacts-go-stubbornly-undeleted/trackback.
11. Charles Kadushin, interview with Blau, August 15, 2008.
12 Charles Kadushin, "The Friends and Supporters of Psychotherapy: On Social Circles in Urban Life," *American Sociological Review* 31 (December 1966): 786–802; Kadushin, "The Small World, Circles, and Communities," in *Making Connections* (New York: Oxford University Press, forthcoming).
13. Toni Antonucci, interview; Robert Kahn and Toni Antonucci, "Convoys over the Life Course: Attachment, Roles, and Social Support," in *Life-Span Development and Behavior*, edited by P. B. Baltes and O. Brim (New York: Academic Press, 1980): 254–83; Toni Antonucci, "Hierarchical Mapping Technique," *Generations* 10 (1986): 10–12; Toni Antonucci, Hiroko Akiyama, and Keiko Takahashi, "Attachments and Close Relationships Across the Life Span," *Attachment and Human Development* 6 (2004): 353–70.
14. Bernie Hogan, Juan Antonio Carrasco, and Barry Wellman, "Visualizing Personal Networks: Working with Participant-Aided Sociograms," *Field Methods* 19 (May 2007): 116–44; Ray Pahl and Liz Spencer, *Rethinking Friendship* (Princeton, N.J.: Princeton University Press, 2006).
15. Ray Paul, interview with Blau, July 19, 2006; Bernie Hogan, email to Blau, August 30, 2007.
16. Antonucci limits her assessment to social partners who are important in the participant's life and finds people list an average of ten to twenty people in their three circles. Hogan and his colleagues ask about "very close ties" ("people with whom you discuss important matters, with whom you regularly keep in touch, or who are there for you when you need help") as well as "somewhat close ties" ("people who are more than casual acquaintances, but not very close") and find their respondents

have as many as thirty such ties. For studies that also include peripheral relationships, see H. Russell Bernard et al., "Comparing Four Different Methods for Measuring Personal Social Networks," *Social Networks* 12 (1990): 179–215; Christopher McCarty et al., "Comparing Two Methods for Estimating Network Size," *Human Organization* 60 (Spring 2001): 28–39; and Peter Killworth et al., "Estimating the Size of Personal Networks," *Social Networks* 12 (1990): 289–312. These papers cover many of the methods used to estimate the overall size of people's networks. Each approach has its shortcomings, not the least of which is that some studies only look at subtypes of networks. Emotional support and instrumental (practical) support, to name two different, but often overlapping, types of networks, are part of the "global network"—everyone you know—while the "effective network" is comprised of people you can find if you need to. Depending on what they're looking for, researchers also use different definitions of "knowing." Is it someone you simply know by name, by face, or is some interaction necessary? What time span are we talking about? For example, in H. Russell Bernard and his colleagues' study of effective networks, "knowing" was defined this way: "You know the person and they know you by sight or by name; you can contact them in person, by telephone, or by mail; and you had contact with the person in the last two years." Hence, there is often wide variation in reports of global network size—overall, numbers range from as low as 20 (from a study of support networks) to a high of 5,053. Clearly, there are individual variations in network size, but different methods also tend to elicit different numbers. The "high" estimate, for example, is based on how many names participants recognized in a phone book, but a similar study showed that it also mattered which city's phone book was used!

17. Katherine L. Fiori, Toni C. Antonucci, and Kai S. Cortina, "Social Network Typologies and Mental Health Among Older Adults," *The Journals of Gerontology: Psychological Science* 61 (2006), 25–32; H. Litwin and S. Shiovitz-Ezra, "Network Type and Mortality Risk in Later Life," *Gerontologist* 46 (2006): 735–43.
18. Wellman and Wortley, "Different Strokes from Different Folks: Community Ties and Social Support," *American Journal of Sociology* 96 (1990): 558–88.
19. Ethan Watters, *Urban Tribes: A Generation Redefines Friendship, Family, and Commitment* (New York: Bloomsbury, 2003), and interview with Blau, April 15, 2008.
20. Burt, "The Social Capital of Structural Holes."

21. Claude Fischer, *To Dwell Among Friends: Personal Networks in Town and City* (Chicago, Il.: University of Chicago Press, 1982).
22. Dottie Mayhew, Joan Seaver, and Chris Wright, interviews with Blau, October 17, 2006.
23. Raymond Chau, interview with Blau and follow-up emails, December 2007–January 2008.
24. "Effects of the Asian Financial Crisis on Hong Kong," *Asia Society*, May 1998, http://www.igcc.ucsd.edu/pdf/afc_hongkong.pdf.
25. Laura L. Carstensen, "The Influence of a Sense of Time on Human Development," *Science* 312 (2006): 19–21; L. L. Carstensen, D. M. Isaacowitz, and S. T. Charles, "Taking Time Seriously: A Theory of Socioemotional Selectivity," *American Psychologist* 54 (1999): 165–81; S. T. Charles and J. R. Piazza, "Memories of Social Interactions: Age Differences in Emotional Intensity," *Psychology and Aging* 22 (2007): 300–309.
26. B. L. Fredrickson and L. L. Carstensen, "Choosing Social Partners: How Old Age and Anticipated Endings Make People More Selective," *Psychology and Aging* 5 (1990): 335–47. The other groups studied were "young" (between eleven and twenty-nine, average age twenty-three) and "middle-aged" (between thirty and sixty-four, average age forty-six).
27. Carstensen, "The Influence of a Sense of Time on Human Development"; Carstensen, Isaacowitz, and Charles, "Taking Time Seriously"; Charles and Piazza, "Memories of Social Interactions."
28. Helene H. Fung, Laura L. Carstensen, and Amy M. Lutz, "Influence of Time on Social Preferences: Implications for Life-Span Development, *Psychology and Aging* 14 (1999): 595–604. In a survey conducted in 1996, a year before the handover of Hong Kong to Communist China, older people again chose family and younger respondents opted for acquaintances. But when the survey was replicated *two months before the handover*, a time when anxiety affected old *and* young, everyone preferred family.
29. Helene H. Fung and Laura L. Carstensen, "Goals Change When Life's Fragility Is Primed: Lessons Learned from Older Adults, the September 11 Attacks and SARS," *Social Cognition* 24 (2006): 248–78. In the SARS study, three groups were tested at the peak of the outbreak—young (aged 18–35), middle-aged (36–55), and older (56 and over)—and in each group, familiar social partners were favored.
30. Ibid.
31. Graham Spanier, interview with Blau, July 12, 2006, and subsequent emails.

32. John F. Welch, "Letter to Share Owners, *GE 2000 Annual Report*, http://www.ge.com/annual00/letter/index.html.
33. In 2006 and 2007, Blau interviewed several people regarding the history of Swiffer: at Procter & Gamble, Craig Wynett, director of Corporate New Ventures, Gordon Brunner, former chief technology officer and board member, now retired, and Karl Ronn, global R&D director, Home Care; and at Design Continuum, Harry West, Ph.D., vice president of strategy and innovation and former MIT professor; Naomi Korn Gold, senior strategist, and David Chastain, vice president, Program Development.
34. "Procter's Gamble: Durk Jager Attempts Turnaround at Procter and Gamble," *The Economist* (U.S.), June 12, 1999. http://www.highbeam.com/doc/1G1-54885178.html.
35. "Using the Net for Brainstorming, *Business Week Online*, December 13, 1999, www.businessweek.com/1999/99_50/b3659021.htm; Diana Day, "Raising Radicals: Different Processes for Championing Innovative Corporate Ventures," *Organization Science* 5 (1994): 148–72, cited in Mark Granovetter, "The Impact of Social Structure on Economic Outcomes, *Journal of Economic Perspectives* 19 (Winter 2004): 33–50; Duncan Watts, "Innovation, Adaptation, and Recovery," in *Six Degrees: The Science of a Connected Age* (New York: W. W. Norton, 2003), 253–89.
36. George Anders, "Management Leaders Turn Attention to Followers," *Wall Street Journal*, December 24, 2007. Anders cites two recent books, *Followership* by Barbara Kellerman at Harvard's Kennedy School of Government, and *The Starfish and the Spider* by entrepreneurs Ori Brafman and Rod Beckstrom. Among others, Anders interviewed Shari Ballard, Best Buy's executive vice president, Retail Channel Management, who routinely asks store managers and employees to come up with suggestions for sales promotions tailored to local tastes—information which cannot be gleaned at the executive level.
37. Burt, "The Social Capital of Structural Holes."
38. It's typically a long way from a bright idea to a finished product. Once P&G settled on the "diaper on a stick" concept, the responsibility of testing various nonwoven materials for the mop head fell to Naomi Korn Gold, a sophomore at MIT who interned at Design Continuum that summer. Some of the materials were so revolutionary, P&G had her ship the dirty remnants back to Cincinnati. (It is not a myth that technology thieves raid the garbage bins of companies and its contractors.) To standardize these experiments, Gold concocted batches of "typical dirt"—a

mix of flour, sand, oils, and dead skin donated by a local podiatrist. Her mop was specially weighted to apply precisely the same amount of pressure per swipe. Gold's findings were painstakingly recorded and included in DC's final report.

39. Avan R. Jassawalla and Hemant C. Sashittal, "An Examination of Collaboration in High-Technology Product Development Processes, *Journal of Product Innovation Management* 15 (1998): 237–54; Jassawalla and Sashittal, "Cultures That Support Product Innovation Processes," *Academy of Management Executive* 16 (2002); and Blau's interviews with the authors who are at the Jones School of Business, State University of New York, Geneseo.
40. Randal C. Archibold, "Western States Agree to Water-Sharing Pact," *New York Times*, December 10, 2007. In the western United States, where reservoirs are at their lowest level in years, similarly disparate groups of "stakeholders"—residents, real estate developers, manufacturers, environmentalists, wildlife advocates, the Interior Department, and all levels of state and local agencies—have spent years trying to reach a consensus.
41. Thomas Homer-Dixon, "Terror in the Weather Forecast," *New York Times*, op-ed contribution, April 24, 2007.
42. Eva Schiffer, multiple interviews with Blau and emails, November 2007–January 2008. The manual for the toolbox and other information about Net-Map are on Eva Schiffer's blog: http://netmap.ifpriblog.org.
43. In "The Social Capital of Structural Holes," Burt notes that "only insiders, 'the right kind of people,' have direct access to the social capital of brokerage. Outsiders have to borrow. Among senior managers, for example, insiders are typically older men; outsiders include women and young men. The outsider proposing an idea that bridges groups has to borrow social capital in the sense that she has to work through a strategic partner, a person who has the social capital of a network that spans structural holes." Of course, some women and young people are very skillful brokers. However, in Pat Jones's case, she was a newcomer to the school and a woman. It stands to reason that she would have to garner support from more influential players.

3 Beyond the Confines of the Familiar

1. Jenny Joseph, "Warning," reprinted in *The Red Hat Society: Fun and Friendship After Fifty* by Sue Ellen Cooper (New York: Warner Books, 2004).

2. Walter J. Carl and Steve Duck, "How Relationships Do Things with Us," lead chapter in *Communication Yearbook* 28, edited by P. Kalbfleisch (New Brunswick, N.J.: International Communication Association, 2004), 1–35.
3. Office of the First Lady, White House press release, October 28, 2004, http://www.whitehouse.gov/news/releases/2004/10/20041028-15.html.
4. Sue Ellen Cooper, email to Blau, May 14, 2006.
5. William James, *The Principles of Psychology* (New York: Dover, 1950; original work published 1890), quoted in Peggy Thoits and Lauren K. Virshup, "Me's and We's: Forms and Functions of Social Identities," in *Fundamental Issues*, edited by R. D. Ashmore and L. Jussim (New York: Oxford University Press, 1976).
6. Kenneth J. Gergen, *The Saturated Self* (New York: Basic Books, 1991).
7. Kenneth Gergen interview with Blau, August 31, 2006.
8. Marilyn B. Brewer and Wendi Gardner, "Who Is This 'We'?: Levels of Collective Identity and Self Representations," *Journal of Personality and Social Psychology* 71 (1996): 83–93.
9. Carl and Duck, "How Relationships Do Things with Us."
10. Lynn Smith-Lovin, "Self, Identity, and Interaction in an Ecology of Identities," in P. J. Burke et al., *Advances in Identity Theory and Research* (New York: Plenum, 2003): 167–78.
11. Peggy A. Thoits, "Personal Agency in the Accumulation of Role-Identities," presented at "The Future of Identity Theory and Research: A Guide for a New Century" conference, University of Indiana, Bloomington, April 2001, 179–93.
12. Jan E. Stets and Peter A. Burke, "A Sociological Approach to Identity," chapter for *Handbook of Self and Identity*, edited by Mark Leary and June Tangney (New York: Guilford Press, 2003), 128–52. http://www.people.fas.harvard.edu/-johnston/burke.pdf.
13. Lynn-Smith Levin, "The Strength of Weak Identities: Social Structural Sources of Self, Situation, and Emotional Experience," 70 (June 2007): 106–24.
14. Gergen, interview.
15. Thoits, "Personal Agency in the Accumulation of Role-Identities."
16. Peggy A. Thoits, "Identity Structure and Psychological Well-Being: Gender and Marital Status Comparisons," *Social Psychology Quarterly* 55 (September 1992): 236–56; and Peggy Thoits, emails to Blau.
17. Rose Laub Coser, *In Defense of Modernity: Role Complexity and Individual Autonomy* (Palo Alto, Calif.: Stanford University Press, 1991).

18. Ibid.
19. Arlie Hochschild, *The Unexpected Community: Portrait of an Old Age Subculture* (Berkeley: University of California Press, 1973), xii.
20. K. J. Kiecolt, "Stress and the Decision to Change Oneself: A Theoretical Model," *Social Psychology Quarterly* 57 (1994): 49–63, in Stets and Burke, "A Sociological Approach to Identity."
21. Thoits, "Personal Agency in the Accumulation of Role-Identities."
22. Doug Davis, interview with Blau, November 4, 2006, January 24 and 27, 2008.
23. K. E. Norman, "Alternative Treatments for Disseminated Intravascular Coagulation," *Drug News Perspect* 17 (May 2004): 243–50. http://www.ncbi.nlm. nih.gov/pubmed/15334173.
24. Ladd Wheeler and Kunitate Miyake, "Social Comparison in Everyday Life, *Journal of Personality and Social Psychology* 62 (1992): 760–73; K. D. Locke, "Status and Solidarity in Social Comparison: Agentic and Communal Values and Vertical and Horizontal Directions," *Journal of Personality and Social Psychology* 84 (2003): 619–31.
25. Hochschild, *The Unexpected Community*, 58–63.
26. Brewer and Gardner, "Who Is This 'We'?: Levels of Collective Identity and Self Representations."
27. Scott E. Page, *The Difference: How the Power of Diversity Creates Better Groups, Firms, Schools, and Societies* (Princeton, N.J.: Princeton University Press, 2007), 1–2.
28. Scott E. Page, interview with Blau, February 5, 2008.
29. Barbara Green, interview with Blau, August 13, 2006, and December 30, 2007.
30. Tamar Lewin, "When Richer Weds Poorer, Money Isn't the Only Difference," *New York Times*, May 19, 2005.
31. Bonnie H. Erickson, "Culture, Class, and Connections," *American Journal of Sociology* 102 (July 1996): 217–51; "Cultural Literacy: E. D. Hirsch Tells Reporters Why Knowledge Matters," *The Hechinger Report*, Fall–Winter 2007, 11. We coined the phrase "culture smarts" to specifically refer to knowledge of the culture in its many forms. Sociologists use the broader term "cultural capital" to include cultural knowledge, beliefs, values, educational degrees, and skills that confer status and privilege. E. D. Hirsch, an education scholar, uses the phrase "cultural literacy" to mean "the knowledge taken for granted when people like us, who are well-enough educated to be newspaper reporters, or lawyers, or doctors—when we can take for granted when we're writing to a general

literate audience or talking to each other. It's what you need to know, as it were, to be able to talk to strangers and to understand strangers in the common sphere—that's the public sphere that holds the language community together."

32. Erickson, "Culture, Class, and Connections."
33. Bonnie Erickson, interview with Blau, November 4, 2006.
34. Nan Lin, *U.S. 2004–5 National Survey on Social Capital*, "The Summary of Social Capital USA 2005 (Wave 1)," August 2006.
35. Diplomat who prefers to remain anonymous, interview with Blau, June 3, 2007.
36. Apologies to Mark Granovetter. In an email to Blau, he agreed with the concept of a loop, not the phrase itself, although he understood that the alliteration was irresistible to a journalist. "I think of ties as weak or strong, but I don't know what it means for a tie to be 'loose.' I suppose there is an opposite usage, where people say that they are 'tight,' meaning close. But I never heard anyone saying that they and someone else were 'loose.' I think the usage arose from Elizabeth Bott's use of 'close-knit' and 'loose-knit' networks, where the latter were networks where a lot of people's friends don't know one another. I later argued that this was more likely when ties were weak. So I think of 'loose' as referring to the 'knit' of networks, and weak/strong as referring to the ties themselves."
37. Mark Granovetter, "The Impact of Social Structure on Economic Outcomes," *Journal of Economic Perspectives* 19 (Winter 2004): 33–50.
38. Wendy Pollack, "Why Wall Street's Top Women Rarely Lose Their Star Power," *Wall Street Journal*, January 25, 2008. http://blogs.wsj.com/informedreader/2008/01/25/why-wall-streets-top-women-rarely-lose-their-star-power/trackback.
39. Mark Granovetter, emails, February 7–9, 2008.
40. Malcolm Gladwell, "Disclosure Statement," website, http://gladwell.com/disclosure.html.
41. Florence Passy, "Social Networks Matter. But How?" in *Social Movements and Networks: Relational Approaches to Collective Action*, edited by Mario Diani and Doug McAdam (New York: Oxford University Press, 2003), 21–48.
42. Jim Kates, interview with Blau, February 12, 2008. Kates, "June 1964," Veterans of the Civil Rights Movement website, http://crmvet.org/info/katesexp.htm.
43. Doug McAdam, *Freedom Summer* (New York: Oxford University Press, 1988).

44. Ibid.
45. Doug McAdam, interview with Blau, September 6, 2007.
46. McAdam, interview.
47. Chude Allen, interview with Blau, December 6, 2007. Jim Kates and another movement veteran, Jane H. Adams, also noted that when it came to activism, their casual acquaintances, not their best friends, were more likely to be involved.
48. Brewer and Gardner, "Who Is This 'We'?: Levels of Collective Identity and Self Representations."
49. Duncan J. Watts, *Six Degrees: The Science of a Connected Age* (New York: W. W. Norton, 2003).
50. Elizabeth DeVita-Raebu, "If Osama's Only 6 Degrees Away, Why Can't We Find Him?: The Famous 6 Degrees Separation Theory Fades Under Scrutiny," *Discover*, February 2008. http://discovermagazine.com/2008/feb/if-osama.s-only-6-degrees-away-why-can.t-we-find-him.
51. Peter Sheridan Dodds, Roby Muhamad, and Duncan J. Watts, "An Experimental Study of Search in Global Social Networks," *Science*, August 8, 2003, 827–29.
52. Sue Ellen Cooper, *The Red Hat Society: Fun and Friendship After Fifty* (New York: Warner Books, 2004).
53. Janna Quitney Anderson and Lee Rainie, "The Future of the Internet II," Pew Internet & American Life Project, September 24, 2006, http://www.pewinternet.org/PPF/r/188/report_display.asp.
54. David Godes and Dina Mayzlin, "Firm-Created Word-of-Mouth Communication: Evidence from a Field Test," HBS Marketing Research Paper No. 04-03, August 2007, http://papers.ssrn.com/sol3/papers.cfm?abstract_id=569361.
55. DeVita-Raebu, "If Osama's Only 6 Degrees Away. . . ."
56. W. G. Mangold, F. Miller, and G. R. Brockway, "Word-of-Mouth Communication in the Service Marketplace," *Journal of Services Marketing* 13 (1999): 73–89. The second most prevalent reason was that the subject came up organically in a conversation—a discussion of weekend plans leads to restaurant talk, a health complaint to a medical recommendation. Interestingly, satisfaction or dissatisfaction with a service is cited less often than these other reasons.
57. Emanuel Rosen, *The Anatomy of Buzz: How to Create Word-of-Mouth Marketing* (New York: Doubleday Currency Books, 2000), 15–16.
58. Reneé Dye, "The Buzz About Buzz," *Harvard Business Review* 78 (2000): 139–46.

59. Pew Internet Survey, Internet Activities, September 2007, http://www.pewinternet.org/trends/Internet_Activities_2.15.08.htm.
60. Walter J. Carl, "What's All the Buzz About?: Everyday Communication and the Relational Basis of Word-of-Mouth and Buzz Marketing Practices, *Management Communication Quarterly* 19: 601–34; Keller Fay Group in Cooperation with BzzAgent, "The More, the Better: Creating Successful Word-of-Mouth Campaigns," Keller Fay Group LLC, October 2006. Carl found that 80% of word-of-mouth were face-to-face interactions; Keller Fay, looking specifically at word-of-mouth agents, found that 99% talked about products in person—91% said it's the method they use most often, but that they use other channels as well, including phone, email, instant and/or text messaging, online chats, or blogs.
61. Andrea C. Wojnicki and David B. Godes, "Word-of-Mouth and the Self-Concept: The Effects of Satisfaction and Subjective Expertise on Inter-consumer Communication," August 2004, http://64.233.167.104/search?q=cache:h21oYzEFeWMJ:rotman.utoronto.ca/marketing/Wojnicki.doc+Renee+Dye,+%22The+Buzz+About+Buzz%22&hl=en&ct=clnk&cd=2&gl=us&ie=UTF-8.
62. Dave Balter and John Butman, *Grapevine: The New Art of Word-of-Mouth Marketing* (New York: Penguin Books, 2005), 17–18.
63. Celia W. Dugger, "Mothers of Nepal Vanquish a Killer of Children," *New York Times*, April 30, 2006.
64. Carl and Duck, "How Relationships Do Things with Us."

4 Good for What Ails Us

1. George Plimpton, *Shadow Box: An Amateur in the Ring* (New York: Putnam, 1977).
2. Art Buchwald, *Too Soon to Say Goodbye* (New York: Random House, 2007).
3. George A. Bonanno, "Loss, Trauma, and Human Resilience: Have We Underestimated the Human Capacity to Thrive After Extremely Aversive Events?" *American Psychologist* 59 (2004): 20–28.
4. Thomas Perls, "The Different Paths to 100," *American Journal of Clinical Nutrition* 83 (2006): 484–87S supplement.
5. Liburd C. Leandris and Joe E. Sniezek, "Changing Times: New Possibilities for Community Health and Well-Being," *Preventing Chronic Disease* 4 (July 2007): 1–5. http://www.cdc.gov/pcd/issues/2007/jul/07_0048.htm.

World Health Organization, "Launch of the Chronic Disease Report." Mauritius Institute of Health, March 7, 2006. http://209.85.165.104/search?q=cache:uCeW3mh2ycEJ:www.who.int/dg/lee/speeches/2006/mauritius_chronic_disease/en/index.html+chronic+disease+increases&hl=en&ct=clnk&cd=1&gl=us&ie=UTF-8.

6. "Chronic Disease Overview," National Center for Chronic Disease Prevention and Health Promotion website: http://cdc.gov/nccdphp/overview.htm). Renee Brown, a statistician at NCCDPHP, which is part of the Centers for Disease Control and Prevention, interviewed by Blau on March 12, 2008, grants that these figures are growing. This is confirmed in Gerard Anderson and Jane Horvath, "The Growing Burden of Chronic Disease in America, *Public Health Reports* 119 (May–June 2004): 263–69.
7. Anne Harrington, *The Cure Within: A History of Mind-Body Medicine* (New York: W. W. Norton, 2008).
8. Bonanno, "Loss, Trauma, and Human Resilience."
9. Dan P. McAdams, "The Psychology of Life Stories," *Review of General Psychology* 5 (2001): 100–22.
10. Harrington, *The Cure Within.*
11. Ellen Conser, research assistant to Sheldon Cohen, interview with Blau and email, July 10, 2008.
12. Sheldon Cohen et al., "Social Ties and Susceptibility to the Common Cold," *JAMA* 277 (June 25, 1997): 1940–44.
13. Sheldon Cohen, Benjamin H. Gottlieb, and Lynn G. Underwood, "Social Relationships and Health," in *Social Support Measurement and Intervention: A Guide for Health and Social Scientists*, edited by Cohen et al. (New York: Oxford University Press, 2000): 3–25.
14. L. F. Berkman and S. L. Syme, "Social Networks, Host Resistance, and Mortality: A Nine-Year Follow-up Study of Alameda County Residents," *American Journal of Epidemiology* 109 (1979): 186–204.
15. Sheldon Cohen and Edward P. Lemay, "Why Would Social Networks Be Linked to Affect and Health Practices?" *Health Psychology* 26 (2007): 410–17; Howard Litwin and Sharon Shiovitz-Ezra, "Network Type and Mortality Risk in Later Life," *The Gerontologist* 46 (December 2006): 735–43; J. S. House, K. R. Landis, and D. Umberson, "Social Relationships and Health," *Science* 241 (1988): 540–44.
16. Ibid.
17. Sarah D. Pressman and Sheldon Cohen, "Use of Social Words in Autobiographies and Longevity," *Psychosomatic Medicine* 69 (2007): 262–69.

18. Several social scientists have studied support networks in older adults. Integrated networks are best; having a family-only network is second best. Of older adults who have only *one* source of support, those who had family ties fared better than older adults who are dependent solely on acquaintances and formal paid providers. Lisa Berkman's study of social networks in Berkeley also found that ties to spouses, friends, and relatives were better predictors of longevity than church or group member ties. However, every type of relationship helped deter mortality. See Berkman and Syme, "Social Networks, Host Resistance, and Mortality"; K. L. Fiori, T. C. Antonucci, and K. S. Cortina, "Social Network Typologies and Mental Health Among Older Adults," *Journal of Gerontology: Psychological Sciences* 61B (2006): 25–32; and G. C. Wenger, "Social Networks and the Prediction of Elderly People at Risk," *Aging and Mental Health* 1 (1997): 311–20.
19. John Cacioppo, interview with Blau, March 15, 2008.
20. John Cacioppo and William Patrick, *Loneliness: Human Nature and the Need for Social Connection* (New York: W. W. Norton, 2008), 14.
21. Henry Perlman (pseudonym), interview with Blau, August 8, 2006, and April 15, 2008.
22. Cohen and Lemay, "Why Would Social Networks Be Linked to Affect and Health Practices?"
23. Sheldon Cohen et al., "Social Relationships and Health," 2000.
24. Bella DePaulo, *Singled Out: How Singles Are Stereotyped, Stigmatized, and Ignored, and Still Live Happily Ever After* (New York: St. Martin's Press, 2006). According to the 2004 U.S. Census, 44% of Americans are single. http://www.census.gov.
25. John Cacioppo, email to Blau, December 2, 2008; Louise C. Hawkley, Michael W. Browne, and John T. Cacioppo, "How Can I Connect with Thee?: Let Me Count the Ways," *Psychological Science* 16 (2005): 798–804.
26. Barry Wellman and S. Wortley, "Different Strokes from Different Folks: Community Ties and Social Support," *American Journal of Sociology* 96 (1990): 558–88.
27. R. Sosa et al., "The Effects of a Supportive Companion on Perinatal Problems, Length of Labor, and Mother-Infant Interaction," *New England Journal of Medicine* 303 (1980): 597–600. See Kathryn D. Scott, Gale Berkowitz, and Marshall Klaus, "A Comparison of Intermittent and Continuous Support During Labor: A Meta-Analysis," *American Journal of Obstetrics & Gynecology* 180 (May 1999): 1054–59 for a more recent

meta-analysis of *doulas*, which found that having a continuous *doula* was more helpful than an intermittent one.

28. James Pennebaker, "Writing About Emotional Experiences as Therapeutic Process," *Psychological Science* 8 (1997): 162–66.
29. Yasushi Kiyokawa et al., "Partner's Stress Status Influences Social Buffering Effects in Rats," *Behavioral Neuroscience* 118 (2004): 798–804.
30. T. Kamarck, S. Mannuck, and J. Jennings, "Social Support Reduces Cardiovascular Reactivity to Psychological Challenge: A Laboratory Model," *Psychosomatic Medicine* 52 (1991): 42–58.
31. G. E. Miller, S. Cohen, and A. K. Ritchey, "Chronic Psychological Stress and the Regulation of Pro-inflammatory Cytokines: A Glucocorticoid-resistance Model," *Health Psychology* 21 (2002): 531–41.
32. Y. L. Michael et al., "Social Networks and Health-Related Quality of Life in Breast Cancer Survivors: A Prospective Study," *Journal of Psychosomatic Research* 52 (May 2002): 285–93.
33. Sylvia Mackey, multiple interviews with Blau in 2007 and 2008.
34. Sheldon Cohen, "The Pittsburgh Common Cold Studies: Psychosocial Predictors of Susceptibility to Respiratory Infectious Illness," keynote presentation at the 8th International Congress of Behavioral Medicine, Mainz, Germany (August 25–28, 2004), *International Journal of Behavioral Medicine* 12 (2005): 123–31.
35. Jennifer L. Wolff and Judith D. Kasper, "Caregivers of Frail Elders: Updating a National Profile," *The Gerontologist* 46 (June 2006): 344–56; Debra K. Moser and Kathleen Dracup, "Role of Spousal Anxiety and Depression in Patients' Psychosocial Recovery After a Cardiac Event," *Psychosomatic Medicine* 66 (2004): 527–32; P. Langeluddecke et al., *Journal of Psychosomatic Research* 33 (1989): 155–59; "Family Caregivers Often Neglect Their Own Health," *CA: A Cancer Journal for Clinicians* 56 (2005): 5–6.
36. Wolff and Kasper, "Caregivers of Frail Elders: Updating a National Profile"; R. Schulz and S. R. Beach, "Caregiving as a Risk Factor for Mortality: The Caregiver Health Effects Study," *JAMA* 282 (1999): 2215–19.
37. Mary E. Liming Alspaugh et al., "Longitudinal Patterns of Risk for Depression in Dementia Caregivers: Objective and Subjective Primary Stress as Predictors," *Psychology and Aging* 14 (March 1999): 34–43.
38. Carolyn C. Cannuscio et al., "Employment Status, Social ties, and Caregivers' Mental Health," *Social Science & Medicine* 58 (April 2004): 1247–56.

39. I. Kawachi and L. F. Berkman, "Social Ties and Mental Health," *Urban Health* 78 (2001): 458–67.

40. Richard M. Cohen, *Blindsided: Living a Life Above Illness: A Reluctant Memoir* (New York: HarperCollins, 2004), 215–16.

41. Gunhild O. Hagestad, *Falling Out of Time: Reflections from an Illness Journey* (2008, in press).

42. Richard M. Cohen, *Blindsided,* 224.

43. Niall Bolger et al., "Close Relationships and Adjustment to a Life Crisis: The Case of Breast Cancer," *Journal of Personality and Social Psychology* 70 (1996): 283–94.

44. Richard Cohen, interview with Blau, March 18, 2008.

45. Richard M. Cohen, *Blindsided,* 175.

46. Jerri Nielsen, *Icebound: A Doctor's Incredible Battle for Survival at the South Pole* (New York: Miramax Books, 2002), 6.

47. Paul A. Toro, "A Comparison of Natural and Professional Help," *American Journal of Community Psychology* 14 (1986): 147–59; Emory L. Cowen, "Help Is Where You Find It: Four Informal Helping Groups," *American Psychologist* 37 (1982): 385–95.

48. Donald C. McKensie, "Abreast in a Boat: A Race Against Breast Cancer," *Canadian Medical Association Journal* 159 (1998): 376–78.

49. Catherine Sabiston, interview with Blau, March 26, 2008; Catherine M. Sabiston, Meghan H. McDonough, and Peter R. E. Crocker, "An Interpretive Phenomenological Examination of Psychosocial Changes Among Breast Cancer Survivors in Their First Season of Dragon Boating," *Journal of Applied Sport Psychology* 20 (2008): 425–40.

50. Sheldon Cohen, "Social Relationships and Health," *American Psychologist* 59 (November 2004): 676–84.

51. William White, "The History and Future of Peer-based Addiction Recovery Support Services," prepared for the Substance Abuse and Mental Health Services Administration Consumer and Family Direction Initiative Summit, March 22–23, 2004, Washington, D.C., http://www.bhrm.org/P-BRSSConcPaper.pdf.

52. Melinda Blau, "Recovery Fever," *New York,* September 9, 1991.

53. Michelle Visca, interview with Blau, February 27, 2008.

54. "Harris Poll Shows Number of 'Cyberchondriacs'—Adults Who Have Ever Gone Online for Health Information—Increases to an Estimated 160 Million Nationwide," Harris Poll, July 31, 2007, http://www.harrisinteractive.com/harris_poll/index.asp?PID=792.

55. Heidi Donovan, interview with Blau, December 4, 2006.

56. Greta E. Greer, director, Survivor Programs, American Cancer Society, interview with Blau, March 18, 2008.
57. Sheldon Cohen et al., "Social Relationships and Health," 2000.
58. K. P. Davidson, J. W. Pennebacker, and S. S. Dickerson, "Who Talks?: The Social Psychology of Illness Support Groups," *American Psychologist* 55 (2000): 205–17.
59. Jason E. Owen et al., "Use of Health-Related and Cancer-Specific Support Groups Among Adult Cancer Survivors," *Cancer* 69 (2007): 2580–89.
60. Richard Cohen, interview.
61. Sabiston, interview.
62. Bonanno, "Loss, Trauma, and Human Resilience."
63. Sheldon Cohen et al., "Social Relationships and Health," 2000.
64. Carolyn E. Cutrona and Valerie Cole, "Optimizing Support in the Natural Network," in *Social Support Measurement and Interventions*, edited by S. Cohen, L. G. Underwood, and B. H. Gottlieb (New York: Oxford University Press, 2000).
65. Judith Snow, interview with Blau, April 9, 2008; Mary O'Connell, "The Gift of Hospitality: Opening the Doors of Community Life to People with Disabilities," Community Life Project Center for Urban Affairs and Policy Research, Northwestern University; René R. Gadacz, *Re-Thinking Dis-Ability: New Structures, New Relationships* (Edmonton: University of Alberta Press, 1995), 185–89.
66. Laura Halliday, interview with Blau, March 6, 2008.
67. Elizabeth Edwards, *Saving Graces: Finding Solace and Strength from Friends and Strangers* (New York: Broadway Books, 2006); E. Edwards, book-signing talk, Barnes & Noble, New York City, October 2, 2006; and interview on *Today*, September 20, 2006.
68. Henry Perlman, interview.
69. Steve McCeney, interview with Blau, April 11, 2008.
70. Cindi Gibbs, interview with Blau, March 18, 2008.
71. Peggy A. Thoits, "Personal Agency in the Stress Process," *Journal of Health and Social Behavior* 47 (December 2006): 309–23.
72. Sheldon Cohen, "Social Relationships and Health," 2004.
73. Thoits, "Personal Agency in the Stress Process."
74. Peggy A. Thoits and Lyndi N. Hewitt, "Volunteer Work and Well-Being," *Journal of Health and Social Behavior* 42 (June, 2001): 115–31; S. L. Brown et al., "Providing Social Support May Be More Beneficial Than Receiving," *Psychological Science* 14 (2003): 320–27.

75. Sheldon Cohen, "Social Relationships and Health," 2004.
76. Dan Buettner, *The Blue Zones: Lessons for Living Longer from the People Who've Lived the Longest* (Washington, D.C.: National Geographic Press, 2008).
77. Jennifer Lodi-Smith and Brent W. Roberts, "Social Investment and Personality: A Meta-Analysis of the Relationship of Personality Traits to Investment in Work, Family, Religion, and Volunteerism," *Personality and Social Psychology Review* 11 (2007): 68–86; Brent W. Roberts, Dustin Wood, and Jennifer L. Smith, "Evaluating Five Factor Theory and Social Investment Perspective on Personality Trait Development," *Journal of Research in Personality* 39 (2004): 166–84. To document his social investment theory, Roberts "meta-analyzed" data from ninety-four studies that looked at how certain personality traits played out at work, in the family, and in religious and volunteer settings—all venues that involve consequential strangers. Even investment in family roles includes casual relationships—people your partner and your children know.
78. Brent Roberts, interview with Blau, November 7, 2006.
79. Astrid Matthysse, multiple interviews with Blau and emails, March and April 2008.
80. Cacioppo and Patrick, *Loneliness*, 18.
81. American Diabetes Association, *Feria de Salud por Tu Familia*, 2007. Statistics based on information from the Centers for Disease Control and Florida Charts. http://www.diabetes.org/communityprograms-and-localevents/whatslocal-detail.jsp?id=LOCALINFOITEM_352528&zip=33135&title=.

5 Being Spaces

1. Karen Robinovitz, interview with Blau, August 8, 2006, and follow-up emails. Karen has come a long way since her move to the West Village; see http://karenrobinovitz.com.
2. Jane Jacobs, *The Death and Life of Great American Cities* (New York: Random House, 1961), 50–54. Humanistic geographer David Seamon uses the phrase "place ballet," which suggests how our movements in and around a place are "choreographed" into the fabric of our daily lives. For a discussion of "place attachment," see Mark S. Rosenbaum et al., "A Cup of Coffee with a Dash of Love: An Investigation of Commercial Social Support and Third-Place Attachment," *Journal of Service Research* 10 (August 2007).
3. Barbara B. Brown, Carol M. Werner, and Irwin Altman, "Relationships

in Home and Community Environments: A Transactional and Dialectic Analysis," in *The Cambridge Handbook of Personal Relationships*, edited by Anita L. Vangelisti and Daniel Perlman (Cambridge: Cambridge University Press, 2006), 673–93.

4. Richard Florida, *Who's Your City: How the Creative Economy Is Making Where to Live the Most Important Decision of Your Life* (New York: Basic Books, 2008).
5. Brown, Werner, and Altman, "Relationships in Home and Community Environments."
6. "Being Spaces," trendwatching.com, http://64.233.167.104/custom?q=cache:07cxsJIHhM0J:www.trendwatching.com/trends/brand-spaces.htm+being+space&hl=en&ct=clnk&cd=1&gl=us&ie=UTF-8.
7. Thomas Sander, executive director of Robert Putnam's Saguaro Seminar: Civic Engagement in America, email to Blau, September 25, 2008. Sander used the term "hybrid ties" to describe "the most promising forms of technology to build social capital" in that they "combine virtual and real strands." See also Barry Wellman, "Personal Relationships: On and Off the Internet," in *The Cambridge Handbook of Personal Relationships*, edited by Anita L. Vangelisti and David Perlman (Cambridge: Cambridge University Press, 2006), 709–23.
8. Ray Oldenburg, interview with Blau, October 27, 2006, and follow-up emails.
9. Ray Oldenburg, *The Great Good Place: Cafés, Coffee Shops, Bookstores, Bars, Hair Salons and Other Hangouts at the Heart of a Community* (New York: Marlowe & Company, 1999).
10. Oldenburg, *The Great Good Place*, 65.
11. Reiner Evans, email to Blau, November 5, 2006.
12. Sheila Hoffman, Braeburn resident, interview with Blau, April 24, 2008, and follow-up emails.
13. Dana Behar, multiple interviews and follow-up emails with Blau, April–May 2008.
14. Although community gardens can be found everywhere today, only in Seattle are they called "P-patches." According to "The History of the P-Patch Program" on Seattle. gov, the "P" stands for Picardo, the family that launched a movement in the early seventies by giving a piece of its farmland to nearby residents who were willing to work it. Today, the P-patch program in Seattle includes more than 60 gardens with over 1,900 plots on 12 acres of land throughout the city. http://www.ci.seattle.wa.us/neighborhoods/ppatch/history.htm.
15. Julia Werman, interview with Blau, June 3, 2008. Also Raakhee Mir-

chandani, "Multi Culture," *New York Post*, October 7, 2006; Eric Wilson, "Mixed-Culture Zoning," *New York Times*, October 19, 2006; Sembar Debessai, "Bringing 818 to the 212," *Daily News* L.A. Edition, December 13, 2006; "Openings," *New York*, October 16, 2006.

16. Brown, Werner, and Altman, "Relationships in Home and Community Environments."
17. National Trust Main Street Survey, October 2001; and Kennedy Smith, currently principal and cofounder of Community Land Use and Economics—the CLUE Group—in Washington, D.C., interview with Blau, May 9, 2008.
18. Marcelle S. Fischler, "Super-Duper Markets: Stores Race to Offer More," *New York Times*, July 30, 2006.
19. Gregory P. Stone, "City Shoppers and Urban Identification: Observations on the Social Psychology of City Life," *American Journal of Sociology* 60 (1954): 36–45.
20. Annie Cheatham, "Annie's Garden," in Ray Oldenburg, *Celebrating the Third Place: Inspiring Stories About the "Great Good Places" at the Heart of Our Communities* (New York: Marlowe & Company, 2001): 9–24.
21. Fred Kent, interview with Blau, May 1, 2008.
22. Oldenburg, *The Great Good Place.*
23. Roger Yu, "Hotels Ditch Imposing Desks for Friendly 'Pods,'" *USA Today*, October 26, 2006.
24. Elena Gatti, interview with Blau, June 1, 2007.
25. Tom Rath, *Vital Friends* (New York: Gallup Press, 2006), and interview with Blau, October 23, 2006.
26. Kristina Shevory, "The Workplace as Clubhouse," *New York Times*, February 16, 2008.
27. Sue Shellenbarger, "Rules of Engagement: Why Employers Should—and Increasingly Do—Care About Creating a Great Workplace," *Wall Street Journal*, October 1, 2007.
28. Lyn Lofland, *A World of Strangers* (Prospect Heights, Il.: Waveland Press, 1985).
29. Ibid.
30. Anthony M. Orum, "All the World's a Coffee Shop: Reflections on Place, Identity and Community," *Reconstruction: Studies in Contemporary Culture: Rhetorics of Place* 5 (2005). http://reconstruction.eserver.org/053/orum.shtml.
31. Oldenburg, *The Great Good Place.*
32. Toby Rosenbaum, interview with Blau, May 15, 2008.

33. Margo Maine, Ph.D., psychologist, founding member of the Academy for Eating Disorders, past president of the National Eating Disorders Association, and author of *The Body Myth: Adult Women and the Pressure to Be Perfect*, interview with Blau, May 15, 2008, and email, June 16, 2008. Maine stresses that geriatric anorexia is not the same as anorexia nervosa. The former can be "a result of depression, or medical issues which cause malaise and limit involvement in the world and is sometimes medication-related (certain drugs affect taste, appetite, and digestion), but does not necessarily have anything to do with a desire to be thin, or body image issues as anorexia nervosa does."
34. Lofland, *A World of Strangers.*
35. Mark S. Rosenbaum, "Exploring the Social Supportive Role of Third Places in Consumers' Lives," *Journal of Service Research* 9 (August 2007): 59–72; Rosenbaum et al., "A Cup of Coffee with a Dash of Love," 2007.
36. Mark S. Rosenbaum and Carolyn A. Massiah, "When Customers Receive Support from Other Customers," *Journal of Service Research* 9 (February 2007): 1–14.
37. Ibid.
38. See Rosenbaum, "A Cup of Coffee with a Dash of Love," 2007, for a review of various conceptualizations of person-to-place attachments.
39. Rosenbaum, "Exploring the Social Supportive Role of Third Places in Consumers' Lives," 2006; and Rosenbaum et al., "A Cup of Coffee with a Dash of Love," 2007.
40. Paul Saginaw and Ari Weinzweig, interviews with Blau, May 26, 2006.
41. Corey Kilgannon, "If OTB Goes, So Would a Relic of a Grittier City," *New York Times*, February 22, 2008.
42. Julie A. Willett, *Permanent Waves: The Making of the American Beauty Shop* (New York: New York University Press, 2000).
43. Lanita Jacobs-Huey, *From the Kitchen to the Parlor: Language and Becoming in African American Women's Hair Care* (New York: Oxford University Press, 2006).
44. Richard Florida, *The Rise of the Creative Class: and How It's Transforming Work, Leisure, and Everyday Life* (New York: Basic Books, 2002).
45. Emory L. Cowen et al., "Hairdressers as Caregivers I: A Descriptive Profile of Interpersonal Help-Giving Involvement," *American Journal of Community Psychology* 7 (1979): 633–48; Emory L. Cowen, "Help Is Where You Find It: Four Informal Helping Groups," *American Psycholo-*

gist 37 (1982): 385–95; Paul A. Toro, "A Comparison of Natural and Professional Help," *American Journal of Community Psychology* 14 (1986): 147–59.

46. "Softball History," SportsKnowHow.com, http://www.sportsknowhow.com/softball/history/softball-history.shtml.
47. Allison Munch, interview with Blau, May 20, 2008.
48. Allison Munch, "Everyone Gets to Participate: Floating Community in an Amateur Softball League," in *Together Alone: Personal Relationships in Public Places*, edited by Calvin Morrill, David A. Snow, and Cindy White (Berkeley: University of California Press, 2006), 111–33. "Astros" is the pseudonym Munch used for the team.
49. Barbara B. Brown, interview with Blau, May 15, 2008.
50. Munch, "Everyone Gets to Participate."
51. Erving Goffman, *Behavior in Public Places: Notes on the Social Organization of Gatherings* (New York: Free Press, 1963).
52. Edward T. Hall, *The Hidden Dimension* (New York: Anchor Books, 1966). Hall pointed out that these distances were based on observations of predominantly white, middle-class natives of the Northeastern Seaboard of the United States. Among other ethnic groups and cultures one might find evidence of different "proxemic patterns."
53. Goffman, *Behavior in Public Places.*
54. Khaled Hosseini, *A Thousand Splendid Suns* (New York: Riverhead Books, 2007).
55. "The U.S. Health Club Industry: Industry Estimates as of January 2008," International Health, Racquet, and Sportsclub Association Industry Fact Sheet, http://cms.ihrsa.org/index.cfm?fuseaction=page.viewPage.cfm&pageId=18822.
56. Jamie Heller, "So Close . . . and So Separate," *Wall Street Journal*, October 21, 2006.
57. Irwin Altman and William W. Haythorn, "Interpersonal Exchange in Isolation," *Sociometry*, 28 (December 1965): 411–26; Irwin Altman and Dalmas A. Taylor, *Social Penetration: The Development of Interpersonal Relationships* (New York: Holt, Rinehart & Winston, 1973), 82–84, 111–12.
58. Mark L. Knapp and Anita L. Vangelisti, *Interpersonal Communication and Human Relationships*, 5th edition (Boston, Mass.: Allyn & Bacon, 2005).
59. Irwin Altman, Anne Vinsel, and Barbara B. Brown, "Dialectic Conceptions in Social Psychology: An Application to Social Penetration and

Privacy Regulation," in *Advances in Experiential Social Psychology*, edited by L. Berkowitz (New York: Academic Press, 1989), 107–59; Brown, Werner, and Altman, "Relationships in Home and Community Environments."

60. Altman and Taylor, *Social Penetration*.
61. Zick Rubin, "Disclosing Oneself to a Stranger, Reciprocity and Its Limits," *Journal of Experimental Social Psychology* 11 (1975): 233–60.
62. Scott Heiferman, interview with Blau, October 7, 2006.
63. "What is Meetup?" Meetup.com fact sheet, http://static4.meetupstatic.com/pdf/meetup-about-one-page-1.pdf.
64. Katelyn Y. A. McKenna and Gwendolyn Seidman, "Considering the Interactions: The Effects of the Internet on Self and Society," in *Computers, Phones, and the Internet: Domesticating Information Technology*, edited by Robert Kraut, Malcolm Brynin, Sara Keisler (New York: Oxford University Press, 2006), 279–95.
65. Keith Hampton and Neeti Gupta, "Community and Social Interaction in the Wireless City: Wi-Fi use in Public and Semi-Public Spaces, *New Media & Society* 10 (2008).
66. Azi Barak and Orit Gluck-Ofri, "Degree and Reciprocity of Self-Disclosure in Online Forums," *CyberPsychology & Behavior* 10 (2007): 407–17.
67. John Suler, "The Online Disinhibition Effect," *CyberPsychology & Behavior* 7 (2004): 321–26.
68. McKenna and Seidman, "Considering the Interactions: The Effects of the Internet on Self and Society."
69. Barak and Gluck-Ofri, "Degree and Reciprocity of Self-Disclosure in Online Forums"; McKenna and Seidman, "Considering the Interactions: The Effects of the Internet on Self and Society."
70. Ibid.
71. Ibid.
72. Roger Hobbs, "Instant Message, Instant Girlfriend," *New York Times*, May 25, 2008.
73. McKenna and Seidman, "Considering the Interactions: The Effects of the Internet on Self and Society."
74. Ibid. In this review of studies that looked at the effects of Internet use, the authors cite a 2002 study which found that the "critical mediator of whether an individual would form close Internet relationships was his or her responses to a 'real me' scale." Those who were better able to express important aspects of themselves and their personalities online—their "real me"—were more likely to form relationships online, to integrate

those relationships into real life as well, and to maintain those ties two years later. See also K. Y. A. McKenna, A. S. Green, and M. E. J. Gleason, "Relationship Formation on the Internet: What's the Big Attraction?" *Journal of Social Issues* 58 (2002): 9–31.

6 The Downside

1. Juju Chang and Gail Deutsch, "When Good Neighbors Go Bad: Neighborhood Spats Can Turn Ugly and Violent," ABCnews .com, June 22, 2006, http://abcnews.go.com/2020/Entertainment /Story?id=1928359&page=1.
2. Paul Kellogg (pseudonym), interview with Blau, July 11, 2008.
3. Steve Farkas et al., *Aggravating Circumstances: A Status Report on Rudeness in America* (New York: Public Agenda, 2002).
4. Maureen Crane et al., "The Causes of Homelessness in Later Life: Findings from a 3-Nation Study," *Journal of Gerontology* 60B (May 2005): S-152–59.
5. Kira S. Birditt, Karen L. Fingerman, and David M. Almeida, "Age Differences in Exposure and Reactions to Interpersonal Tension: A Daily Diary Study," *Psychology and Aging* 20 (2005): 330–40. The list of family relationship types, which accounted for 60% of daily interpersonal tensions, included spouse/partner, child, and other family members (parent, sibling, grandchild, grandparent, other relative). The nonfamily relationship category included were friend, neighbor, coworker, fellow student, boss, teacher, employee, supervisor, group or organization member, client, customer, patient, service provider, and acquaintance.
6. Karen S. Rook, "The Negative Side of Social Interaction: Impact on Psychological Well-Being," *Journal of Personality and Social Psychology* 46 (1984): 1097–1108.
7. Loraleigh Keashly, "Interpersonal and Systemic Aspects of Emotional Abuse at Work: The Target's Perspective," *Violence and Victims* 16 (January 1, 2001): 233–68.
8. Christine L. Porath and Christine M. Pearson, "On the Nature, Consequences and Remedies of Workplace Incivility: No Time for 'Nice'? Think Again," *Academy of Management Executive* 19 (February 2005): 7–18.
9. Loraleigh Keashly and Joel H. Neuman, "Bullying in the Workplace: Its Impact and Management," *Employee Rights and Employment Policy Journal* 8 (2004): 335–73.

10. Porath and Pearson, "On the Nature, Consequences and Remedies of Workplace Incivility."
11. Robert I. Sutton, *The No Asshole Rule: Building a Civilized Workplace and Surviving One That Isn't* (New York: Warner Business Books, 2007).
12. Gary Namie, interview with Blau, July 1, 2008.
13. Director of a psychotherapy institute, interview with Blau, June 30, 2008. Regarding time spent mediating workplace set-tos, see J. Connelly, "Have We Become Mad Dogs in the Office?" *Fortune*, November 28, 1994, an article cited by many scholars who study bullying. In 1991, Accountemps, a New York City firm that provides temporary financial workers, found that executives from the nation's 1,000 largest companies spent over 13% of their time—the equivalent of six and a half weeks a year—resolving conflicts between workers. One can only wonder how much higher that figure might be today.
14. See Keashly and Neuman, 2004; and Sutton, *The No Asshole Rule.* In anywhere from 50 to 80% of cases, depending on which definition is used, perpetrators hold superior positions over the victim, and 20 to 50% are roughly the same rank.
15. Estimates of "upward bullying" range from 2 to 27% of cases. See Sara Branch, Sheryl Ramsay, and Michelle Barker, "Managers in the Firing Line: Contributing Factors to Workplace Bullying by Staff—An Interview Study," *Journal of Management and Organization* 13 (2007): 264–81.
16. Kelly Naybor (pseudonym), interview with Blau, June 30, 2008. Other names and details also have been changed.
17. Ellen Roth (pseudonym), interview with Blau, October 14, 2006. Other names and details also have been changed.
18. Air traffic controllers Chuck Adams stationed in Grand Forks, North Dakota, Wally Briggs in Lexington, Kentucky, Kenny Ellis in South Haven, Mississippi, Donna Lenhardt in Chicago, Illinois, and Mike Patterson in Evansville, Indiana, interviews with Blau, October–November 2007.
19. Rena L. Repetti, "Short-Term Effects of Occupational Stressors on Daily Mood and Health Complaints," *Health Psychology* 17 (1993): 125–31.
20. Air traffic controllers, interviewed by Blau.
21. Chuck Adams, interview.
22. Repetti, interview with Fingerman, July 2006.
23. Rena L. Repetti and Jennifer Wood, "Effects of Daily Stress at Work on Mothers' Interactions with Preschoolers," *Journal of Family Psychology* 11 (1997): 90–108.

24. N. Wager, G. Fieldman, and T. Hussey, "The Effect on Ambulatory Blood Pressure of Working Under Favourably and Unfavourably Perceived Supervisors," *Occupational and Environmental Medicine* 60 (2003): 468–74.
25. *Larry King Live,* memorial show on George Carlin, CNN, June 23, 2008, http://www.cnn.com/video/#/video/bestoftv/2008/06/24/lkl.carlin.long.cnn.
26. Ronald S. Burt, "Bandwidth and Echo: Trust, Information, and Gossip in Social Networks," in *Networks and Markets: Contributions from Economics and Sociology*, edited by Alessandra Cadella and James E. Rauch (New York: Russell Sage Foundation, 2001).
27. E. Tory Higgins, "Achieving 'Shared Reality' in the Communication Game: A Social Action that Creates Meaning," *Journal of Language and Social Psychology* 11 (1992): 107–31.
28. Luke Bridges (pseudonym), interview with Blau, June 28, 2008. Other names and details have also been changed.
29. Jennifer K. Bosson et al., "Interpersonal Chemistry Through Negativity: Bonding by Sharing Negative Attitudes About Others," *Personal Relationships* 13 (2006): 135–50.
30. Burt, "Bandwidth and Echo."
31. Frans B. M. de Waal, "How Animals Do Business," *Scientific American* 292 (April 2005).
32. Anthony Giddens, *The Consequences of Modernity* (Stanford, Calif.: Stanford University Press, 1990).
33. Ronald S. Burt, *Brokerage and Closure: An Introduction to Social Capital* (New York: Oxford University Press, 2005).
34. Marc Knez and Duncan Simester, "Firm-wide Incentives and Mutual Monitoring at Continental Airlines," *Journal of Labor Economics* 19 (2001): 743–72.
35. Loraleigh Keashly, interview with Blau, July 8, 2008, and emails, July–September 2008.
36. Burt, "Bandwidth and Echo."
37. Allyson Beatrice, *Will the Vampire People Please Leave the Lobby? (True Adventures in Cult Fandom)* (Naperville, Il.: Sourcebooks, 2007), and interview with Blau, June 21, 2008.
38. Marc Feldman, *Playing Sick: Untangling the Web of Munchausen Syndrome, Munchausen by Proxy, Malingering, and Factitious Disorder* (New York: Brunner-Routledge, 2004), and interview with Blau and emails, September 2008.

39. John Suler, "The Online Disinhibition Effect," *CyberPsychology & Behavior* 7 (2004): 321–26.
40. Bella M. DePaulo et al., "Lying in Everyday Life," *Personality and Social Psychology* 70 (1996): 979–95; Bella M. DePaulo, Wendy L. Morris, and R. Wyelin Sternglanz, "The Clash of Two Noble Intentions: Truthfulness and Kindness," in *Feeling Hurt in Close Relationships*, edited by L. Vangelisti (New York: Cambridge University Press, 2009).
41. Bella M. DePaulo and Deborah A. Kashy, "Everyday Lies in Close and Casual Relationships," *Journal of Personality and Social Psychology* 74 (1998): 63–79.
42. Dianne M. Tice et al., "When Modesty Prevails: Differential Favorability of Self-Presentation to Friends and Strangers," *Journal of Personality and Social Psychology* 69 (1995): 1120–38.
43. Robert S. Feldman, Erik J. Coats, and Jason C. Tomasian, "Nonverbal Deception Abilities and Adolescents' Social Competence: Adolescents with Higher Social Skills Are Better Liars," *Journal of Nonverbal Behavior* 23 (Fall 1999): 237–49.
44. Brent Weiss and Robert S. Feldman "Looking Good and Lying to Do It: Deception as an Impression Management Strategy in Job Interviews," *Journal of Applied Social Psychology* 36 (April 2006): 1070–86.
45. DePaulo et al., "Lying in Everyday Life."
46. Robert Feldman, interview with Blau, July 7, 2008.
47. Robert S. Feldman, James A. Forrest, and Benjamin R. Happ, "Self-Presentation and Verbal Deception: Do Self-Presenters Lie More?" *Basic and Applied Social Psychology* 24 (June 2002): 163–70.
48. Robert Feldman interview; DePaulo and Kashy, "Everyday Lies in Close and Casual Relationships."
49. Charles F. Bond Jr. and Bella M. DePaulo, "Accuracy of Deception Judgments, *Personality and Social Psychology Review* 10 (2006): 214–34.
50. Ibid.
51. Bella DePaulo, interview with Blau, June 21, 2008.
52. Beatrice, interview.
53. Barbara B. Brown, Carol M. Werner, and Irwin Altman, "Relationships in Home and Community Environments: A Transactional and Dialectic Analysis," in *The Cambridge Handbook of Personal Relationships*, edited by Anita L. Vangelisti and Daniel Perlman (Cambridge: Cambridge University Press, 2006), 673–93. Irwin Altman, Anne Vinsel, and Barbara B. Brown, "Dialectic Conceptions in Social Psychology: An Application to Social Penetration and Privacy Regulation," in *Advances in Experi-*

ential Social Psychology, edited by L. Berkowitz (New York: Academic Press, 1981): 107–59; and Barbara Brown, interview with Blau, May 16, 2008.

54. Dana Cummings (pseudonym), interview with Blau, March 26, 2006.
55. Brown et al., "Relationships in Home and Community Environments."
56. Irwin Altman, interview with Blau, May 14, 2008.
57. Ibid.
58. Kathy E. Kram and Monica C. Higgins, "A New Approach to Mentoring: These Days, You Need More Than a Single Person. You Need a Network," *Wall Street Journal*, September 22, 2008.
59. Laura Wander (pseudonym), interview with Blau, June 14, 2008. Other names and details also have been changed.
60. Michael Sunnafrank and Artemio Ramirez Jr. , "At First Sight: Persistent Relational Effects of Get-Acquainted Conversations," *Journal of Social and Personal Relationships* 21 (2004): 361–79.
61. Katherine Morgensen (pseudonym), interview with Blau, July 12, 2008. Other names and details also have been changed.
62. K. D. Vohs, R. R. Baumeister, and N. J. Ciarocco, "Self-Regulation and Self-Presentation: Regulatory Resource Depletion Impairs, Impression Management and Effortful Self-Presentation Depletes Regulatory Processes," *Journal of Personality and Social Psychology* 88 (2005): 632–57.
63. Brian A. Nosek, Mahzarin R. Banaji, and Anthony G. Greenwald, "Harvesting Implicit Group Attitudes and Beliefs from a Demonstration Web Site," *Group Dynamics Theory, Research, and Practice* 6 (2002): 101–15; Mahzarin Banagi, interview with Blau, July 9, 2008, and subsequent emails.
64. Banagi, interview.
65. Jennifer A. Richeson and J. Nicole Shelton, "Negotiating Interracial Interactions: Costs, Consequences, and Possibilities," *Current Directions in Psychological Science* 16 (2007): 316–20.
66. Thomas F. Pettigrew and Linda R. Tropp, "A Meta-Analytic Test of Intergroup Contact Theory," *Journal of Personality and Social Psychology* 90 (2006): 751–83; Pettigrew and Tropp, "Does Intergroup Contact Reduce Prejudice?: Recent Meta-Analytic Findings," in *Reducing Prejudice and Discrimination*, edited by S. Oskamp (Mahwah, N.J.: Lawrence Erlbaum, 2000), 93–114.

7 The Future of Consequential Strangers

1. Silent Rave in New York, announcement on Facebook, http://www.facebook.com/group.php?gid=24032096712.
2. Howard Rheingold, *Smart Mobs: The Next Social Revolution* (New York: Perseus Books, 2002).
3. Ellen Gamerman, "The New Pranksters," *Wall Street Journal*, September 12, 2008.
4. John Schwartz, "New Economy: In the Tech Meccas, Masses of People, or 'Smart Mobs,' Are Keeping in Touch Through Wireless Devices," *New York Times*, July 22, 2002.
5. Neil Howe and William Strauss, "The Next 20 Years: How Customer and Workforce Attitudes Will Evolve," *Harvard Business Review* 41 (July–August 2007); Howe and Strauss, *Millennials Rising: The Next Great Generation* (New York: Vintage Books, 2000).
6. Richard T. Sweeney, "Reinventing Library Buildings and Services for the Millennial Generation," *Library Administration & Management* 19 (Fall 2005): 165–75. Sweeney notes that demographers "disagree about the end date of Generation X and the beginning date of the Millennials. The Municipal Research and Services Center of Washington put them between 1979 and 1994, the U.S. Census Bureau between 1982 and 2000, and the book *Millennials: Americans Under Age 25* uses 1977 as a start date. Sweeney therefore considers 1979 "a good compromise." Additionally, we must note that social scientists typically do not include more than ten years in definition of a "cohort"—for example, the baby boomers are often treated as two generations—early and late—in recent social scientific work.
7. Howe and Strauss, "The Next 20 Years."
8. Robert D. Putnam, "Robert Putnam Commentary: The Rebirth of American Civic Life," *Boston Globe*, March 2, 2008; Tom Sander, executive director, Saguaro Seminar: Civic Engagement in America, email to Blau, September 25, 2008.
9. Betsy Israel, "The Overconnecteds," *New York Times*, November 5, 2006.
10. Hannah Seligson, "All Together Now," *Wall Street Journal*, September 12, 2008.
11. Nan Lin, "Building a Network Theory of Social Capital," *Connections* 22 (1999): 28–51.
12. Richard T. Sweeney, interview with Blau, November 24, 2008; Claire

Raines, "Managing Millennials," excerpt from *Connecting Generations: The Sourcebook for a New Workplace* (Menlo Park, Calif.: Crisp Publications, 2003). Other names for this generation, according to Raines, include Echo Boomers, the Boomlet, Nexters, Generation Y, the Nintendo Generation, Digital Generation, and in Canada, the Sunshine Generation. But according to an ABCnews.com poll, most of those born between 1980 and 2000—the age range Raines uses—prefer the term "Millennials." http://www.generationsatwork.com/articles/millenials.htm.

13. John Cassidy, "Me Media: How Hanging Out on the Internet Became Big Business," *The New Yorker*, May 15, 2006.
14. Seligson, "All Together Now."
15. Jonathan Dee, "The Tell-All Campus Tour," *New York Times Magazine*, September 21, 2008.
16. "America's Children in Brief: Key National Indicators of Well-being, Federal Interagency Forum on Child and Family Statistics, Washington, D.C., 2008, http://www.childstats.gov/pdf/ac2008/ac_08.pdf.
17. Edward Wyatt, "Generation Mix: Youth TV Takes the Lead in Diversity Casting," *New York Times*, August 21, 2008.
18. Reed W. Larson et al., "Changes in Adolescents' Interpersonal Experiences: Are They Being Prepared for Adult Relationships in the Twenty-first Century?" *Journal of Research on Adolescence* 12 (2002): 31–68.
19. Gustavo Pérez Firmat, *Life on the Hyphen: The Cuban-American Way* (Austin: University of Texas Press, 1994).
20. Tim Dickinson, "The Machinery of Hope: Inside the Grass-Roots Field Operation of Barack Obama, Who Is Transforming the Way Political Campaigns Are Run," RollingStone.com, March 20, 2008, http://www.rollingstone.com/news/coverstory/obamamachineryofhope.
21. Andrew Kohut et al., "Trends in Political Values and Core Attitudes, 1987–2007—Political Landscape More Favorable to Democrats," Pew Research Center for the People and the Press, news release, March 22, 2007. The poll also found that "the most secular Americans" are under age thirty—19% of those born after 1976 do not identify with a religious tradition. http://people-press.org/reports/pdf/312.pdf.
22. Larson et al., "Changes in Adolescents' Interpersonal Experiences."
23. Ibid.
24. See Richard Florida, *The Rise of the Creative Class: And How It's Transforming Work, Leisure, Community, and Everyday Life* (New York: Basic Books, 2002). Other writers who have used different terms also describe roughly the same privileged and culturally "hip" segment of society: Paul H. Ray

and Sherry Ruth Anderson, *The Cultural Creatives: How 50 Million People Are Changing the World* (New York: Three Rivers Press, 2000); and David Brooks, *Bobos in Paradise: The New Upper Class and How They Got There* (New York: Basic Books, 2000).

25. Michael Ventura, interview with Blau, September 25, 2008.
26. Michael Ventura, "The New Social Mind," *Psychotherapy Networker*, May–June 2008.
27. Jason Alderman et al., "The Most Conservative and Liberal Cities in the United States," Bay Area Center for Voting Research, 2005, alt.coxnewsweb.com/statesman/metro/081205libs.pdf.
28. Bill Bishop with Robert G. Cushing, *The Big Sort: Why the Clustering of Like-Minded America Is Tearing Us Apart* (Boston, Mass.: Houghton Mifflin, 2008).
29. Jim and Christine Hourihan, multiple interviews with Blau, July–September 2008.
30. Ray Pahl, "Hidden Solidarities That Span the Globe," *The New Statesman* 134 (January 17, 2005).
31. Putnam, "The Rebirth of American Civic Life."
32. Howe and Strauss, "The Next 20 Years."
33. Sarah Abruzzese, "Peace Corps Looks for Older Volunteers," *New York Times*, November 25, 2007.
34. Kevin E. Cahill, Michael D. Giandrea, and Joseph F. Quinn, "Retirement Patterns from Career Employment," *The Gerontologist* 46 (2006): 514–23; Cahill, Giandrea, and Quinn, "A Micro-level Analysis of Recent Increases in Labor Force Participation Among Older Men," U.S. Bureau of Labor Statistics, Office of Productivity and Technology, working paper 400 (2006).
35. Morris A. Okun and Josef Michael, "Sense of Community and Being a Volunteer Among the Young-Old," *Journal of Applied Gerontology* 25 (2006): 173–88; Margaret Gerteis, head writer, and the Conference Planning Committee at the Harvard School of Health, "The Outlook for Volunteering," in *Reinventing Aging: Baby Boomers and Civic Engagement*, Center for Health Communication, Harvard School of Public Health–MetLife Foundation Initiative on Retirement and Civic Engagement (2004), 19–24, http://www.reinventingaging.com.
36. David Brooks, "The Social Animal," *New York Times*, September 12, 2008.
37. "Aquarius," from *Hair*, lyrics by James Rado and Gerome Ragni, music by Galt MacDermot.

38. Mary Washington, pseudonym for a survivor of Hurricane Katrina, discussion with Blau, Susan Valentine, and Karima Gebel, fellow volunteers with the Louisiana Local Aid Project of Western Massachusetts, November 12, 2005.
39. Violet Simmons, pseudonym for a survivor of Hurricane Katrina, interview with Blau, September 11, 2008.
40. Robert D. Putnam and Lewis M. Feldstein with Don Cohn, *Better Together: Restoring the American Community* (New York: Simon & Schuster, 2003).
41. Pahl, "Hidden Solidarities That Span the Globe."
42. Molly Josephs and Jennifer Landes, "Samba Drums Told to Beat It at Sagg Main: Impromptu Gatherings Said to Draw 1,500," *East Hampton Star*, August 7, 2008; Richard Siegler, interview with Blau, September 22, 2008.
43. Sarah Kramer, "In Strangers, Centenarian Finds Literary Lifeline, *New York Times*, August 1, 2008.
44. Michelle Slatella, "Dear Stranger: It's 4 a.m. Help!," *New York Times*, August 28, 2008.

Appendices

1. Lynne McAllister Jones and Claude S. Fischer, "Studying Egocentric-Networks by Mass Survey," working paper no. 284, Institute of Urban and Regional Development, University of California, Berkeley, January 1978; Claude S. Fischer, *To Dwell Among Friends: Personal Networks in Town and City* (Chicago, Il.: University of Chicago Press, 1982).
2. Used by permission of Nan Lin, Department of Sociology, Duke University, *U.S. 2004–5 National Survey on Social Capital,* "The Summary of Social Capital USA 2005 (Wave 1)," August 2006.
3. Bonnie H. Erickson, "Culture, Class, and Connections," *American Journal of Sociology* 102 (July 1996): 217–51.

INDEX

Page numbers beginning with 225 refer to notes.